Search Engine Optimization
for Flash

Todd Perkins

Beijing · Cambridge · Farnham · Köln · Sebastopol · Taipei · Tokyo

Search Engine Optimization for Flash
by Todd Perkins

Published by O'Reilly Media, Inc., 1005 Gravenstein Highway North, Sebastopol, CA 95472.

O'Reilly books may be purchased for educational, business, or sales promotional use. Online editions are also available for most titles (*http://safari.oreilly.com*). For more information, contact our corporate/institutional sales department: (800) 998-9938 or *corporate@oreilly.com*.

Editor: Steve Weiss

Production Editor: Loranah Dimant

Copyeditor: Audrey Doyle

Proofreader: Nancy Reinhardt

Indexer: Fred Brown

Cover Designer: Karen Montgomery

Interior Designer: David Futato

Illustrator: Robert Romano

Printing History:

March 2009: First Edition.

RepKover.
This book uses RepKover™, a durable and flexible lay-flat binding.

ISBN: 978-0-596-52252-0

[M]

1236364650

Adobe Developer Library

Adobe Developer Library, a copublishing partnership between O'Reilly Media Inc., and Adobe Systems, Inc., is the authoritative resource for developers using Adobe technologies. These comprehensive resources offer learning solutions to help developers create cutting-edge interactive web applications that can reach virtually anyone on any platform.

With top-quality books and innovative online resources covering the latest tools for rich-Internet application development, the *Adobe Developer Library* delivers expert training straight from the source. Topics include ActionScript, Adobe Flex®, Adobe Flash®, and Adobe Acrobat®.

Get the latest news about books, online resources, and more at *http://adobedeveloper library.com*.

Table of Contents

Foreword

If a SWF falls onto the Web and there's no search engine to crawl it, does it make a sound?

To put it another way, what's the point of producing all that great artwork, animation, writing, and ActionScript programming if no one can find your Adobe Flash and Flex applications on the Web?

For years, the biggest misconception about Flash was that it was just a toy for making cool "skip intro" animations. The rise of Rich Internet Applications, enabled by Flash and Flex, has fully dispelled that myth.

Today's big misconception is that Flash-based applications are SEO-unfriendly and can't be indexed by search engines. This book will help shatter that myth into tiny little pieces.

Admittedly, we have traveled a long potholed road on the way to Flash searchability. Years ago, Macromedia Flash 4 took the first steps along that road by letting you export all the static text in a Flash application into the HTML wrapper file published with the SWF file. Later Macromedia offered a swf2html utility that extracted all the static text and links from a SWF file so that search engines could index it all.

The problem with those approaches is that Flash content is dynamic by nature. The static text in a SWF file often doesn't tell you much. Sometimes all the static text exported from a SWF file just amounts to something like "loading loading loading loading loading." (Try that search in Google today and see how many SWF files or pages show up in the results.)

It became clear that to make Flash SEO work, you needed to apply lots of different tools. You needed to take a holistic approach, optimizing every aspect of your website, including the text in your SWF files, the text on your web pages, the titles and URLs of your web pages, and so on.

More recently, in 2008, Adobe and Google cooperated to deliver a quantum improvement in SWF search indexing. Adobe produced a "headless" version of the Flash Player (codenamed "Ichabod") that can simulate all of the visual states of a Flash or Flex application, and extract the text or URL content that is present in the application at each state. Google developed a sort of "virtual user" technology that uses that player to quickly grab and index text content from each application state. Adobe has also made the "headless" Flash Player available to other search engine companies so that they can develop similar Flash indexing capabilities.

This represents a great advancement in the ability of search engines to extract and index content from Flash files. But still it's just one (much improved) tool in the Flash SEO toolbox.

You still need to optimize all aspects of your website, not just the SWF files. You still need to try every search optimization trick in the book and see what works best for your site. Luckily, Flash and Flex developers now have "the book." There are a raft of techniques to try here, and great guidance about when each technique will be useful.

The best SEO solutions involve HTML techniques, JavaScript techniques, and Flash/Flex techniques. This book covers all of those bases. It takes you from general SEO principles to very specific code examples and site optimization exercises.

Search engine optimization is not a one-time project; it's an ongoing process. As the search engine algorithms evolve, so must your sites and applications. This book provides a great starting set of tools for your Flash SEO toolbox. Now it's up to you to apply them, and get your Flash and Flex websites found.

—Robert L. Dixon, Adobe Systems Inc., Content Architect, Flash Platform

Preface

Introduction to Search Engine Optimization (SEO)

Search Engine Optimization, or *SEO*, is extremely popular in the web design and web marketing world. The following sections discuss what SEO is, and how it relates to Flash content.

Understanding SEO and Reasons to Use SEO

Search Engine Optimization (SEO) refers to making web content visible to search engines like Google, Yahoo!, and MSN. You may be thinking, "Can't the search engines just find everything anyway," but there's actually a complex science of making content visible or easily found by search engines. In fact, there are many businesses solely devoted to optimizing websites. The process of optimizing a site for search engines involves a lot of thought and specific coding and coding practices. There are actually many deciding factors, which we'll talk about in great detail throughout the rest of this book.

Understanding SEO and Flash

HTML, video, and images are indexed by search engines and stored so you can easily find them in a web search. Recently, Adobe announced that some search engines (namely Google and Yahoo!) have been given a special version of the Flash Player that allows them to search through and index textual information found in Flash content.

Even though search engines can index some Flash content, it still takes special strategies to make the content more visible on the Web. One of the most popular websites, YouTube.com, uses a Flash-based video player, and is extremely visible on the Web. Part of the site's success in terms of visibility is attributed to its HTML and other content on each page that work together to effectively to make the Flash content more visible to search engines. So, although a

YouTube video may have very little searchable text, search engines know what's in a video based on its HTML title and description. At least at this point, Flash SEO is less about making your Flash movie visible, and more about using effective, searchable HTML to make the content within your Flash movie easy for search engines to find.

Understanding SEO and Web Standards

One aspect of SEO is making your site *unobtrusive*, or painless for the user to navigate in terms of requiring the user to download plug-ins or change settings in their browser. The idea is that the user should still be able to view the content on the site without being forced to do tasks they may not want to do. *Web standards*, put out by the *World Wide Web Consortium*, or *W3C*, mandate how websites should be built and organized to be most effective in portraying the content they contain. The W3C has stated that all sites should be accessible. That means that people going to your site should be able to view the content of your site regardless of whether they have the Flash Player or JavaScript enabled.

You may be thinking, "Wait a minute. I'm designing *Flash* content, so why do I want to make my site viewable to someone who *doesn't have Flash*?" Of course you want people to see your sweet Flash animation or use your awesome application, but having content only usable by certain groups of people alienates others who might otherwise view your site. Think about it this way: The more traffic you drive to your site, the more money you make...or the more popular you become...or the more people read about your opinion on the last episode of your favorite TV show. Now if you can simultaneously get more people on your site and still appease the W3C gods, there's no reason *not* to do it.

What You Should Know Before Reading This Book

Before reading this book, you should already be familiar with using a web browser, your operating system, and some applications and programming languages. Throughout the book, we'll be writing lots of ActionScript, HTML, JavaScript, CSS, and even PHP code.

If you're not an expert coder, don't sweat it. We're not going to be writing an endless amount of code, and I'll explain in detail the code that we do write, so you'll be able to understand how it's working. Here's a look at what I recommend you already know.

Flash CS4

You should be familiar enough with Flash to know how to navigate a Timeline, and work with Movie Clip symbols. You should also be comfortable with the Flash interface, be able to use the drawing tools, and be familiar with the Properties Panel and other common panels used in Flash development.

ActionScript 3.0

ActionScript 3.0 is the native language of Flash CS4, and is used to build interactive Flash applications. If you're not a programming wizard, that's OK, but you should at least have a basic knowledge of ActionScript 3.0. If you don't, an intermediate knowledge of ActionScript 2.0 will do...I guess (joking). Your knowledge should include knowing what variables, functions, and events are and how to use them in a Flash application.

HTML

HTML is the language of the Web, and it is used on nearly every web page to define the content of the page. Though we're not going to hand code entire websites in this book, you should be familiar with at least the basics of HTML. For example, you should know enough not to freak out if I mention anchor tags (HTML links), tables, div tags, and HTML metadata. Other than that, you should be comfortable with basic HTML terminology such as the difference between tags and attributes.

JavaScript

JavaScript is used to control interactivity in a web page, and to manipulate HTML content. I'm not a JavaScript guru, and I don't expect you to be either. You should be familiar with creating variables and functions. Other than that, I'll explain everything as we go. If you already know that much ActionScript and aren't familiar with JavaScript at all, you won't need to learn any JavaScript since it's nearly the same at that level.

Cascading Style Sheets (CSS)

CSS is used to control the style and layout of web pages and is a key tool in web design. Don't worry about being a CSS all-star either, although it could help you out a lot in the long run. We're only going to be writing simple CSS, but we'll talk a lot about the importance of it throughout the book.

PHP

PHP is a powerful, server-side language. In other words, PHP code has finished running before you ever see the HTML page, and it can be used to display data from a database. You don't have to know anything about PHP before reading this book, but it will definitely help.

Setting Up Your Software

You'll need a computer that can run Adobe Flash CS4 or a later version of Flash (specs available at *http://www.adobe.com/products/flash/systemreqs*) and the current version of the Flash Player installed in your web browser (download the Flash Player at *http://www.adobe.com/go/getflash*).

Adobe Flash CS4

To create Flash content, you'll need a copy of Adobe Flash. In order to write and run ActionScript 3.0 code, you'll need Adobe Flash CS4 or a later version. If you don't have that, you can download a fully functional trial of the latest Flash version free on the Adobe site (*http://www.adobe.com/go/getflash*).

Dreamweaver CS4 or a Plain-Text Editor

Other than Flash CS4, I'm going to be using Adobe Dreamweaver CS4 for writing HTML, JavaScript, CSS, and PHP code. If you don't already have a copy of Dreamweaver, you can download a free trial version from the Adobe site (*http://www.adobe.com/dreamweaver*). You can also use a plain-text editor like TextEdit (Mac) or Notepad (Windows) and save your code files with the appropriate extensions. TextEdit and Notepad are both installed with all versions of Mac OS X and the Windows platform, respectively. It's important that you don't use a word processing program, like Microsoft Word, to write your code because word processing programs typically add extra data to text files that make them unusable in a web browser.

Understanding the Facts About Flash and SEO

There are plenty of rumors, myths, and semi-myths about Flash and SEO floating around on the Web. The following are some facts about Flash content on the Web.

Is Flash Content Searchable?

Many, if not most, people in the world of web design think Flash content is not searchable. Are they right? It really depends on what you mean by "searchable." At the time of this writing, search engines Google and Yahoo! are able to index text compiled into a Flash movie, as well as any HTML code that is automatically generated by Flash. And although *Flash movie itself* is not extremely searchable, any content inside a Flash movie can still be made very *visible* by using the right tactics.

 Google indexes SWF files on the Web. In Google, you can search specifically for SWF files by searching for `filetype:swf` + `"search example"`, and the results will search page URLs and static text in Flash movies. The problem with using this method for Flash SEO is that users are unlikely to perform a search for a particular file type to find your site. Further, the pages found in a Google search are links to actual SWF files, not HTML pages, so you have significantly less control over what the user will see even if they do end up finding your Flash movie.

What About SWF Metadata?

In Flash, for a few versions now, you have been able to add metadata information like a title and description to your Flash movies. This metadata gets embedded in your Flash movies to make them potentially visible to search engines. Sadly, SEO in Flash isn't that easy, because search engines don't currently index this information.

What Should I Expect to Learn in This Book?

It's important to understand that this book isn't a portal to a magical future where Flash content is perfectly indexed by search engines, but rather the book is a tool for you to make your Flash content visible regardless of whether Flash movies are indexed.

The book is your key to understanding how to use Flash effectively on the Web so your pages that contain Flash movies will be clearly visible to search engines. After you set up your web pages to effectively store Flash movies, it doesn't matter how or even if search engines index Flash content. And if, at some later day, search engines *do* index Flash movies, your Flash content will be *even more* searchable!

Who This Book Is For

If you are interested in making your Flash content more visible on the Web, this book is for you. If you run an honest site that needs all of its content (Flash and non-Flash) known to the world, this book is for you too. This book is really for anyone interested in SEO, anyone who currently uses Flash on a site, anyone who plans on using Flash, or anyone who won't use Flash for SEO reasons. Further, this book is for people who are already familiar with web design, but who may or may not be web design gurus. Essentially, this book is for you to beef up your web development skills regardless of whether you're a beginner or a pro.

Websites

After you've learned the techniques necessary to most effectively use Flash content on the Web, where do you go for the latest tips?

The Web is constantly changing, and so are the standards for using all different types of content on the Web. Here are some websites that I look to daily for up-to-date search engine optimization trends and techniques:

SEOmoz (http://www.seomoz.org/)
> This site has an amazing blog that is updated daily and provides access to industry trends, as well as information about using Flash on the Web.

All Things Adobe—The Chad and Todd Podcast (http://www.chadandtoddcast .com/)
> This is my video podcast's website, dedicated to providing video training for all Adobe products, including Flash. Here, you'll find useful (and free!) training about Flash on the Web.

Lynda.com (http://www.lynda.com/)
> This site is an amazing resource for video training. Not only will you find thousands of hours of software training, but you will also find training on SEO.

Who This Book Is Not For

This book is not for people who want to learn SEO for non-cool purposes, like phishing, or other shady web practices that attract people to your site for unholy reasons. Other than that, this book is not for people who want to learn web design from scratch. In other words, this is not a book on how to use Dreamweaver, Flash, or any other web design tools or languages. In fact, I'm going to assume you have at least some familiarity with web design before you start reading this book. See Table P-1.

Table P-1. Key terms defined

Term	Definition
Flash	Used as a general term to refer to Flash movies. Also the environment used to create Flash movies, such as Flash CS4.
Flash Player	Refers to a plug-in in a web browser required to play Flash movies.
SWF, Flash movie, Flash content, Flash application	Used synonymously to refer to content created in Flash.
Flash Video	Flash's native video file format, also known as FLV.
ActionScript 3.0	The native programming language of Flash CS4 and Flash Player 9 and above.
ActionScript 2.0	Native programming language of Flash Player 7 and 8.
HTML	Hyper Text Markup Language.
JavaScript	Generally used to control the behavior of a web page and to manipulate HTML data.
CSS	Cascading Style Sheets. A web standards compliant language used to style the content and layout of a web page.
PHP	A very powerful scripting language that can write HTML content as output.
SEO	Search Engine Optimization. Refers to the process of optimizing a web page for visibility to search engines.
Metadata	A definition or description of some data that helps provide context to the user. In terms of HTML, it refers to keywords and description for a page. In Flash, metadata holds information about a title and description of the content within the Flash movie.
Search engine	Refers to a website or web application that stores data from websites all over the Internet so that they may easily be found. Popular search engines include Google.com, Yahoo.com, and MSN.com.
Unobtrusive	As it relates to web design, refers to setting up a site that doesn't force the user to download plug-ins or change browser settings to view the content of the site.
W3C	World Wide Web Consortium. International standards organization for the Web.
Web Standards	A set of recommended best practices to use when developing websites, set out by the World Wide Web Consortium (W3C) at w3.org.

Conventions Used in This Book

The following typographical conventions are used in this book:

Italic

> Indicates new terms, URLs, email addresses, filenames, and file extensions.

`Constant width`

> Used for program listings, as well as within paragraphs to refer to program elements such as variable or function names, databases, data types, environment variables, statements, and keywords.

`Constant width bold`

> Shows commands or other text that should be typed literally by the user.

`Constant width italic`

> Shows text that should be replaced with user-supplied values or by values determined by context.

 This icon signifies a tip, suggestion, or general note.

 This icon indicates a warning or caution.

Using Code Examples

This book is here to help you get your job done. In general, you may use the code in this book in your programs and documentation. You do not need to contact us for permission unless you're reproducing a significant portion of the code. For example, writing a program that uses several chunks of code from this book does not require permission. Selling or distributing a CD-ROM of examples from O'Reilly books does require permission. Answering a question by citing this book and quoting example code does not require permission. Incorporating a significant amount of example code from this book into your product's documentation does require permission.

We appreciate, but do not require, attribution. An attribution usually includes the title, author, publisher, and ISBN. For example: "*Search Engine Optimization for Flash*, by Todd Perkins. Copyright 2009 Todd Perkins, 978-0-596-52252-0."

If you feel your use of code examples falls outside fair use or the permission given above, feel free to contact us at *permissions@oreilly.com*.

Safari® Enabled

When you see a Safari® Enabled icon on the cover of your favorite technology book, that means the book is available online through the O'Reilly Network Safari Bookshelf.

Safari offers a solution that's better than e-books. It's a virtual library that lets you easily search thousands of top tech books, cut and paste code samples, download chapters, and find quick answers when you need the most accurate, current information. Try it for free at *http://mysafaribooksonline.com*.

How to Contact Us

Please address comments and questions concerning this book to the publisher:

O'Reilly Media, Inc.
1005 Gravenstein Highway North
Sebastopol, CA 95472
800-998-9938 (in the United States or Canada)
707-829-0515 (international or local)
707-829-0104 (fax)

We have a web page for this book, where we list errata, examples, and any additional information. You can access this page at:

http://www.oreilly.com/catalog/9780596522520

To comment or ask technical questions about this book, send email to:

bookquestions@oreilly.com

For more information about our books, conferences, Resource Centers, and the O'Reilly Network, see our website at:

http://www.oreilly.com

CHAPTER 1

SEO Fundamentals

When you create a website, you want people to visit it. Your intent may be to make money by selling something on your site, by advertising something on your site, or through some other means. To drive traffic to your site, you need to effectively communicate the information in your site to search engines. Connecting your site to search engines correctly will help more people find your site, and eventually will result in whatever you want your website to accomplish for you.

This chapter focuses on establishing a good relationship with search engines and getting people to get to (and stay at) your site. To do these things, it's essential that you understand the relationships between search engines, your searchers, and your site.

Understanding How Search Engines Work

To create websites that are optimized for search engines, you'll need to understand the basics of how search engines work. Search engines have several facets that you should be familiar with, and you'll need to know the meaning of some key terms associated with the world of SEO. The following sections explain the basics of how search engines work.

Spiders

Search engines are powered by *spiders*—software that's designed to search for words throughout the Web. Spiders aren't physical creatures, nor are they robots. They're programs or applications.

Spiders are sent to web servers that are widely used. They go through pages on the server, following each link they find. This gets the spiders all over the Web very quickly. Spiders can search (or *crawl*) through hundreds of pages per second.

As the spiders go through the Web, they grab words on every web page, along with the context in which the words are used. For example, a spider could find the word *math* in a page's title, in a heading, or in a link. Based on the context of a word, the word is given more weight or relevance. As an example, words in a page's title get more weight than a random word used only once on the page.

 The way spiders view your pages is different from the way people view them. Spiders see pages as regular old HTML content, as though they were rendered by a text-only web browser such as Lynx (*http://lynx.isc.org/*). They cannot see images, click through Flash animations, or see text that's only viewable using JavaScript, as people can.

After the spiders capture the text and context data, that information is encoded (or compressed) and stored for you (or anyone) to find by performing a web search on sites you are likely to be very familiar with, such as Google, Yahoo!, and MSN.

Search Engine Results Pages (SERPs)

Search engine results pages, also known as *SERPs*, are the pages that show up when you do a web search on a site such as Google. When you perform a web search, pages show up based on how the information in your *keyword query* (the word(s) or phrase you're searching for) matches the information indexed by spiders (and the weight or relevance of said information) for that particular query. Figure 1-1 shows an example of a SERP for the keyword query *socks*.

SEO Versus SEM

SERPs are divided into two parts: paid results and non-paid results. Non-paid results are ranked based on the algorithms of the search engine spiders, as we already discussed. These results are often referred to as *organic search results*.

Paid results are based on several factors, most of which relate to the amount of money paid for the spot in the search results area. In other words, a higher spot typically costs more money. Popular keywords are more expensive than less popular keywords, because there's more competition to be at the top of a popular keyword search.

Generating organic results in SERPs is known as *search engine optimization*, or *SEO*. The process of doing research to rank high in organic search results as well as paid ads is called *search engine marketing*, or *SEM*.

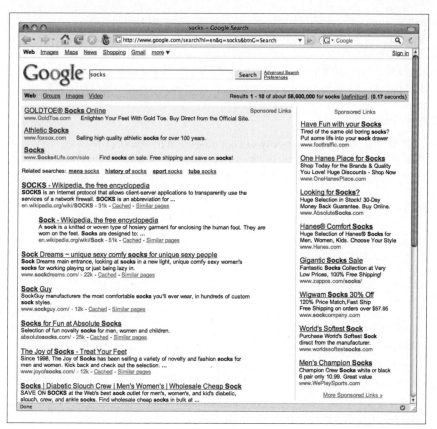

Figure 1-1. SERP generated from a search for socks

 Similar to SEO, SEM is a very broad topic. If you want to learn more about SEM, look in the webmaster sections of Google, Yahoo! or MSN.

What ads are paid?

Search engines are typically kind enough to let us know which results are paid advertising and which are organic. In this way, people can make informed decisions regarding what links they want to follow. For example, you may be looking for a great restaurant in a given area, and would prefer to make your choice based on what other people have said about the restaurant, rather than choosing the restaurant that paid for the top spot.

So, how do you know which ads are paid and which are organic? Figure 1-1 shows example search results from Google in a search for *socks*.

Notice the highlighted box near the top of the page in Figure 1-1. At the top right of that box are the words *Sponsored Links*. These ads are the highest paid for and most clicked ads of the sponsored ads. The rest of the sponsored ads are in the right column of the page, where you'll also notice the words *Sponsored Links*.

Who clicks the paid ads?

So, how many people actually click the paid ads? Reports tend to vary and change on a monthly basis, but typically it's somewhere in the ballpark of 10 percent to 15 percent clicking paid ads, with the other 85 percent to 90 percent clicking the organic search results. So, the great thing for us is that most people go with organic SEO over paid links anyway.

Should I pay for ads?

Although most people click the organic ads, it may be a good move for you to go with paid ads. This is especially true in a competitive market. For example, you may have a ton of competitors, but have a high turnover of site visits that result in sales. In that case, it may be worth it to pay for ads in favor of getting more business. Also remember that if your page is buried several pages deep in the SERPs, the vast majority of searchers won't ever see it. Statistics show that only around 20 percent of searchers move past the first page in search results, and that only about half of those searchers move on to the third page.

Page Rank, Relevance, and Popularity

When you perform a search on the Web, several factors determine the order of the results that you see. Regarding this, some key terms you should be familiar with are *page rank*, *relevance*, and *popularity*.

Page rank

Page rank refers to where links to your page stand in the SERPs. Page rank is decided based on a page's popularity and relevance.

Relevance

Relevance is how well a page matches your search query. For example, in a search for *pink fuzzy socks*, a page that specializes in pink fuzzy socks is more relevant than a page that sells a variety of socks, among them pink fuzzies.

Popularity

Popularity is measured by how many other pages link to your page. The popularity of a page can increase or decrease based on the other pages that link to it. For example, a link to your page from Amazon.com will increase your page's popularity (as well as page rank for that matter), whereas a link from Spamlinkfarm.com (or any site with a poor reputation) is more likely to hurt your page's standing.

You can also measure popularity in the opposite direction, with *outbound links* (links from your site to other sites). If you have links to Spamlinkfarm.com, or any other site with a bad reputation, search engines may view your site as being less credible.

Understanding Black Hat SEO

When optimizing your sites, understand that there are known acceptable practices called White Hat SEO (including all SEO methods taught in this book), as well as known unethical practices called Black Hat SEO. To avoid getting your pages removed from search engine indexes, and to be a proper citizen in the web design realm, never use any Black Hat techniques to boost your results in the SERPs. One Black Hat technique is to hide keywords from humans and reveal them to search engines using cascading style sheets (CSS). For example, a site may have keyword-rich text hidden using CSS or use CSS to make keyword-dense text at a font size so small it isn't readable by humans. Another example of Black Hat SEO is *cloaking*, which involves inserting code into web pages that delivers different content to search engines than it does to people. Again, always avoid Black Hat SEO, and be sure to research any methods that seem to be Black Hat.

Getting into a Searcher's Mind

Before you even start writing the content of your site, you need to understand how people actually search for content.

How do you establish trust with a site on the Web? I look for blog articles by searching for a specific question, rather than searching for Flash Blog. If I go to a blog and see that the design is awesome, the site is easy to navigate, and (most important) the site has answers to questions I might have in the future, I bookmark that site. If a site has poor design or poor usability, I see the site as less authoritative, so I bookmark and visit that site often only if it regularly provides answers to my questions.

Likely Visitors to Your Site

Before you optimize your site, you should know who you expect to visit your site. If your site is a high-tech blog about the geekiest stuff in the world, you might be safe in assuming that everyone who comes to your site is going to have the latest version of his browser. On the other hand, a search engine's site is likely to have people from all kinds of backgrounds, so the search engine site must be optimized for people with ancient versions of web browsers; the goal of the search engine is to ensure that the most people possible can use its services.

Along those lines, the demographic of your site's users can help you to know what plug-ins people have installed. This is especially important in terms of Flash content. I have a podcast site (*http://www.chadandtoddcast.com*) that I use to show people tips and tricks for Flash. Because people are coming to my site to learn the latest Flash tricks, I'm safe in assuming that they have current versions of Flash Player installed in their browsers, and I can put up the most cutting-edge Flash content on my site. A site like YouTube, however, has a much broader audience, including a mobile device audience, and even a video game console audience (the Nintendo Wii supports YouTube video via Flash Player 7). That means the content on YouTube must work on as many devices as possible. Therefore, to make YouTube content accessible to a greater number of people, the site uses an older version of Flash Player to play it.

So, before you even start to optimize your site, make sure you take some time to think about the type of user who will be viewing it. There are four main reasons people will come to your site: to buy, learn, do, or validate. What will your users be looking for on your site, and how can you best meet their needs?

What People Search For

When you're setting up your site for SEO, it's important to understand how people perform web searches. People usually start with general search terms, and then narrow their search as they get more information.

Let's consider an example. Someone planning to buy a computer monitor might start with a search for *computer monitor*. After noticing some popular monitors in the search results, the person might then search for a particular monitor to find more information about that monitor—for instance, the person might change the search from *computer monitor* to *Dell computer monitor*. The searcher may then notice that a particular monitor stands out, and decide to do a search for reviews on that model, ending with a search for *Dell 2209WFP review*. So, in a search starting with a general term such as *computer monitor*, the searcher is often looking for specific information, such as details regarding which monitor to buy.

As a website creator, you'll need to keep this in mind. The more specific you are in defining your products and services, the more likely you are to be found in a search. Sure, a search with broad terms is going to happen more often, but typically people are looking for specific things when they search on the Web. Consider the previous example of a search for *computer monitor*. The results can cover anything from buying and selling monitors, to the history of computer monitors, to configuring the colors on your monitor, and more. Seeing these results when looking for something specific, such as a product review, will cause a searcher to refine her search to fulfill her specific needs.

What does this mean to you? Though it's not bad to have pages that have general content, it's easier to get higher in search results with a more specific page.

Connecting with Your Searchers

What sites will people stay on or come back to? To answer this question, think about the websites that you frequently visit. Why do you go to those sites instead of competing sites? If the site is that of an online retailer, like Amazon.com, it may be because you know that retailer isn't going to rip you off. Maybe you feel safe buying from Amazon because you trust that its site is secure. Maybe you like the design of a particular site more than that of a competing site, or the design of the competing site looks old and outdated, so you don't trust that company as much. You might also visit a site because its information is reliable. You may avoid sites that have content that stinks of Black Hat SEO, or sites that are difficult to navigate.

Common through all of these scenarios is the idea of trust. Your site should be a place that people trust, due to its security, design, layout, and content.

Establishing trust through security

Keeping your site secure is a must, especially if you have a quickly growing site. Users need to feel safe on your site. This is crucial in terms of making purchases, but it also applies in other areas. Rapidly growing sites, such as MySpace.com, for example, have often been the target of hacking. Preventing hacking through solid code and password protection of pages is a must.

 We'll discuss solid code practices and protecting pages with passwords in more detail in Chapter 2.

In addition to protecting against hackers, your site should be as free as possible from spam. Spam can sneak in by way of comments on a blog, posts in a forum, and even profiles in a social network. To safeguard your site, you can install CAPTCHA, a picture-recognition-based registration package for posting comments and creating profiles.

 We will discuss how to install CAPTCHA in Chapter 2.

Establishing trust through design

High-quality site design is not just a more aesthetically pleasing experience for users; it can also add great credibility and trust to your site. One excellent example of a site that utilizes high-quality design is the Apple website, *http://www.apple.com/*. You can find other examples of good site design at *http://csszengarden.com/*. When creating the layout and design of your site, understand that it needs to be a positive experience for as many people as possible. Go out of your way to make sure your main content and navigation are easy to look at, good looking, of quality design, and are viewable by everyone.

One characteristic of a high-quality site is that it has easy-to-read text. This means the text on your site should not be on a busy or low-contrast background. In other words, keep lighter text on darker backgrounds and darker text on lighter backgrounds. A lot of sites with high-quality design use black or dark gray text on a white background. Avoid placing animated graphics close to text that you want a visitor to read, because animations can distract users' eyes when they are trying to read the content of your site.

Another important factor in high-quality design is the navigation of your site. Have you ever had trouble navigating a site? Sites that are hard to navigate are a huge turnoff to nearly everyone. If a searcher has difficulty navigating your site, she's likely to leave and unlikely to return. Make your navigation easy to find and easy to use. Have the most commonly used links on the home page of your site, nice and obvious for everyone to find. Avoid "mystery meat" navigation, navigation that forces your users to think about where your navigation is, or where the content might be located. If you have many pages on your site, consider using a subnavigation system to make all pages as easily accessible as possible. It is always best to avoid Flash-based navigation unless you provide some plain HTML as an alternative. That may sound like heresy to you, but remember that not everyone has Flash Player installed in his browser, and that a Flash navigation system that doesn't use text fields cannot be indexed. Some browsers (especially on mobile devices) don't even have

Flash Player plug-ins and may never have them. If your site requires Flash and does not provide an HTML alternative, you automatically lose much of the business and traffic you could otherwise get.

The Apple website makes great use of graphics. The photography is top-notch, and the design for the images is always astounding. Many sites have high-quality images, which add a lot to the aesthetics of the site. Be sure to use high-quality graphics on your site if you choose to use graphics. Whether you create them yourself or buy them from stock photography/graphics sites, make sure to use graphics that are visually pleasing. Even if it takes a little more time to get your site up, you won't regret it.

Establishing trust through content

It goes without saying that the content of your site should be of high quality, but what does that mean? Even though one of the purposes of your site may be to make money, it's not the best idea to have your site content screaming that message to visitors. Lots of sites have a large number of ads compared to content. If your ad-to-content ratio is off balance, consider removing some ads or adding more content.

High-quality content is content created for people, not search engines. Your pages should be written to give information your visitors consider valuable, not just to attract search engines. That means your pages should not be saturated with keywords or other things that make it obvious that you created your pages for search engines.

 For more information about creating high-quality content, see Chapter 2.

Connecting through community

These days, almost every site has a community. That is to say, people make comments on the site's blog, or sites offer ways in which users can interact with each other in some way. Why? Not only does this often make a site more interesting, but it also keeps people coming back.

Make your site something people can get addicted to. Think of MySpace and Facebook. People come to these sites and spend hours on them, because they want to interact with their friends, and see what other people are saying. These are multibillion-dollar sites that rely solely on community. As you browse the Web, note the communities on websites such as blogs and social networking sites, and consider ways in which you can add a sense of community to yours.

Not all sites require a community, but close examination of your site may reveal opportunities to build a community. If you're selling products, you can have a way for people to rate and review them. Write a blog that people can comment on or offer a way for people to subscribe to your site so that they can receive notification when you update it.

Connecting with the locals

Another way to connect to your searchers is to provide local search information to the search engines. Local searches apply to websites whose intent is to drive customers into a retail store or service station. If your site has that purpose, make sure to submit any local information you have, such as your business address and phone number, to the search engines.

 For more information about the process of submitting a local site to search engines, see Chapter 2.

You and SEO

With an understanding of the ways in which people and search engines conduct searches, you can begin to plan your SEO for your website. Planning a website, or redesigning a website for SEO purposes, requires that you consider important factors such as the design, layout, and usability of your site. The following subsections give insight into some of the most important features of top-notch SEO websites.

Effectively Choosing Keywords

Earlier in this chapter, I mentioned that searchers tend to search starting with broad terms, and then refine their search results by choosing more specific keywords to search for. Knowing that you want to optimize your site for specific keyword queries, you will have to judiciously pick the keywords you choose to associate with your site. But how do you choose those keywords? Further, how can you know which specific keywords are better than others?

Highly competitive keywords

Understand that some keywords, such as *news* and *software*, are not the best to use, even if all kinds of people are searching for those terms. When you use terms that are too broad in scope, you're likely to get buried in all the competition and never show up at all (or show up too far down the line to matter).

Other than the fact that the most common keywords are highly competitive, remember that more common keywords are typically general terms, so choosing them usually isn't the best decision anyway. As I mentioned earlier, choosing incredibly common keywords will result in you competing with sites you don't even need to compete with.

Unique keywords

I was in a punk band for several years. The name of my band was a made-up word—*wedgekase*. Don't ask me what it means. Do a search for that word and you won't find anything other than information about my band (there isn't much out there, by the way). You might not make up a word as wacky as *wedgekase*, but think of the word *iPod*, or any of Apple's programs that begins with a lowercase *i*. No one confuses them with anything else, because they're invented words. In other words, they're unique, so they have little or no competition. If your company, your product, or your site uses an invented word, or words no one is using, you're automatically at the top of the SERPs when you use that keyword effectively on your site.

Use online tools to see what people are searching for

Some tools on the Web can help you see what people are searching for, and you can base your keywords off that information. Following are three popular methods for finding keywords:

Google AdWords

Google AdWords is a paid service that allows you to get your ads into Google's search results. Though the service costs money and does not make your ads show up in organic search results, you can use the free AdWords keyword selector (*https://adwords.google.com/select/Keyword ToolExternal*) to see the popularity of search terms, including the monthly volume of searches for related queries as well as the relative number of competitive ads. You can then optimize your site based on that information.

Brainstorm

Consider meeting with some people from your company (or just putting in some "thought time" if your company is just you) to brainstorm some ideas for keywords. Take the time to consider what keywords you want to use to bring traffic to your site. Remember that unique keywords will help you rise to the top. Of course, you can do this in conjunction with online keyword help tools such as Wordtracker.

Hire outside help

Many SEO experts out there can help you come up with effective keywords for your site. You don't necessarily need to hire someone to find keywords for you, but you might find it helpful if you're having trouble coming up with them. Remember that you need to have the appropriate keywords and phrases throughout your content and page titles to get people on your site, so it may be worth it to pay for help if you're having trouble finding effective keywords.

Important Parts of a Site

Earlier in this chapter, I mentioned that high-quality sites often have some common features like security, quality design, and community. When you're designing your website, you should keep those in mind. Here are some other important aspects of your site that you may not have considered.

Design

In addition to gaining trust, as I mentioned earlier in this chapter, high-quality design on a site can say something about your site's content. Professional design shows people that you can afford to create an attractive-looking site, and therefore that you must mean business. Granted, not every well-designed site is legitimate, but design can definitely give you an edge over your competitors and enhance your brand.

Typography

One important aspect of your site's design is the *typography* used. Typography refers to all aspects of text in your site, including fonts, font sizes, and the layout of text. When using HTML, make sure the fonts you use are viewable by everyone who views your site, and that you include lists of fonts in your design in case someone doesn't have the main font you want him to see.

In Chapter 2, we'll discuss creating lists of fonts in detail. For information about common fonts used on the Web, see the following article: *http://www.wildwoodinteractive.com/rc_common_fonts.php*.

When using Flash, remember that it's more important for someone to be able to read the fonts you use than it is for the font to look cool. If someone has trouble reading text in your Flash movie, he may leave your site.

Another good practice for typography is to make fonts big enough so that everyone can view them. Font sizes run a little smaller on a Mac than on a PC, so make sure to test your site on both platforms if you can.

You can also group your content into related sections and use headings to organize them. Remember that people reading content on the Web typically skim more often than they read everything, so making the process easier using grouping will give you a better site. Another thing you can do to make your site content easier to read is to make sure blocks of text are not in wide columns. Opinions vary as to how wide columns of text should be, but most agree that columns should be somewhere between 400 and 600 pixels wide.

 See Chapter 2 for more information about controlling the width of text columns.

Accessibility

The more traffic you get, the better. When designing your site, keep accessibility in mind. Creating an accessible site will allow the most people to view your content through the most means possible. If you can design a version of your site for mobile devices, you can get more traffic than if you design it only for computers. Keep this in mind when publishing Flash content. Some devices support less robust versions of Flash (such as Flash Player 7 or Flash Lite), so it's best to use cutting-edge Flash in the computer version of your site and target your Flash content to mobile devices based on the version of Flash Player the mobile device is running. You can set this up using HTML and JavaScript. When a user requests a page, you can use HTML and JavaScript to check what type of reader or browser a person is using, and display content that can be read by it. Though it may take a little more time to create all the content of your site, it can also generate more traffic.

Additionally, and perhaps more importantly, content should be accessible to all people. Consider having closed captioning for Flash movies on your sites for those who are hearing impaired, and a way to adjust font sizes for those who are visually impaired.

 For more details about how to write the code for an accessible site, see Chapter 2.

Usability

Even if your site is accessible to all people on all devices, people may choose to leave your site quickly if the layout is not easy to use. Usability is an extremely important aspect of web design, and it is essential in SEO. Your site should be easy to navigate and should not require plug-ins (including Flash) or JavaScript to move through it. If you must use Flash or JavaScript for navigation in your site, you should include some text-only navigation as well. That way, people without Flash or JavaScript can still navigate through your pages.

You often can increase the usability of a site dramatically by simply changing some text. If your site requires that people do something, such as create an account before using your services, you can make the text that tells them what to do extremely obvious and easy to read. For example, consider popular blog sites such as Blogger and WordPress. The main feature of these sites is blog creation, so when you go to their home pages (*http://www.blogger.com* for Blogger, shown in Figure 1-2), you'll see a large portion of the page calling you to the action of creating a blog, and outlining the steps you need to take to create one.

Figure 1-2. Blogger's home page with an excellent call to action

When creating your site, make usability a priority. Even a site that is flawless in every other regard can lose great amounts of traffic due to bad usability.

Usability is a very broad topic, and entire books are devoted to it. For more information about usability, and for examples of adding it to your site, see Chapter 2.

Site search

One great feature that almost every (if not every) high-quality site has is the ability to search the site. Site searches are especially important when you have a lot of content in your site. But regardless of your site's size, it can't hurt to add a search bar. Don't worry if you don't know how to write the code to perform a search of your site; there are plenty of free tools you can use to add this capability pretty easily.

 Chapter 2 provides detailed information about adding a search bar to your site.

Ways to Track SEO on Your Site

Search engines want your site to be optimized and accurately represent the information they contain, so many search engines have a plethora of tools for you to track SEO. One tool is Google Analytics, which you can find at *http://www.google.com/analytics/*. This tool shows you how many people get to your site from Google and what search queries they used to find your site.

Keeping Up with the Latest Info

As an SEO wizard, you'll want to keep up with the latest information on the topic. This is especially important in the world of SEO, or anything technology-related, because technology is always changing. What works today might not work so well 10 years from now. That's why you have to keep up the good work and follow the leaders in this field. Here's a look at some great places to check often to make sure you're staying up-to-date.

The following sites have information straight from the source (Google and MSN) on creating SEO sites:

- *http://www.google.com/webmasters/*
- *http://webmaster.live.com/*

The best place to go for facts is to the source of the information (i.e., Google and MSN). If you want opinions from professionals in the industry, you can find some great blogs and whitepapers at these sites:

- *http://www.seomoz.org/*
- *http://searchenginewatch.com/*
- *http://www.enquiro.com/*

You can also find some great forums on these sites:

- *http://www.cre8asiteforums.com/*
- *http://www.highrankings.com/forum/*
- *http://forums.digitalpoint.com/*

Key Terms Used in This Chapter

Table 1-1 contains the terms that were introduced in this chapter and gives you their definitions.

Table 1-1. Key terms used in this chapter

Term	Definition
Algorithm	An automated system for working with data. In search engines, refers to how spiders view and analyze page data.
CAPTCHA	A picture-based system used when filling out forms on the Web for preventing spam.
Keyword query	A search term made in a search engine.
Organic search results	Non-paid results that show up in SERPs.
Outbound/inbound links	Links that are from your site to another site (outbound) or from another site to your site (inbound).
SEM	Search engine marketing. Involves all paid search results.
SERPs	Search engine results pages. Pages that are displayed after a keyword query is performed in a search engine.
Spider	Software robot that captures and stores data from web pages.
Typography	The art of type. Refers to fonts, font colors, font sizes, and font layout.
Webmaster	The head person (or people) in charge of maintaining or creating a website.

Creating an SEO Website

Most of your role in search engine optimization (SEO) deals with how you write the HTML code for your website. To optimize your website for search engines, you'll need to have a few handy tricks up your sleeve. This chapter is practice for you to begin writing HTML code that's optimized for search engines. In addition, you'll learn how to communicate directly to search engine spiders by creating a sitemap and a *robots.txt* file.

Search Engines and HTML Code

The most important factor for determining your page rank in the search engine results pages (SERPs) is based on your HTML code. Let me say that again: your HTML code is the most important factor in your page's rank, credibility, and potential to be searchable. With the right HTML code, your rank will soar. Following are examples of HTML code that can impact where your page ranks in the SERPs.

Page Titles

As far as HTML is concerned, the most important factor in SEO is the title of your page. The *page title* is the heading at the top of the browser window when people view a page, and it's defined by the title element, or title tag, in the HTML of a page.

You probably don't spend much time staring at the top of your browser window, so how could a page's title matter so much? Page titles are crucial in SEO because they're the biggest text in the SERPs. Figure 2-1 shows the SERP for the keyword query *science*. Notice the text "Science for Kids" and all the large, blue, underlined links on the SERP. Those are page titles. Page titles are the most obvious form of communication to your searchers.

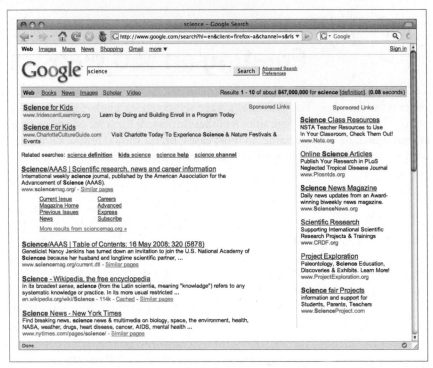

Figure 2-1. Example of title element shown in a SERP

Adding page titles to HTML code

You insert page titles into HTML in a title element within the head element, or *head tag*:

```
<head>
    <title>This is the title of the page</title>
</head>
```

Here's what a page title looks like in the context of a simple HTML page:

```
<html>
<head>
    <title>This is the title of the page</title>
</head>
<body>
    This is the body of the page
</body>
</html>
```

Choosing an effective page title

The page title is the most crucial element on which to focus because it is the most prominent part of your listing in the SERPs. It is also the only element over which you have complete control. If you don't have time to come up with the most effective page title possible, you should at least give your page a title. If you don't, it may be named "Untitled Document" or the name of your HTML file. This can do great harm to the SEO of your site.

The most prominent part of a page title should be a keyword connected to the content on the page. For example, a page selling shoes might have the keywords "Buy Shoes" in a page title. Another important element of a page title is your *brand*, or website name. In most cases, brand should follow keywords with some separating character(s). For example, a site called *Buysomeshoeshere.com* might advertise shoes in a page title as such: "Buy Shoes | buysomeshoeshere.com".

 Of course, you can use vertical pipes (|) as separators, along with colons (:), hyphens (-), greater than (>) or less than (<) symbols, or any other characters or combination of characters without regard to SEO.

Although branding is typically less important in a page title than keywords, at times you may find better results by putting your brand name first. For example, if your brand is what drives traffic to your site, you may want it first in your page title.

Working with Links

Links build the Web by connecting pages. They're key in SEO because they communicate information to spiders about a particular link. The following section explains the various aspects of a link, which you should be familiar with for optimization purposes.

Writing links

Links in HTML are fairly simple. You create them using the `<a>` (which stands for anchor) tag. A link must contain at least one attribute, `href`, which represents the location of the link, or where the link is directed. Inside the opening and closing anchor tags, you can place the link text, or the text the site visitor clicks to activate the link. Here's what a link to *http://www.somesite.com* looks like in HTML code:

```
<a href="http://www.somesite.com">This is a link to some site</a>
```

Understanding the link voting system

When spiders are crawling your pages, links on your pages act as votes for the pages to which they're linked. This voting process connects a URL with keywords. For example, the following link tells spiders that *http://www.amazon .com* is a site that has something to do with the phrase "buy dvds" because of the link text:

```
<a href="http://www.amazon.com">buy dvds</a>
```

Links to your site are great, especially if the text used in the links from other sites includes keywords you want associated with your site.

Working with link attributes

HTML allows you to connect links with keywords, which can be a great help for SEO and accessibility purposes. You can connect keywords to links via the `<a>` tag's `title` attribute. Consider the following example:

```
<a href="http://www.amazon.com" title="Buy my DVDs online">you can buy
my DVDs online</a>
```

In this example, the keyword is "DVDs" and the link text is "you can buy my DVDs online". Using the `title` attribute, the example tells search engines that the keyword for this link is "DVDs," so the search engines won't be left to turn the entire phrase within the link text into keywords associated with the link.

Another useful link attribute and value is `rel="nofollow"`. Using `nofollow`, you can tell search engine spiders not to follow a certain link. Links that aren't followed don't count for or against you. That way, you can link to any site you want on your pages for any number of reasons without losing any credibility with search engines.

Here's what the HTML code looks like when you use `rel="nofollow"`:

```
<a href="http://www.somerandomsite.com" title="basketball game"
rel="nofollow">look at what this guy had to say about it</a>
```

Inbound links

Links coming from another site (or even from elsewhere within your site) to your site are called *inbound links*. You typically don't have full control over what link text is used in inbound links (other than from search engines and from your own site). Inbound links from low-quality or spam sites will reduce your page's rank, whereas links from high-quality sites can increase your page rank. Of course, the text of the inbound link and the keywords connected to your page can affect your page rank as well. For example, if multiple people set up a link to your website using the link text "worst site ever," your page may be affected poorly because your site will be more likely to show up in searches for "worst site".

Outbound links

Outbound links are links from your site to external websites. The quality and quantity of outbound links in your pages can affect the page's SEO. Obviously, links to spam sites can decrease your legitimate page's credibility, since a vote associated with an illegitimate site makes it more likely that your site is illegitimate as well. If you want to use links to illegitimate sites for some reason, make sure to tell the spiders not to follow the links by using the `nofollow` attribute.

Link limits

As I just mentioned in the previous section, the *quantity* of links on your pages can negatively affect your pages. Too many unique links make it appear to search engines that your page is simply a spam link farm. To stay in line, it's best to keep the number of unique links on a page at or below 100.

Headings

Heading tags have six levels, starting with heading 1 (the `h1` element, which is the largest) and ending with heading 6 (the `h6` element, which is the smallest). Search engines put considerable weight on page headings that contain keywords, especially bigger headings such as `<h1>` and `<h2>`. Smaller headings don't have the same search value, but all headings can still provide a great way to group the information on your pages.

Creating h1, h2, and h3 elements

Adding a heading to an HTML file is pretty simple. You can add headings anywhere within the **body** element. Here's what a heading 1 element looks like in HTML code:

```
<h1>Here's a heading 1 heading</h1>
```

Other than the tag name, there's no difference between any of the heading tags:

```
<h2>Heading 2, in all its glory!</h2>
<h6>No special code for other headings, like this h6</h6>
```

Bold/Strong Text

Bold text, or text within `<b>` (bold) or `<strong>` tags, tends to add extra weight when it contains keywords to which you want to give special attention. Both `<b>` and `<strong>` elements carry the same weight as far as SEO is concerned.

 The `<b>` tag is deprecated in XHTML, and there are important reasons for it. Using the `<strong>` element favored over using the `<b>` element for to separate style from structure. Another reason the `<strong>` tag is preferred is because of HTML semantics. For example, you may want some text to stand out to readers and search engines, but you may not want it to appear in bold. By choosing `<strong>` over `<b>`, you aren't necessarily telling a web browser that the content should be displayed in bold, thus separating semantics (code that associates a tag with the content it should contain, such as `<h1>` tags for headings, `<p>` for paragraphs, etc.) from presentation. Of course, regardless of which element you use, you can still control the look of the content using CSS.

Creating bold and strong elements

Both `<b>` and `<strong>` elements are very easy to use in HTML. Here's what bold `<b>` text looks like in HTML:

```
<b>This is some bold text</b>
```

And here's what `<strong>` text looks like:

```
<strong>Here's some strong text</strong>
```

Emphasized Text

Emphasized text, or text within `<i>` (italic) or `<em>` tags, gives a little boost as well if you wrap keywords in them. Both `<i>` and `<em>` text carry the same weight in SEO. You don't need to overuse these for SEO purposes (or overuse any HTML tags, for that matter), but they can help nonetheless.

 Just like the `<strong>` tag is preferred over the `<b>` tag for semantic reasons and because of deprecation, the `<em>` tag is preferred over the `<i>` tag for the same reasons. Also, you can control the style of both (be it italic, or anything else) via CSS.

Creating emphasized elements

Like <b> and <strong> elements, <i> and <em> elements are easy to use. Simply wrap the text you want to emphasize in the proper opening and closing tags. Here's an example of using the <i> tag in HTML:

```
<i>This text is what? Italic</i>
```

Here's an example of the <em> tag:

```
<em>This text is emphasized</em>
```

Images

Include information about the images you place on your pages to improve SEO as well as accessibility on your site. The big secret in image SEO is the use of the alt attribute. The alt attribute, besides associating keywords with an image for SEO purposes, tells the browser what text to display (or read) if an image is not viewable. For example, if a person is browsing your site using a *screen reader*. A *screen reader* is a computer program typically used by the visually impaired that converts text to speech. If a person is browsing your site this way, the screen reader will read the alt text for the person.

The alt text should contain keywords that are relevant to the image to be useful for SEO.

Images and the alt attribute in HTML

Images are fairly simple to use in HTML code, and they can be useful tools for SEO as well. You can connect keywords to images through filenames and the alt attribute. Simply use the <img> tag and set the value of the src attribute to the path of the image file. Here's an example of an image element in HTML, displaying a file called *dog.jpg*:

```
<image src="dog.jpg"/>
```

Here's what an image reference with a connected keyword via the alt attribute looks like in HTML code:

```
<img src="dog.jpg" alt="Dog"/>
```

As we will discuss later in this chapter, you can also include keywords in your image filenames to better optimize your site. Here, the filename *dog.jpg* further emphasizes the connection of the word *dog* to this image.

Metadata

Metadata includes information about a web page, including its description and associated keywords. Early in the days of the Web, metadata was all the rage, and it was the most important part of SEO for a page. Today, metadata has somewhat lost its flair—especially keyword metadata. Even so, it's best to include metadata on your pages, especially in the page description.

Using keyword metadata

Keyword metadata is a list of keywords to associate with your web page. Again, this is not the SEO powerhouse it used to be, but it can help a little. If you need keywords, you can use the keywords you're already using in your site for SEO purposes. If you don't have those keywords planned out already, follow the keyword creation tips in Chapter 1 to create somewhere between three and eight of them.

Google does not use meta keywords, but other popular search engines, such as Yahoo!, still claim to utilize them.

Keywords in HTML code

Adding metadata keywords to your HTML code, like just about everything else in HTML, is pretty straightforward. Simply insert a <meta> tag inside the <head> tag, use Keywords as the value for the title attribute. Comma-separate your keywords in the content attribute. Here's an example of keyword metadata in a <meta> tag:

```
<meta name="Keywords" content="dogs,cats,pets" />
```

Creating a metadata description

The metadata description is essential for SEO. A metadata description has more weight than keywords do, plus a page's metadata description is often used as a description on the SERPs. Other information is also sometimes used as a description on an SERP. More about that below. Each page's description should be unique to that page. If you're using a web page creation tool, such as Dreamweaver, make sure your page descriptions can be changed on each page instead of being confined to one description in a template.

Metadata descriptions in HTML code

Like keyword metadata, description metadata uses the `<meta>` element with the `title` and `content` attributes. In a description, the `title` element has a value of `Description`. Here's an example of a metadata description:

```
<meta name="Description" content=
"For centuries, dogs and cats have been used as pets" />
```

Controlling spiders via metadata

Earlier I mentioned that the SERPs *often* use description metadata. Sometimes, however, search engines use other information for page descriptions.

One source of these descriptions is directory listings, which we'll discuss in detail later in this chapter. If you want to be in control of your page descriptions, you can tell spiders not to grab an external description for your page.

Writing the code to tell spiders not to use directory information for your page descriptions is simple. The `<meta>` tag gives you the power to speak directly to search engine spiders. Use the `<meta>` tag as you would for a page's keywords or description; for `name` give a value of `robots`, and for `content` give a value of `noodp` (short for "no open directory project"). Here's an example of the code:

```
<meta name="robots" content="noodp" />
```

Yahoo! has its own directory, and it requires a different command to tell its spiders to use your descriptions over the descriptions in its directory. Luckily, it's nearly identical to the previous code. To tell Yahoo! not to use its directory listings for your page's description, use the following code:

```
<meta name="robots" content="noydir" />
```

Another way spiders (specifically, Google) change the description of your page is by showing a snippet of your page under your page title in the SERPs. Though this isn't necessarily a bad thing, because your content should reflect your description, you don't have control over which snippets are used. If you want to make sure your meta description shows rather than a snippet, you can give instructions to Google's spiders.

Telling Google's spiders not to use snippets for your page descriptions is easy. Just use the `<meta>` tag with a value of `robots` for `name` and a value of `nosnippet` for `content`. Your code should look like this:

```
<meta name="robots" content="nosnippet" />
```

 You can also use `robots` metadata to tell spiders not to index a page. I discuss this in more detail later in this chapter.

File Sizes

Your HTML files, excluding images or linked file sizes, should not exceed 150 KB. Large HTML files can hurt page rankings.

If a file or folder name contains keywords for which a user searched, those keywords are bolded in that file or folder name. Searchers are much more likely to click on a link if they see a page filename containing their desired keywords bolded.

For those reasons, it's important to name all the files and folders in your website effectively.

When naming files and folders, don't use spaces to separate words. If you need to separate them, use hyphens. You *can* use underscores as well, but it's not a best practice because there is some research showing that search engines don't separate words that are separated with underscores. For example, a person may have to search for *purple_monkey_dishwasher* to find your file *purple_monkey_dishwasher.html*, whereas separating the filename using hyphens would allow a person to search for the words separately. Also, underscores might get lost when manually copied if the link text happens to be underlined.

Though it's irrelevant to SEO, it's also easier to say the word "dash" than "underscore" if you're telling someone a URL.

Understanding file and folder syntax

When you browse to *www.randomsite.com/*, you're actually viewing the file that's configured as the default file for that site, such as *http://www.randomsite.com/index.html*. If no default file is specified, web servers automatically look for one of three filenames within a folder: index, default, or home.

For your links, you may not want someone to see the actual filename of your page if it's something such as *index.html* or *default.php*. Rather, you may want just a folder name to be visible. For example, you may want the URL to look like *www.randomsite.com/random-folder/* instead of *www.randomsite.com/random-folder/index.html*. In your site, you can do that by removing the name of the file from your link. It's a best practice to tell a web browser that */random-folder/* is a folder, by ending the link with a forward slash (/), even though browsing to a folder without a trailing slash will still navigate to that folder.

It can be bad for SEO when a file is buried in a long folder structure. When you're setting up the structure of your site, make sure files aren't buried more than four folders deep.

Consolidating URLs

Currently, search engines may see *http://yoursite.com* (no *www*) and *http://www.yoursite.com* as two different sites. Because of that, your rankings could be split in half. To capture all the rankings and maintain them in one site, you can use some server-side code to direct all visits to display either the *www* (recommended) URL of your site or the non-*www* URL. The process varies a little depending on which server you're using.

The following example shows how to redirect URLs using servers running Apache. For servers without Apache, visit your website's control panel and see information about how to redirect URLs.

URL rewriting works on Apache and IIS servers. Here's how it works on servers running Apache, which is most likely the case on your server: Begin by creating a blank text file, and name it *.htaccess* (the period [.] is the first character in the filename). If your operating system doesn't allow you to create a file beginning with a period, you can change the filename after you upload it, so name it *htaccess.txt*. Open the file in a plain-text editor, such as Notepad (Windows), TextEdit (Mac), or Dreamweaver. Then, add the following code to the file, swapping *yoursite.com* with your actual site:

```
Options +FollowSymLinks
RewriteEngine on
RewriteCond %{HTTP_HOST} .
RewriteCond %{HTTP_HOST} ^yoursite\.com [NC]
RewriteRule ^(.*)$ http://www.yoursite.com/$1 [R=301,L]
```

Modify the code on the last line by removing the *www* if you don't want *www* in your site's consolidated URL.

Once you have that code, save the file and upload it to your site's root directory using ASCII format (not binary, which may be the default) in your FTP program. If you're not sure how to ensure that the file is uploaded in ASCII, see the Preferences section of your FTP software. Also, you may need to tell your FTP program to show hidden files (typically via Preferences) to view *.htaccess*. Make sure to change the file's name to *.htaccess* if you started out calling it *htaccess.txt*. After the file is uploaded, visit your site without entering *www* at the beginning of your site address in your web browser and notice the *www* URL display in the browser window.

 The exercises at the end of this chapter provide examples of consolidating URLs.

Don't Forget the Content

More important than anything in SEO is the content of your page. Why do you go to any page on the Web? It's because of the information contained in the page, its content. Make sure your page isn't bloated with too many keywords or excessive content that's built only for search engines. It's important that your page is attractive to people, not just search engines. It needs to make sense to the end user: the human being who's looking for the information you provide.

On the other hand, if your content doesn't actually contain your keywords, you should rework your content or your keywords, or both, to make sure your keywords accurately represent your content.

Always remember that the real goal of SEO is to accurately portray the information on your pages, and when you do that properly, you'll inevitably create quality content.

Sitemaps

Sometimes your web pages can get lost in the mix because there aren't many links to them, because they're new pages, or because of the content contained within the pages (i.e., dynamic content, Flash content, AJAX, or other media). Search engines can find out about these pages through a *sitemap*, a file containing information about pages on your site that you want search engines to index. Sitemap files can be in XML or plain-text format, and they require a special syntax to work properly.

 XML, or eXtensible Markup Language, is somewhat similar to HTML, which is used to represent data in a simple, organized, universally accessible way. XML files are simply text files that contain XML code, saved with the *.xml* extension.

Plain-text files refer to files created in a text editor that contain only text, and have a *.txt* extension.

Along with using a sitemap to tell search engines about your pages, you can optionally add extra information about each page. The information can include when the page was last modified, how often the page is updated, and how the page's importance ranks in relation to the other pages on your site.

 Many search engines, including Google, Yahoo!, and MSN, follow the sitemap standards at *http://www.sitemaps.org*. You can find more information on sitemaps and sitemap standards on that site.

Why You Need a Sitemap

Sitemaps are great for pages that are more difficult for search engines to index. This includes pages with Flash, AJAX, and dynamic content. If you have pages that utilize any of these technologies, it's a good idea to create a sitemap. Although it's not guaranteed that search engines will index every page in your sitemap, creating one won't hurt your rankings, so you may find it makes sense to create one.

Creating a Sitemap

All you need to create a sitemap is a plain-text editor, such as TextEdit on the Mac or Notepad on the PC. As I mentioned earlier, there are two types of sitemaps: XML and plain text. The creation process is slightly different depending on which type of sitemap you decide to create.

 Some websites, such as *http://www.xml-sitemaps.com/*, create sitemaps for you by giving you cut-and-paste text to put into an XML file and upload to your site. This is a great option, especially if you want to create a sitemap quickly.

Creating an XML-Based Sitemap

Following is an example of an XML-based sitemap.

File: *sitemap.xml*

```
<?xml version="1.0" encoding="UTF-8"?>
<urlset xmlns="http://www.sitemaps.org/schemas/sitemap/0.9">
    <url>
        <loc>http://www.yoursite.com/page1.html</loc>
        <lastmod>2008-01-01</lastmod>
        <changefreq>hourly</changefreq>
        <priority>1</priority>
    </url>
```

```
<url>
    <loc>http://www.yoursite.com/page2.html</loc>
    <lastmod>2008-02-01</lastmod>
    <changefreq>weekly</changefreq>
    <priority>0.5</priority>
</url>
<url>
    <loc>http://www.yoursite.com/page3.html</loc>
    <lastmod>2008-03-01</lastmod>
    <changefreq>monthly</changefreq>
    <priority>0.2</priority>
</url>
</urlset>
```

Here's a walkthrough of the preceding code.

```
<?xml version="1.0" encoding="UTF-8"?>
```

This line is standard as the first line in an XML file, and it includes information about the XML version used in the file and how the text data is encoded.

```
<urlset xmlns="http://www.sitemaps.org/schemas/sitemap/0.9">
...(code not shown here)
</urlset>
```

This code defines a set of URLs for your sitemap, in the urlset element. The xmlns attribute defines an *XML namespace*, a syntax standard unique to the URL value. This namespace is the http://www.sitemaps.org/schemas/sitemap/0.9 namespace.

```
<url>
    ...(code not shown here)
</url>
```

The url tag defines a URL in your sitemap. Except for the required URL location element, all other elements are optional.

```
<loc>http://www.yoursite.com/page1.html</loc>
```

The loc element contains the location of a URL in your sitemap. In this example, the URL is *http://www.yoursite.com/page1.html*. Each url element must at least contain the loc element.

```
<lastmod>2008-01-01</lastmod>
```

This element, lastmod, contains the date that the URL from the loc element, was last modified. The format for the date is YYYY-MM-DD, or a four-digit year, a two-digit month, and a two-digit date, separated by hyphens. This date represents January 1, 2008.

```
<changefreq>weekly</changefreq>
```

The changefreq element refers to how often the page is updated, or its change frequency. For example, this code declares that the URL is updated weekly. Valid values for changefreq are as follows:

- always
- hourly
- daily
- weekly
- monthly
- yearly
- never

It's important to note that declaring your page's change frequency doesn't necessarily mean search engine spiders will index your page as often as they're updated. This is more of a guideline for them. In fact, spiders will occasionally crawl pages that have a value of never, just in case any changes have been made.

```
<priority>0.2</priority>
```

The priority element dictates a page's importance relative to other pages in your sitemap. This element has a default value of 0.5, and it ranges from 0 to 1. Giving your pages higher-priority ratings doesn't mean the pages will rank higher than other sites in search engine results. Rather, this is for the sitemap to choose which pages on your site are more important than their pages on your site. This is a means of controlling which of your pages get priority over your other pages in the results pages. Pages with higher priority will show up higher than pages with lower priority.

 All major search engines (Google, Yahoo!, and MSN) use the same sitemap syntax, so you don't have to create a unique sitemap for each search engine.

In summary, remember to declare the XML version and the encoding, keep url elements in a urlset element, make sure to declare the namespace, and include at least the loc element inside each url.

 You can declare a maximum of 50,000 URLs in a sitemap.

If you have a lot of URLs in your sitemap, you may want to consider creating multiple sitemaps and linking them together. You can find instructions for doing that at *http://www .sitemaps.org*.

Warning: special characters

When creating an XML sitemap, or any XML file, for that matter, certain characters aren't allowed because they're reserved XML characters. To use these characters in an XML file, characters such as <, for example, you must *escape* them by using special syntax to represent them. Table 2-1 shows which characters must be escaped and how to escape them.

Table 2-1. Characters that must be escaped

Character	Escape code
&	&amp;
' (single quote)	&apos;
" (double quote)	&quot;
<	&lt;
>	&gt;

Most likely, the only character escaping you'll need to do when creating a sitemap is for a dynamic URL. For example, you may want to include a page that keeps track of a person's username and ID, so your page URL may look like this:

```
http://www.yourwebsite.com/index.php?user=someone&id=83736
```

To separate URL parameters, `user` and `id` in this case, you need to use an ampersand (&). To escape an ampersand, use the escape code &. Your sitemap code would then need to look like this:

```
<loc>http://www.yourwebsite.com/index.php?user=someone&amp;id=83736</loc>
```

 Even though problems with escaping characters may not be immediately obvious to you, and may not cause errors when you submit your sitemap, it's important to double-check your URLs to make sure the proper characters are escaped.

Creating a Plain-Text Sitemap

A plain-text sitemap is much simpler than an XML sitemap, but it offers you less control. Using a plain-text sitemap lets you specify one URL on each line.

Following is an example of a plain-text sitemap.

File: *sitemap.txt*

```
http://www.yoursite.com/page1.html
http://www.yoursite.com/page2.html
http://www.yoursite.com/page3.html
```

Your plain-text sitemap should contain only the URLs for the pages on your site. Don't include header, footer, or any other text in your plain-text sitemap.

Placing Your Sitemap

Your sitemap should be in the highest directory level that you want to be indexed. For example, if you want your entire site to be indexed, you'd put your sitemap in your root directory. If your domain was Yoursite.com (*http://Your site.com*) and your sitemap file was called *sitemap.xml*, the URL to your sitemap would be:

```
http://www.yoursite.com/sitemap.xml
```

 Search engines will automatically look for a sitemap called *sitemap.xml* at the root directory of your server, so if you put it here you can skip the process of submitting your sitemap.

Sometimes you may only want part of your site to be indexed. For example, you may have several folders on your web server that are password-protected and one folder for the public to view. In this case, you'd put your sitemap in the public folder. Here's an example of what the URL to your sitemap would be if you were to call the sitemap file *sitemap.xml* and the public folder *public*:

```
http://www.yoursite.com/public/sitemap.xml
```

Submitting a Sitemap

For Google, you can log in to your Webmaster Tools account (assuming you've created an account) at *http://www.google.com/webmasters* and give Google the URL to your sitemap. The process is the same for MSN. Log in to Webmaster Tools at *http://webmaster.live.com*, and submit your website and sitemap URL. To submit your sitemap to Yahoo!, go to *https://siteexplorer.search.yahoo.com/ submit*, submit your site, and submit your sitemap in the Submit Site Feed area.

Once you've submitted your sitemap, the search engines will do the rest of the work for you. Although it's not guaranteed that submitting a sitemap will force spiders to crawl all of your pages, it still gives you more control over what pages are indexed and how they rank in relation to other pages on your site.

 Again, search engine spiders automatically look for sitemaps called *sitemap.xml* at the root level of your website.

Preventing Spiders from Indexing Pages

You may not want spiders to crawl all the pages of your site, but simply omitting those pages in your sitemap doesn't mean spiders won't crawl them. For that reason, search engines have a way for you to communicate to spiders, telling them to ignore certain pages of your site while crawling.

> Why wouldn't you want spiders to crawl through all the pages of your site? One reason is to keep spiders from indexing duplicate pages. If spiders find duplicate pages on your site, the pages can potentially be viewed as spam, and that could get you banned from search engines.
>
> You might have duplicate pages for many reasons. For example, you may be creating a new version of your site, and you may be using the same content in multiple pages for testing purposes.

You can communicate with search engine spiders through a text file, which you can create and store on your web-hosting server. The file, *robots.txt*, contains information about pages the spiders shouldn't index. It's essentially the exact opposite of a sitemap.

> The information to block pages in the *robots.txt* file is a request only search engine spiders follow. If you're requesting that search engines not search your pages because the pages contain confidential information, it's best to store those pages in a password-protected directory on your server. That way, spambots and other malicious web predators don't have access to those pages.

Creating a robots.txt File

You can create the *robots.txt* file, or have a search engine, such as Google, create it for you. Information about each process is available via the Google site in the Webmaster Tools section, which you can find at *http://www.google .com/webmasters/*. The Help section contains information about creating your own *robots.txt* file. Through the Tools section, you can create an account for your website and Google will create the file for you. Full documentation for *robots.txt* files is available at *http://www.robotstxt.org*.

Search engines' Webmaster Tools are a great resource for you in building a website. They can provide you with useful information about SEO, as well as additional great web-building tips and tricks straight from the horse's mouth.

Once you have the *robots.txt* file, follow the instructions on the Google, Yahoo!, or MSN webmaster site to test the file and get it onto your website.

Your *robots.txt* file can also contain information about where your sitemap is stored.

Here's an example of a simple *robots.txt* file:

File: *robots.txt*

```
User-Agent: *

Allow: /

User-Agent: Googlebot

Allow: /index.php

Allow: /

User-Agent: Googlebot-Mobile

Disallow: /not-for-mobile.php

Allow: /
```

This file is designed for Google spiders, and it was created via Google Webmaster Tools. Here, User-Agent refers to a specific robot. At the top of the code, the User-Agent is set to *, referring to all robots, or all spiders. Rules for all spiders are general rules, and are overridden by any rules that are more specific. For example, the / after Allow: means that all spiders may index all files. Below that, however, there are specific instructions for spiders such as Googlebot and Googlebot-Mobile. Because these instructions are more specific, they override the general instructions for all robots.

You can use the terms spider and robot interchangeably. Spiders and robots are both user-agents. For a complete list of user-agents, visit *http://www.user-agents.org*.

When you create your own *robots.txt* file on a site such as Google's Webmaster Tools, you have an easy-to-use interface for helping you select which pages to allow access to and which ones to disallow, as shown in Figure 2-2.

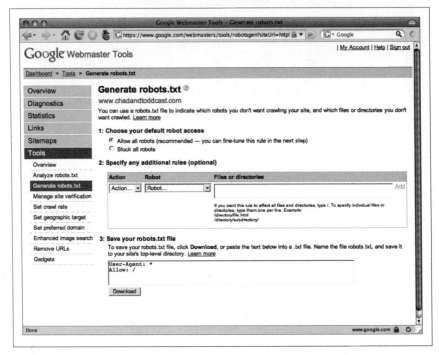

Figure 2-2. Generating a robots.txt file using Google's Webmaster Tools

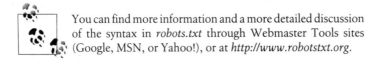 You can find more information and a more detailed discussion of the syntax in *robots.txt* through Webmaster Tools sites (Google, MSN, or Yahoo!), or at *http://www.robotstxt.org*.

Placing the robots.txt File

Once you've created your *robots.txt* file, you can simply put that file at the root directory of your website, so the path to the file would be *http://www.<your-domain.com>/robots.txt*.

Verifying That robots.txt Is Working

Webmaster Tools sites (e.g., Google, MSN, and Yahoo!) provide ways for you to determine whether your *robots.txt* file is working properly. Google's

Webmaster Tools, for example, has a page called "Analyze robots.txt" that will tell you how the file is working.

Other Ways to Prevent Files from Being Indexed

Using *robots.txt* is only one of many methods you can use to keep pages out of search engine indexes. If it's crucial for your pages not to be indexed at all, make sure to use some of these methods to supplement using the *robots.txt* file. Because there are so many ways to prevent pages from being indexed, it may be difficult to choose the best way for your needs. To make sure pages don't show up in the SERPs, it's best to use a combination of different methods (or all of them), because each method serves a particular purpose.

Using noindex in metadata

A quick and easy (although not the most reliable) way to prevent pages from being indexed is to use metadata. Insert the following code into the <head> tag in an HTML page to tell a search engine spider not to index an entire page:

```
<meta name="robots" content="noindex"/>
```

This code is very simple, but you can't trust it fully to protect pages from being found in the SERPs. For example, if the page is already indexed, it'll remain indexed. Also, not all search engine spiders will obey this command. Currently, Google, Yahoo!, MSN, and Ask.com support the noindex meta value. Usually, this method is best used to supplement other index prevention methods.

Password-protecting pages

One of the best ways to keep spiders from indexing pages if they haven't been indexed already is to use server code to password-protect them. The exact method for doing this varies from one server type to another. For example, you can employ password protection on web servers that run Apache by using an *.htaccess* file. By password-protecting pages, you ensure that spiders won't crawl them anymore. This method is excellent for pages that haven't been crawled already, but if the page has been crawled, you may want to password-protect against future crawls, as well as use another method to prevent indexing or to remove indexed pages from search engine indexes.

 The exercises at the end of this chapter explain password protection using an *.htaccess* file in more detail.

Removing pages from Google's index

Even password-protecting your pages isn't enough to keep those pages out of the SERPs if the pages are already indexed. You also can manually remove pages from search engine indexes. This method ensures that pages won't be indexed and will remove pages that are already indexed. For example, Google's Webmaster Tools site allows you to take pages out of Google's index.

I provide a detailed example of removing pages from Google's index in the exercises at the end of this chapter.

Directory Listings

Another way to get your site out there, although significantly less popular, is by submitting your site to a *directory*, a list of websites indexed and maintained by people, instead of by spiders. In a directory, users browse for websites by categories and subcategories, or through a directory search. You can find the Yahoo! directory at *http://dir.yahoo.com/*. MSN's directory is at *http://specials .msn.com/*. Google uses a different system for its directory, called the Open Directory Project. Google's directory is at *http://www.google.com/dirhp*.

You can learn more about the Open Directory Project at *http: //www.dmoz.org*.

Submitting Your Site to a Directory

Find the submission link on the directory for which you'd like to submit your site. Each search engine has different instructions from there. Mainly, you'll need to enter a title for your site, the site's URL, and a description. Figure 2-3 shows the page for submitting a site to the Open Directory Project at *http://www.dmoz.org/add.html*.

Directories You Should Submit To

The major search engines (Google, Yahoo!, and MSN) currently use different directories. Many of the smaller search engines (e.g., AOL and Ask.com) get their directory information (as well as their indexed pages information) from the bigger engines. For that reason, submitting your site to the major engines is sufficient.

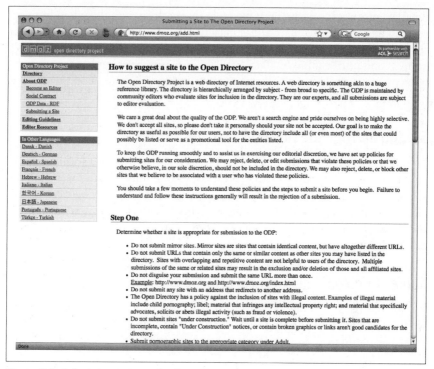

Figure 2-3. Submitting a site to the Open Directory Project

 Earlier I mentioned that directory listings are a less popular venue for SEO. This is because they aren't updated as frequently as the spiders crawl pages. Because of this, I recommend submitting your site to a directory, but putting more of your aggressive SEO energy into your page's keywords and HTML.

Local Searches

One way to get your page up in the SERPs is to optimize it for local searches. For example, you may be an auto parts company in Los Angeles, and the purpose of your website may be to bring customers into your store. Search engines can index the information and *location* of your site to make it easier to find for people searching for businesses in your area.

Benefits of Local Searches

An excellent benefit of local searches is that you can eliminate a lot of your competition based on your location. Another benefit is that you can provide detailed information about your business to search engines that wouldn't necessarily be available to searchers otherwise. For example, if you submit your site to Google's Local Business Center, you can give Google your business's address and phone number. That way, when a searcher searches for a service your business provides, she'll see your business on a map, along with your phone number. This makes your business more visible on the Web.

Setting Up Your Site for Local Searches

To set up your site for local searches, go to a search engine's local area and submit your organization's name, address, phone number, and website. For Google, go to Google's Local Business Center at *http://www.google.com/local/add/*. Yahoo!'s local business center is at *http://listings.local.yahoo.com/csubmit/*, and the MSN local section is at *https://ssl.search.live.com/listings/BusinessSearch.aspx*.

Submitting Your Site for Local Searches

If your business provides services to a local area or multiple areas, you may want to include your page in local searches. The only reason you wouldn't want to submit your site to local search engines is if your business doesn't provide any type of local services.

Your site may have a lot of local competition, especially if you're in a big city. Think of a doctor's office in Los Angeles. If you're trying to optimize your site and you're in a big city, you can narrow the search and eliminate some competition based on how you market your business. Let's say your business is in a Los Angeles suburb. In that case, you might be tempted to use Los Angeles as the location of your business on your website because it's bigger and more well known than your suburb, but remember that the bigger the city you're in, the more competition you have, and the less likely you are to be found. You're actually better off listing your suburb, or section of a city, than the big city. That way, if someone is looking for a business in a specific area, she's more likely to find you because you have less competition.

SEO, Web Standards, and Accessibility

Standards exist on the Web to help guide web developers in creating content that's friendly to all search engines and all people. Most web standards are geared toward helping your sites better communicate the content they contain, and thus become better for SEO and for people viewing your site. Here are some examples of standards on the Web to keep in mind as you develop SEO websites.

Separation of Content, Structure, and Behavior

Websites are made up of three basic parts: *content*, the information on the page, including text you read through a web browser, controlled by HTML; *structure*, the layout, or display, of the content (usually controlled via CSS); and *behavior*, the page's interactivity via JavaScript, Flash, or other interactive media.

Many programmers in all languages separate their content similarly using a programming technique called Model View Controller. With MVC, the model represents the data (HTML), the view represents presentation of the data (CSS), and the controller represents manipulation of data (JavaScript).

It's commonly agreed in the web design world that content, structure, and behavior should remain separate. This way, if a visitor to a site can view only the content of the site, the code doesn't break, keeping the site viewable. When you're designing an SEO website, it's important to keep content, structure, and behavior separate so that you can get your content to as many users in as many ways as possible.

For practice separating content and structure, see the exercise at the end of this chapter. If you want more information about separating behavior, see Chapter 4.

Accessibility

Accessibility and SEO aren't the same, but many good practices in accessibility are also good practices in SEO. For example, making a site that everyone can view, regardless of disability or viewing platform, is great for SEO and accessibility. Adding `alt` text to images is great for both as well. When creating your site, you should be familiar with accessibility standards found on the W3C site, *http://www.w3.org/WAI/*.

If you're much more interested in SEO than accessibility, you don't need to adhere to every detail regarding web accessibility standards. However, it's best to at least be familiar with the standards, because one day all web developers may be required to make all pages completely accessible.

The exercises at the end of this chapter provide more examples of adding accessibility to web pages.

SEO Pitfalls

Although making the right decisions in SEO can improve your site's ranking, making the wrong decisions can damage your ranking. Further, if you make the wrong moves, you may get banned from searches altogether, having your site completely removed from search engine indexes. To avoid that, here are some tips to make sure you adhere to the appropriate SEO guidelines.

Unethical SEO

Unethical SEO, also known as *Black Hat SEO*, refers to bad SEO practices that can get you banned from search engine results, with your site completely removed from the search engines' ndexes. Many things qualify as Black Hat SEO, but they all fall into the same category. Anything that's blatantly written only for search engines and is never intended for human viewing qualifies as Black Hat SEO. This refers to such tricks as white text full of keywords on a white background, text with a font size of zero, and text hidden with CSS.

Good SEO practices are known as *White Hat SEO*.

Avoiding Black Hat SEO isn't too difficult. Simply follow the SEO guidelines laid out in this chapter, and you won't have a problem. To keep your pages from getting banned, just avoid cheating your way to the top of the SERPs.

Too Much Dynamic Data

Many websites are *dynamic*, driven by data from a database or information from forms. You can usually tell whether information on a page is dynamic by viewing the page's URL in your web browser. If the URL contains a question mark (?), that page is dynamic.

If the URL doesn't contain a question mark, the page isn't necessarily static.

Dynamic data won't get you banned from search engines (providing you're not using Black Hat SEO), but unless it is used properly it can harm your search results. If your pages need to contain dynamic data, you should know what gives search engine spiders a hard time. Here's a list of some things that are roadblocks for spiders:

- More than two parameters in a URL
- Pages that are accessible only via login or other input forms
- Pages that require session IDs to be passed through a URL
- Pages that require cookies

One workaround for this is to make sure content that needs to be searchable is not blocked in ways listed above. You can set up your pages in such a way that exposes a page's general and public content to search engines while requiring a login to access information that should not be searchable, such as account information.

Learn how to display dynamic data in static HTML for SEO purposes in Chapter 5.

Excessive JavaScript/AJAX That Controls HTML

If you're a JavaScript junkie, you may be sad to learn that spiders don't execute JavaScript. This isn't a huge deal, unless your important searchable HTML content is hidden from those without JavaScript. For example, if you use Java-Script to create your menus and all of their accompanying HTML code, you might be in trouble. If you have an HTML menu and use JavaScript to show and hide items in the menu, your content will be searchable. Like dynamic, database-driven applications, dynamic JavaScript/AJAX applications can hide searchable content from search engines.

Luckily, also like dynamic content, the workarounds are fairly simple. One is to keep behavior (JavaScript) separated from content (HTML). That way, you don't have to make separate pages for those without JavaScript, providing a seamless experience to all.

You'll be shown more detail about the use of JavaScript/AJAX technologies for SEO in Chapter 4.

Too Much Flash Content

Yes, I know this is a *Flash* book, and that makes it all the more important for you to understand how to most effectively use Flash for SEO. With that said, problems arise when you use too much Flash. How much Flash is too much? It's easy to spot too much Flash when you're visiting a site in a browser that doesn't have Flash. If the site is completely empty and unusable, there may be too much Flash, or your Flash content may not be optimized. In theory, you should be able to go to any Flash site with any browser regardless of whether Flash is installed and still view the same (or at least very similar) content.

As a Flash person, I know there's interactivity in Flash that's hard or impossible to mimic with other technologies. Understanding that, it's OK for you to have some content on your site that requires Flash. Still, people visiting your site who don't have Flash should see information regarding the Flash content. The information should contain details about the Flash content, as well as let people know that Flash Player is required to view the content in all its glory.

Search engines admit to having a hard time indexing Flash content, so you'll have to take special care in the HTML you use to describe and house your Flash movies. One thing Google mentions is that you should avoid using Flash for navigation. If you absolutely must use Flash for navigation, make sure to include an HTML alternative so that spiders can easily crawl through your site.

It's important that you don't use the HTML that Flash generates for you. Flash (at its default setting) uses your FLA filename for the page title and HTML filename, and doesn't give you any searchable content other than static text copied into HTML.

For more information about optimizing Flash content using HTML, see Chapter 3. Also, see Chapters 4 and 5 for tricks on using Flash with JavaScript and PHP, respectively.

Frames

Frames are rectangular sections on web pages that act as windows to other web pages. In HTML, frames are housed by an element called `<frameset>`. Usually, frames are used for layout purposes. As for SEO, frames can be difficult to manage. Because frames use different web pages, spiders crawl frame pages individually. In other words, parts of your pages are indexed separately, rather than as a whole page.

This can create problems for both search engines and people. For example, a person could search for a phrase that's found within only one frame of your site, and following a link in the SERP can take the person to view that page separately from the other frames. Not only would the person see a difference in site layout from the way you intended the site to be viewed, but also the person may be missing key elements of your site, such as navigation.

If you're a frame fanatic, you can still use frames. There are just a few precautions to follow. Make sure to use the `<noframes>` HTML tag, which displays web page content in browsers that don't support frames, and wrap all of your frame content in that tag. That way, all search engines and all people can use your page.

Slicing

Some web creation applications, such as Adobe Fireworks, Illustrator, and Photoshop, use a technique called *slicing* to create web pages. Slicing breaks a large image into smaller images that are organized in HTML frames to create a web page. It's mainly used because it's an easy way to get content on the Web in the same way it's viewed in a desktop application. However, slicing is an SEO vulgarity, and you should avoid it at all costs because it can destroy the most important parts of your web pages.

To understand why slicing can be harmful, consider what's important in SEO. Though you can add filenames and page titles to a sliced HTML page, the rest of the content is made up of images and frames. Images can't include searchable text, so you won't have link text, headings, bold or italic text, or any other kind of searchable text on your pages. Further, slicing uses frames, which hides any of the content that would be searchable from search engine spiders.

 Creating your web pages using slices can be fatal to SEO in your site. Use slices (if you absolutely have to) only on pages that search engines don't need to see.

Monitoring Your Success

It can be difficult to measure your success when optimizing your site, so here are some tips for measuring the success of your SEO efforts.

Number of People Visiting

You can view your site's statistics in a Webmaster Tools center such as Google's Webmaster Tools to see how many people visit your site month by month. Google also shows you how many people visit your site based on certain search queries. You can then put more effort into optimizing your site for those keywords. Also, most web hosts allow some way to track site statistics. Because the process varies for each web host, you may need to contact your web host if there isn't an obvious place to look in your web hosting control panel.

Patience and Time

Because indexing of your site by search engine spiders is something you can't directly control, it may take awhile before your site is even crawled. And even after your site is crawled, it may take awhile (and by *awhile* I mean a few months) before you notice that your pages achieve high results in the SERPs. Be patient when optimizing, and your work will eventually be rewarded.

Poor Results

SEO doesn't guarantee that your page will be ranked number 1 in the SERPs, or even number 10, for that matter. And sometimes even if you follow all SEO techniques you may not yield substantial results, even after "awhile." Don't give up if you don't see the results. At that point, you may want to rework your SEO strategy, targeting different keywords, or reworking your content in a way that attracts more traffic to your site.

Exercises in Creating a Simple SEO Site

In this section, you'll get some practice in SEO and HTML by creating a simple SEO site. Here, you'll review the concepts you read about in the chapter and put them into practice.

Exercise 2-1: Viewing Optimized HTML

In this section, we'll view some sample optimized HTML code and discuss the different parts that relate to SEO as real-world SEO examples. The site you're using is the games mini site that's part of a podcast site.

 This exercise requires a basic knowledge of HTML code.

File: *site/index.html*

1. Open *index.html* in a text editor, such as Dreamweaver, TextEdit, or Notepad. You can also open the page in a web browser to view the page's final layout.

2. The first few lines of code deal with initializing the HTML on the page by explaining the document type and by opening the HTML tag:

```
<!DOCTYPE html PUBLIC "-//W3C//DTD XHTML 1.0 Transitional//EN"
"http://www.w3.org/TR/xhtml1/DTD/xhtml1-transitional.dtd">
<html xmlns="http://www.w3.org/1999/xhtml">
```

3. The <head> tag contains the page title, metadata, and links to CSS and other files. Notice that the title contains the keywords ("Free Online Wii Games"), a separator (|), and then branding ("Wedgekase"). The metadata keywords and description are concise, and are relative to the content on the page while still containing important keywords. From there, there's just a link to the CSS file (*main.css*) and links to the *favicon*. If you're not familiar with favicons, they're the little favorites/bookmark icons you see in your web browser:

```
<head>
<title>Free Online Wii Games | Wedgekase</title>
<meta http-equiv="Content-Type" content="text/html; charset=UTF-8" />
<meta name="Keywords" content="free online games,wii,internet channel,
wedgekase" />
<meta name="Description" content=" Free online games to play with your
Wii via the Internet Channel or your computer with your mouse." />
<link href="styles/main.css" rel="stylesheet" type="text/css"
media="screen" />
<link rel="shortcut icon" href="images/wedgekase-music-favicon.png"
type="image/png" />
<link rel="icon" href="images/wedgekase-music-favicon.png"
type="image/png" />
</head>
```

4. The <body> tag contains the main structure of your HTML page, and the content on the page that the user sees. The <div> tag with an `id` of `container` acts as a wrapper for all visible content:

```
<body>
<div id="container">
```

5. The header section contains the header graphic. Notice that the link for the header graphic is /, which is used to replace a link to *index.html* so that *index.html* isn't used as a link. For the image, notice how the file is named using some keywords and that keywords can also be found in its `alt` text:

```
<div id="header">
<a href="/"><img src="images/wedgekase-music-logo.jpg"
alt="wedgekase,wii games,logo" width="800"
```

```
height="220" /></a>
</div>
```

6. Navigation is fairly simple; it's kept in an unordered list so that it stays connected in case the person viewing the site doesn't have CSS enabled. Here, the Podcast and Artists pages have "#" used for links (this is only because this is a testing site):

```
<div id="navigation">
<ul>
<li><a id="podcast" href="#">Podcast</a></li>
<li><a id="artists" href="#">Artists</a></li>
<li><a id="games" href="/" class="currentPage">Games</a></li>
</ul>
</div>
```

7. The main content in the site is the left side of the page, or main block that includes descriptions for all of the games. It begins with a simple description of this page. The games text, which is an image contained in an `<h1>` tag, includes keywords in its `alt` text:

```
<div id="mainContent">
<h1><a href="/"><img src="images/games.png" alt="wedgekase wii games"
width="107" height="43" class="header" /></a></h1>
<p>These free online games are playable both on the Wii and your
computer. To play games on the Wii, come to this page via the
Internet Channel. For your computer, just use your mouse. Pretend
like you're using a Wii remote and you'll have even more fun!</p>
```

8. The rest of the main content on the page is a set of repeating blocks to display the games, along with descriptions. Each game has a heading (in an `<h2>` tag) with keywords that link to the game (note the use of keywords in the page and folder names), an image for the game (yet again, keywords in the `alt` text), and a brief description:

```
<h2><a href="wii-games/xylophone-master.html">Xylophone Master</a></h2>
<p><a href="wii-games/xylophone-master.html"><img src="images/xylophone-
master.jpg" alt="xylophone, music,game, wedgekase" width="60" height="60"
class="gameThumbnail" /></a>Learn to master playing the xylophone and
simultaneously boost your memory! Listen to the computer play notes
and simply play them back by moving your mouse or Wii remote up and
down over the keys.</p>
<div class="clearFloat"></div>
```

9. After the main content is the sidebar. The sidebar contains quick links to all of the games (again contained in an unordered list), as well as a link to the page's feed in an RSS file. Note the use of keywords in `alt` text, folders, filenames, and link text:

```
<div id="sidebar1">
<h2><a href="#"><img src="images/games-latest.gif"
alt="wedgekase games" width="48" height="19" /></a></h2>
<ul>
<li><a href="wii-games/xylophone-master.html">Xylophone Master</a></li>
```

```
<li><a href="wii-games/meteor-blaster.html">Meteor Blaster</a></li>
<li><a href="wii-games/fun-run.html">Fun Run</a></li>
<li><a href="wii-games/set-the-clock.html">Set the Clock</a></li>
<li><a href="wii-games/hide-and-seek.html">Hide and Seek</a></li>
<li><a href="wii-games/hammer-wielder.html">Hammer Wielder</a></li>
</ul>
<p><a href="rss.xml"><img src="images/subscribe-wedgekase-games.png"
alt="subscribe to wedgekase games" width="110" height="24"
class="subscribeToPodcast" /></a></p>  </div>
<div class="clearFloat"></div>
```

10. The page ends with the footer content. The footer contains text-only links (no images or background images) to act as another means of navigation and copyright information. Text-only alternative navigation is great for SEO (by adding more link text), and it provides another way for users to navigate through your site. This is especially important if your navigation is image-based, because your users may not be able to view images in their browsers:

```
<div id="footer">
<ul>

    <li><a href="#">Podcast</a> | </li>
    <li><a href="#">Artists</a> | </li>
    <li><a href="/">Games</a></li>
</ul>

<ul>
    <li><a href="wii-games/xylophone-master.html">Xylophone Master</a> |
    </li>
    <li><a href="wii-games/meteor-blaster.html">Meteor Blaster</a> |
    </li>
    <li><a href="wii-games/fun-run.html">Fun Run</a> |
<a href="wii-games/set-the-clock.html">Set the Clock</a> | </li>
    <li><a href="wii-games/hide-and-seek.html">Hide and Seek</a> | </li>
    <li><a href="wii-games/hammer-wielder.html">Hammer Wielder</a></li>
</ul>
<p>&copy;2008 <a href="/">wedgekase</a></p>
</div> </div> </body> </html>
```

11. Open the page in a web browser to view the final layout. If CSS is enabled in your browser, you should see something similar to Figure 2-4.

12. The page layout should still be easy to view and well organized if CSS is disabled in the user's browser. That way, your content is viewable to those using browsers without CSS. If you're using Firefox, you can disable CSS by choosing View→Page Style→No Style. Without CSS, the page should resemble Figure 2-5. Notice that the navigation is together, and the body content is organized in the same way it is when CSS is enabled.

Figure 2-4. The Games page with CSS enabled

Exercise 2: Viewing Pages That Contain Flash

Now we'll look at the pages that contain the Flash content. Because they're all generally the same, we'll view only one file.

File: *wii-games/xylophone-master.html*

1. Open *xylophone-master.html* in Dreamweaver, TextEdit, or Notepad.

2. The initial HTML and head data is fairly standard. It contains the opening HTML tag, a page title (keywords and then branding), metadata keywords and a description, and links to external files. Note that the link to the JavaScript file, *AC_RunActiveContent.js*, is the file that Flash creates automatically when you publish HTML via Flash's Publish Settings dialog box.

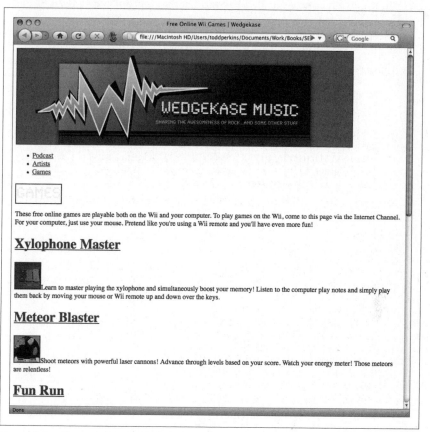

Figure 2-5. The Games page with CSS disabled

```
<html xmlns="http://www.w3.org/1999/xhtml" xml:lang="en" lang="en">
<head>
<meta http-equiv="Content-Type" content="text/html; charset=
iso-8859-1" />
<title>Xylophone Master | Wedgekase Wii Games</title>
<script src="AC_RunActiveContent.js" type="text/javascript"></script>
<link href="../styles/games.css" rel="stylesheet" type="text/css"
media="all">
<meta name="description" content="Move your mouse or WiiMote up and
down to hit the keys on the xylophone in the same order that the
xylophone  master plays them. Prove your coolness to your friends
by getting to the highest level!">
<meta name="keywords" content="xylophone,wii,game,wedgekase">
</head>
```

3. In the <body> tag, the first block of code deals with running JavaScript contained in the file that Flash created. This file tells the web browser to

run the Flash content if the browser has the appropriate version of Flash Player installed:

```
<body bgcolor="#000000">
<div id="game">
<p>
<script language="JavaScript" type="text/javascript">
AC_FL_RunContent(
'codebase','http://download.macromedia.com/pub/shockwave/cabs/flash/
swflash.cab#version=7,0,0,0','width','790','height','610','id',
'Xylophone Master','align','middle','src','xylophone-
master','quality','high','bgcolor','#000000','name','Xylophone
Master','allowscriptaccess','sameDomain','allowfullscreen','false',
'pluginspage', 'http://www.adobe.com/go/getflashplayer',
'movie','xylophone-master' ); //end AC code  </script>
```

4. Next is the actual Flash content in a `<noscript>` block, which simply displays the Flash content if the person viewing the content has JavaScript disabled:

```
<noscript>
<object classid="clsid:d27cdb6e-ae6d-11cf-96b8-444553540000"
codebase="http://download.macromedia.com/pub/shockwave/cabs/flash/
swflash.cab#version=7,0,0,0" width="790" height="610"
id="Xylophone Master" align="middle">
<param name="allowScriptAccess" value="sameDomain" />
<param name="allowFullScreen" value="false" />
<param name="movie" value="xylophone-master.swf" />
<param name="quality" value="high" />
<param name="bgcolor" value="#000000" />
<embed src="xylophone-master.swf" quality="high" bgcolor="#000000"
width="790" height="610" name="Xylophone Master" align="middle"
allowScriptAccess="sameDomain" allowFullScreen="false"
type="application/x-shockwave-flash"
pluginspage="http://www.adobe.com/go/getflashplayer" />
</object>
</noscript>
</p>
</div>
```

5. Last, there's the game's description. Note the use of keywords in the game title, description, and image attributes:

```
<div id="descriptionContainer">
<h1> <a id="showHideDescription" href="#">Xylophone Master Game Details
</a></h1>
<div id="gameDescription">
<p><a href="xylophone-master.html"><img src=".."
/images/xylophone-master.jpg" alt="xylophone,wii,game,
wedgekase" width="60" height="60" class="profilePic"/>
</a>Move your mouse or WiiMote up and down to hit the keys on
the xylophone in the same order that the xylophone master plays them.
Prove your coolness to your friends by getting to the highest level!</p>
</div>
</div>
```

```
</body>
</html>
```

Exercise 3: Setting Up a Google Webmaster Tools Account

For practice working with search engine Webmaster Tools, in this exercise you'll upload your site to your web server and set up a Webmaster Tools account for your site with Google.

 This exercise may be different depending on which web host you use. For more information, see your web hosting account management website.

Files: All Chapter 2 files

1. Upload the site files, with the exception of *.htaccess*, *.htapasswd*, and *private/.htaccess*, to your web server. If you're not sure how to do that, look for instructions on the control panel for your website. You can also upload your site using an FTP program, such as the FireFTP extension for Firefox.

2. Once your site is uploaded, go to the Google Webmaster Central page at *http://www.google.com/webmasters/* (shown in Figure 2-6).

3. From the Google Webmaster Central page, click the link to sign in to the Google Webmaster Tools section.

4. Sign in to Webmaster Tools using your Google account, or create a Google account to sign in.

5. Add your site to your Webmaster Tools account by typing your site's address and clicking Add Site (shown in Figure 2-7).

6. The next step is to verify your account to prove the site you've added is indeed yours. One method is to create an HTML file with the name Google gives you, and upload it to your site. Once your site is verified, you're ready to use Google's Webmaster Tools to help you with SEO.

Exercise 4: Adding a Simple Sitemap

Now it's time to set up the sitemap for your mini site. In this exercise, you'll view and add your sitemap to Google Webmaster Tools.

File: *sitemap.xml*

1. Open *sitemap.xml* in a text editor.

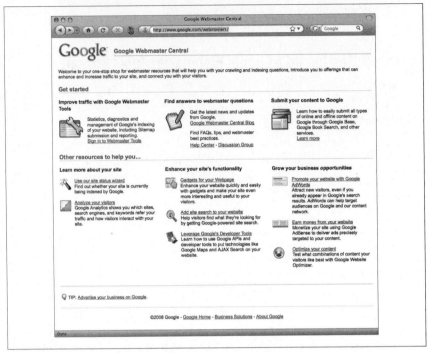

Figure 2-6. Google's Webmaster Central page

2. Notice that the file structure is the same simple structure discussed earlier in this chapter. The file begins with XML version information and a `<urlset>` element:

```
<?xml version="1.0" encoding="UTF-8"?>
<urlsetxmlns="http://www.sitemaps.org/schemas/sitemap/0.9"
xmlns:xsi="http://www.w3.org/2001/XMLSchema-instance"
xsi:schemaLocation="http://www.sitemaps.org/schemas/sitemap/0.9
http://www.sitemaps.org/schemas/sitemap/0.9/sitemap.xsd">
```

3. Each URL is held in a URL tag, which contains the URL and information about the URL. I gave the home page a priority of 1 and the other pages a priority of 0.5:

```
<url>
  <loc>http://games.wedgekase.com/</loc>
  <priority>1</priority>
  <lastmod>2008-06-25T19:20:31+00:00</lastmod>
  <changefreq>daily</changefreq>
</url>
```

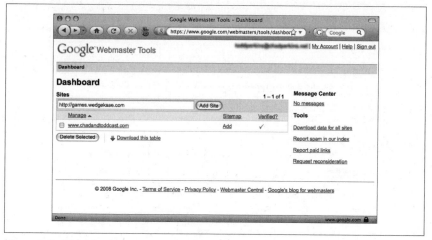

Figure 2-7. Adding a site

 Make sure you change the `<loc>` attributes of the URLs to match your domain. You can do this quickly by using your text editor to perform Find and Replace to replace *games.wedgekase.com* with your domain name. In most text editors, the keyboard shortcut for Find and Replace is Ctrl-F (Windows) or Cmd-F (Mac).

4. The page ends with a closing `<urlset>` tag:

   ```
   </urlset>
   ```

5. Next, you'll tell Google about your sitemap. Log in to your Google Web-master Tools account and click the Sitemap link.

 Remember, if your sitemap is uploaded to *http://www.<yourdomain.com>/sitemap.xml*, search engines will automatically look for it there. Even so, it's best to tell them about it anyway, just to be safe.

6. Click the Add Sitemap button.

7. In the drop-down menu that appears, choose Add General Web Sitemap.

8. Enter your sitemap URL as shown in Figure 2-8, and click the Add General Web Sitemap button to add your sitemap.

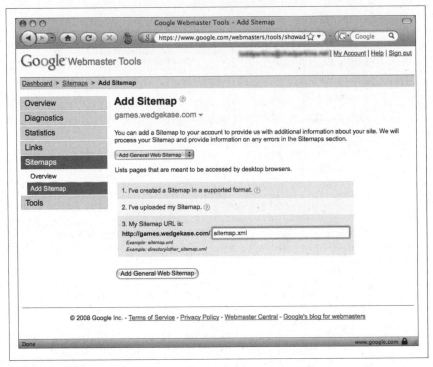

Figure 2-8. Adding a sitemap

Exercise 5: Consolidating Home Page URLs

Now you'll consolidate your home page URLs to make sure your site's rankings aren't divided.

File: *.htaccess*

1. Open *.htaccess* in a plain-text editor.

    Remember, this method will work only with Apache servers. Check your server's Help documents to make sure it accepts *.htaccess* commands before uploading this file.

2. The code in this file simply redirects anyone visiting an acceptable form of your domain name (i.e., without *www*) to your preferred domain name (on the last line):

   ```
   Options +FollowSymLinks
   RewriteEngine on
   RewriteCond %{HTTP_HOST} .
   ```

```
RewriteCond %{HTTP_HOST} ^games.wedgekase\.com [NC]
RewriteRule ^(.*)$ http://games.wedgekase.com/$1 [R=301,L]
```

3. Modify the code to use your domain instead of *games.wedgekase.com*.

4. Upload the file to your domain, making sure to upload the file in ASCII mode.

5. Browse to your site online, using an acceptable, but non-preferred, URL. For example, I would browse to *www.games.wedgekase.com* instead of *games.wedgekase.com*.

6. Notice that you're instantly and seamlessly redirected to your preferred URL. That's it!

Exercise 6: Protecting Private Data

In this exercise, you'll protect your private data by telling search engines not to index your private page and private directory.

File 1: *robots.txt*

File 2: *private.html*

File 3: *private/index.html*

File 4: *private/.htaccess*

1. Open *robots.txt* in a plain-text editor.

2. The code here is pretty simple. The instructions to all spiders are to allow everything in general, but to disallow *private.html* and the *private* folder:

```
User-Agent: *
Allow: /
Disallow: /private.html
Disallow: /private/
```

3. Upload *robots.txt* to your web server at the root of your website.

4. Sign in to your Google Webmaster Tools account. Next, you'll test the *robots.txt* file using Google's Webmaster Tools to make sure the appropriate files are blocked.

5. Click the Tools link to enter the Tools section.

6. Click the "Analyze robots.txt" link.

7. Scroll down to view the code from your *robots.txt* file and find the text field you can use to test URLs.

8. In the test text field, type the URLs to the private file and folder. Your locations should be similar to those shown in Figure 2-9, with your domain in place of games.wedgekase.com (*http://games.wedgekase.com*). Click the

Check button to check whether your private pages are effectively blocked from Google's spiders.

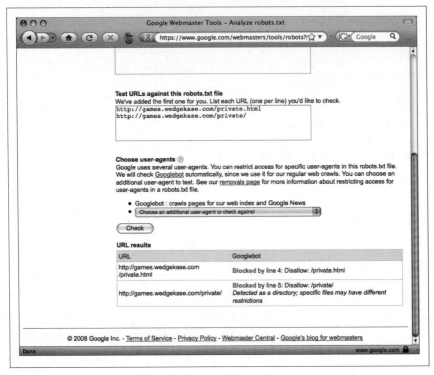

Figure 2-9. *Private files are blocked from Google's spiders*

9. Next, you'll make sure to remove your private files from Google's index. In the Tools section of your Webmaster Tools account, go to the Remove URLs page.

 This method works only for pages that have already been indexed, so this portion of the exercise is mostly for practice.

10. Click New Removal Request.

11. Choose Individual URLs and click Next.

12. Enter `private.html` in the removal area.

13. Click Add.

14. Click Submit to submit the removal request.

15. Repeat steps 10-14 for the *private* folder. Make sure to choose Directories when repeating step 11. You should then see the pages listed as shown in Figure 2-10.

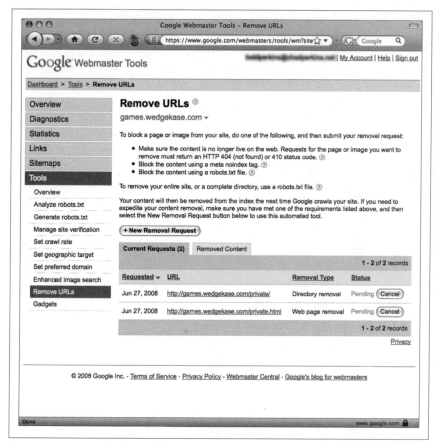

Figure 2-10. Private folder and file pending removal from Google's index

16. Now you'll make sure each page is blocked using robot metadata. Open *private/index.html* and *private.html* in your text editor.

17. Find the following code in each file within the `<head>` tag:

```
<meta name="robots" content="noindex"/>
```

 Although not perfectly effective by itself in keeping pages from being indexed, adding robots metadata can help in achieving your goal.

18. Last, you'll password-protect the private files to make sure they're accessed only by people who are allowed to do so. Start by opening *private/.htaccess* in a text editor.

> You can find detailed information about creating an *.htaccess* file at www.javascriptkit.com/howto/htaccess3.shtml (*http://www.javascriptkit.com/howto/htaccess3.shtml*). This method will work only with Apache servers.

19. The code here password-protects the *private* directory. The top line refers to the location of the file that contains the password information, given as a server path (as opposed to a URL). Make sure to change the server path to reflect a location on your server above your *www* level that is secure. The "AuthName" line is used to name the protected area. The "require user" line is used to define which user(s) can access this page, which of course can be changed. Here, the user is admin:

```
AuthUserFile /privatedir/.htpasswd
AuthGroupFile /dev/null
AuthName "Private Area"
AuthType Basic

require user admin
```

20. Upload *private/.htaccess* if it isn't uploaded already, making sure to use ASCII format.

21. Open *.htpasswd* in a text editor.

22. The code in this file is simple; it has a username and an encrypted password. I used the web application at *http://www.tools.dynamicdrive.com/password/* to generate the password for me.

23. Go to *http://www.tools.dynamicdrive.com/password/* and create an encrypted password based on your username (step 19), and replace the code in *.htpasswd* with the username and password that site gives you.

24. Save and upload the file to the folder you specified in step 19, again making sure the file is uploaded in ASCII format.

25. Visit the *private* folder on your site. Notice that you must enter your username and password to enter that section, as shown in Figure 2-11.

> If your username and password combination isn't working, make sure your *.htpasswd* file is in the location specified in step 19. If you're still experiencing problems, search your web server's Help documents.

Figure 2-11. The private folder is now password-protected

Key Terms Used in This Chapter

Table 2-2 contains the terms that were introduced in this chapter and gives you their definitions.

Table 2-2. Key terms used in this chapter

Term	Definition
Behavior	Interactivity in a web page, which should be created using JavaScript, Flash, or other interactive media
Black Hat SEO	Refers to bad SEO practices that can get you banned from search engine results
Content	The information on a page, which should be contained within HTML
Directory	List of websites and descriptions created and maintained by people, as opposed to spiders
Dynamic website	Site driven by database or form data
Inbound links	Links that are targeted to your website, be they from external sites or from within your own site
Outbound links	Links from your site that lead to external sites
robots.txt	A plain-text file used to tell search engine spiders pages should not be crawled
Sitemap	An XML or plain-text file (usually XML) containing basic information about a site's pages, used to inform search engines that the pages exist and should be crawled
Slicing	A web page creation technique that breaks up a large layout of a page into small images and displays them in frames; typically destructive to SEO
Structure	The display of a page's content, referring to its layout and design, which should be controlled via CSS
Unethical SEO	See *Black Hat SEO*
White Hat SEO	SEO that follows proper SEO guidelines and practices

CHAPTER 3

Creating Optimized Content in Flash

Now that you have some experience creating optimized HTML content, take a look at some techniques to make your Flash content more visible to search engines. This chapter discusses search engine optimization (SEO) mainly from the Flash development perspective, focusing on what you need to do for optimization when creating Flash applications.

Flash SEO Myths

Although they may be legitimate, most of the reasons people don't like Flash are based on outdated myths regarding the technology's SEO capabilities. In this section, we'll look at some of the most prominent myths that create haters out of otherwise normal human folk.

Myth 1: Flash Content Is Bad for SEO

The first myth is that Flash and SEO don't mix. In other words, some people believe that to have an SEO site, you must eliminate most, if not all, Flash content. This is simply not true. Flash content, when used effectively, can work great with SEO. Other media elements, such as images, audio, and video (including video in Flash Player), are searchable based on the HTML content that surrounds them.

Myth 2: Flash Content Isn't Searchable

Another myth about Flash content is that search engines can't search through it to index the information within SWF files. For a long time, this myth was true. Though static text and links in SWF files could be indexed, this was only because Flash added that information to the HTML containing the SWF upon publishing.

Recently, Adobe announced that the Google and Yahoo! search engines received a special version of Flash Player to use in indexing Flash content. This version enables these search engines to crawl through a Flash movie similar to the way they crawl through HTML. As of this writing, Adobe hasn't released details about how this version of Flash Player works, but it has stated that search engines can index all URLs, dynamic or otherwise, and all text that appears in text fields that people can read. What do you have to do to have search engines index your Flash content? Nothing. They're already doing it for all pages being crawled.

 Be careful about placing private data in your Flash applications. Not only can search engines potentially index this data, but also it can be found by people using a SWF decompiler.

Flash SEO Pitfalls and Challenges

Although you can use Flash and still have excellent SEO, and although Flash content is now searchable, there are some things to avoid when creating SEO Flash content. In this section, we'll look at some pitfalls for those of you who are new to Flash SEO, as well as some of the challenges you'll face when developing your Flash applications.

Using Too Much Flash

Many Flash enthusiasts want to create sites entirely in Flash, or sites that use a heavy amount of Flash, using their Flash skills to emulate what's done with HTML. Although it's possible to create an all-Flash site that's optimized for search engines, this is usually discouraged, for a few reasons.

First, optimizing a Flash site using just Flash is possible, but it's difficult to tell how search engines weight different elements. For example, in HTML, you can weight different elements by placing them in heading tags, by making them bold or italic, or by creating links. In Flash, you can place HTML in text fields and use CSS to control how different elements are weighted, but that doesn't necessarily mean the Flash versions of the elements will be weighted the same as the HTML versions. In other words, the same elements may hold different (likely, less) weight in Flash.

Further, to be sure your Flash content is weighted correctly, you should also have an HTML description. That way, since you know for sure that HTML content is indexed, you can be sure that at least a description of the content can appear in search results. For now, it's too early in the game to see whether this can count as duplicate content if your Flash content contains the same information.

If you create a site that's full of content and you wish to have an HTML alternative for those who don't have Flash, you might find yourself needing to create an all-HTML website in addition to your all-Flash site. Not only can this be incredibly time-consuming, but also, as I mentioned earlier, this could count as duplicate content.

The Link Dilemma

One of the advantages of using HTML over Flash for an entire website is that HTML allows links to any page of a site. If you create an all-Flash site, or if an extremely complex Flash application is necessary to make your site usable, people coming to your site might have to navigate through your entire application to view the content they want. At a minimum, they might have to go through a few *pages*, or states, of your application that they don't want to view before viewing the desired content. This isn't necessarily bad for SEO, but it's horrible in terms of user experience.

This link dilemma isn't impossible to fix, but it will take some work and workarounds to create a good user experience. Luckily, the solution isn't too complex. Using some ActionScript along with other technologies, you can create *deep links*, links that take users to specific states of your application. You can also create Flash sites that are made up of multiple web pages, so individual states of the application can be linked to and so your users can use their browser's back and forward buttons.

 You'll learn more about deep linking later in this chapter.

Data Security

Flash, like any other content on the Internet, is prone to hacking. Many tools out there allow others to dig into your Flash applications to find assets you've used, and even extract all of your ActionScript code. In your Flash applications, try to avoid using private data unless you absolutely need to. Even then, keep in mind that through search engines or hacking, your data can potentially be exposed.

Comprehensive instructions for making secure Flash applications are beyond the scope of this book. For more details, search the Web for information on how to secure Flash applications.

Creating SEO Flash Content

Now we'll look at what you can do in Flash to create SEO content. We'll discuss some methods that have been around for a while, as well as some ways to optimize your applications for indexing.

Flash SEO Original Methods

Flash has had built-in tools for SEO ever since Flash MX 2004 was released. Over the years, these features have received some improvements, but they aren't complete SEO powerhouses yet. In this section, we'll talk about each method, and their advantages and disadvantages.

Understanding SWF metadata

SWF files, like HTML, video, and images, can include metadata. You can use this metadata information to give Flash movies titles and descriptions. At this point, search engines, even with the recent advancements of Flash SEO technology, don't index the metadata information. That's not to say you should avoid using it altogether. Rather, you might as well add in the metadata information now, and it may work to your advantage in the future. With the advancements in Flash SEO, it's becoming increasingly likely that this metadata will be used eventually.

The metadata used in SWF files is similar to the metadata used in other Adobe applications, and it contains information about a file that's embedded into the file itself. This is called *XMP metadata*. XMP (*eXtensible Metadata Platform*) metadata can include many different types of information, and even custom information, but what's relevant to SEO is that it can contain a title and a description.

XMP metadata is currently only available in Flash CS4.

Adding metadata to a SWF file

Adding metadata to a SWF file is extremely simple. One way to open the metadata window is to choose File→File Info. Another way to access the window is through the Publish Settings window, which you can access using the Property Inspector or through the window command File→Publish Settings. In the Publish Settings window, click the Flash tab to set options for publishing Flash content. In the Flash tab, click the File Info button next to the Include XMP Metadata checkbox to open the window used to enter XMP metadata into the SWF file (see Figure 3-1).

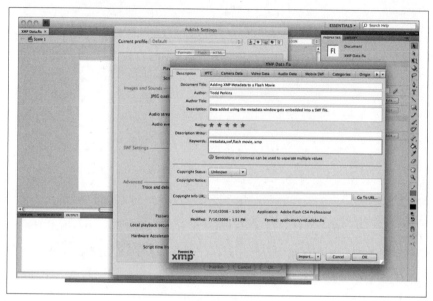

Figure 3-1. Adding XMP metadata to a file

Using the metadata window, you can then add XMP metadata, including title and description information, to your SWF file. Like metadata in HTML, this metadata travels with your SWF file once it's published, providing information about the file's contents.

Viewing XMP metadata

Once XMP data is embedded into a file, you can view the metadata in two ways. You can view it in Adobe Bridge, or view it in a text file created by Flash. Either way, you'll need to turn on the Include XMP Metadata checkbox in Flash's Publish Settings window, add some XMP metadata, and create a SWF file by selecting Control→Test Movie or by Publishing the File.

It's easy to view and edit metadata in Adobe Bridge. To view the data in Bridge, open Bridge and browse to the folder where your SWF file with embedded XMP data is located. Once you're in the proper location, select the SWF file to view its metadata in the Metadata panel (shown at the bottom right of Figure 3-2). While you're in Bridge, you can also edit XMP data by clicking the Edit button (the pencil icon) for a field you'd like to edit.

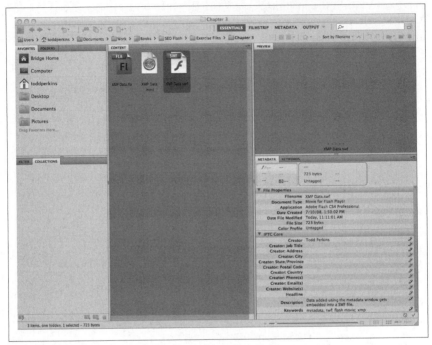

Figure 3-2. Viewing the SWF file's XMP metadata in Bridge

To view metadata as a text file, make sure you select the "Generate size report" checkbox in the Flash tab of the Publish Settings window before you publish your Flash content. After you've published your Flash content, you'll see a plain-text file created in the same folder as your other published content that includes the XMP data. You can view the data (Figure 3-3) by opening the file in any text editor.

Flash text in HTML

Some of the text you enter in Flash will automatically be placed in your published HTML file, and is searchable. This text is limited to text that has been typed manually into a dynamic text field in Flash, without using ActionScript. Though this is a quick and easy way to get Flash text into your HTML code

```
● ○ ○                    XMP Data Report.txt
XMP Data.swf Movie Report
--------------------------

Metadata
--------
Bytes    Value
-----    -----
  703      <rdf:RDF xmlns:rdf="http://www.w3.org/1999/02/22-rdf-syntax-
ns#"> <rdf:Description rdf:about="" xmlns:xmp="http://ns.adobe.com/xap/
1.0/"> <xmp:CreatorTool>Adobe Flash CS4 Professional</xmp:CreatorTool>
<xmp:CreateDate>2008-07-10T13:50:02-07:00</xmp:CreateDate>
<xmp:MetadataDate>2008-07-28T11:28:38-07:00</xmp:MetadataDate>
<xmp:ModifyDate>2008-07-28T11:28:38-07:00</xmp:ModifyDate> </
rdf:Description> <rdf:Description rdf:about="" xmlns:xmpMM="http://
ns.adobe.com/xap/1.0/mm/" xmlns:stRef="http://ns.adobe.com/xap/1.0/
sType/ResourceRef#"> <xmpMM:DocumentID>xmp.did:
0480117407206811AB0892372BFDDE34</xmpMM:DocumentID>
<xmpMM:InstanceID>xmp.iid:0480117407206811AB0892372BFDDE34</
xmpMM:InstanceID>
<xmpMM:OriginalDocumentID>xmp.did:F77F117407206811BEDCDAC3C0267ADE</
xmpMM:OriginalDocumentID> <xmpMM:DerivedFrom rdf:parseType="Resource">
<stRef:instanceID>xmp.iid:F77F117407206811BEDCDAC3C0267ADE</
stRef:instanceID>
<stRef:documentID>xmp.did:F77F117407206811BEDCDAC3C0267ADE</
stRef:documentID>
<stRef:originalDocumentID>xmp.did:F77F117407206811BEDCDAC3C0267ADE</
stRef:originalDocumentID> </xmpMM:DerivedFrom> </rdf:Description>
<rdf:Description rdf:about="" xmlns:dc="http://purl.org/dc/elements/
1.1/"> <dc:format>application/x-shockwave-flash</dc:format> <dc:title>
<rdf:Alt> <rdf:li xml:lang="x-default">Adding XMP Metadata to a Flash
Movie</rdf:li> </rdf:Alt> </dc:title> <dc:creator> <rdf:Seq>
<rdf:li>Todd Perkins</rdf:li> </rdf:Seq> </dc:creator> <dc:description>
<rdf:Alt> <rdf:li xml:lang="x-default">Data added using the metadata
window gets embedded into a SWF file.</rdf:li> </rdf:Alt> </
```

Figure 3-3. Viewing the file in TextEdit

without doing any extra work, relying on this method isn't the best idea, for a few reasons.

For one, you have little control over how Flash translates your dynamic text field's content into HTML. The HTML places the content of your dynamic text field in a <p> tag, giving little structure to the HTML. If you were to hand-write the HTML code, you could organize blocks of text into lists, headings, and so forth.

Next, any links added using the Property Inspector are inserted into the HTML as standard links, using only the href and target attributes. This doesn't allow you to use important SEO attributes, such as title, in your links.

Finally, the HTML version of your Flash text is placed in a comment, so only spiders can view the text. Because the text is visible only to spiders, those who don't have Flash Player installed won't view any alternative content.

Recent Developments on the Flash SEO Front

I mentioned earlier that Adobe announced that Google and Yahoo! will now index Flash movies. This opens the doors to an exciting new frontier in Flash SEO. One of the most important issues with Flash SEO is what content is and isn't indexed. In this section, we'll look at what Flash content search engines index, and how to optimize Flash applications for search.

How does it work? At this point, few details have been released to the public. What we do know is that Adobe created a version of Flash Player made to crawl through Flash applications. What we don't know is, well, everything else.

Understanding what content is searchable

So, what Flash content is searchable? Basically, any text that appears in a text field and any URLs revealed in ActionScript or otherwise are now indexed by search engines. That includes the URLs you want to be indexed, as well as the ones you may not want to be indexed. Essentially, anything in a dynamic text field that a person can see can now be indexed.

Understanding how to make searchable Flash content

To make searchable Flash content, you don't have to do much, if anything at all. Google and Yahoo! are already indexing the content right now. The content indexed is *all* Flash content, not just content published for later releases of Flash Player.

Of course, this news is both triumphant and tragic. Triumphant because search engines are doing all the work and you have to do nothing, and tragic because search engines may end up indexing a lot of private data.

Understanding how to make non-searchable Flash content

Now, you may not want all your Flash text to be indexed. If not for privacy reasons, you may want to have more control over which keywords are used, or you may be using letters as graphical elements. In these cases, simply convert any text to vector outlines (Modify→Break Apart) or import that text as a bitmap graphic. That way, you can have a little more control over which content is indexed and which is not.

Optimizing a Flash application for search

If Flash applications can be searched, it's crucial to understand how the content is indexed relative to how HTML content is indexed. At this point, it's difficult to say, so the best practice currently is to use HTML in dynamic text fields for SEO in Flash, along with CSS or the `TextFormat` class. That way, you have maximum control over the structure and style of your text fields while simultaneously optimizing them.

Using HTML text with CSS in ActionScript 3.0

Using HTML text with CSS in ActionScript 3.0 requires a basic to intermediate knowledge of all three languages. In this section, we'll take a bird's-eye view of how it works.

First, you'll need to have some HTML and CSS code to bring into Flash. Table 3-1 lists the HTML elements and attributes that Flash Player 10 supports, as stated in Flash Help.

Table 3-1. Flash Player 10-supported HTML elements and attributes[a]

Tag	Description
Anchor tag	The `<a>` tag creates a hypertext link and supports the following attributes: `target`: Specifies the name of the target window where you load the page. Options include `_self`, `_blank`, `_parent`, and `_top`. The `_self` option specifies the current frame in the current window, `_blank` specifies a new window, `_parent` specifies the parent of the current frame, and `_top` specifies the top-level frame in the current window.
	`href`: Specifies a URL or an ActionScript `link` event. The URL can be either absolute or relative to the location of the SWF file that's loading the page. An example of an absolute reference to a URL is *http://www.adobe.com*; an example of a relative reference is */index.html*. Absolute URLs must be prefixed with http://; otherwise, Flash treats them as relative URLs. You can use the `link` event to cause the link to execute an ActionScript function in a SWF file instead of opening a URL. To specify a `link` event, use the event scheme instead of the HTTP scheme in your `href` attribute. An example is `href="event:myText"` instead of `href="http://myURL"`; when the user clicks a hypertext link that contains the event scheme, the text field dispatches a `TextEvent` link with its `text` property set to `myText`. You can then create an ActionScript function that executes whenever the `TextEvent` link is dispatched. You can also define `a:link`, `a:hover`, and `a:active` styles for anchor tags by using stylesheets.
Bold tag	The `<b>` tag renders text as bold. A bold typeface must be available for the font used.
Break tag	The ` ` tag creates a line break in the text field. Set the text field to be a multiline text field to use this tag.
Font tag	The `<font>` tag specifies a font or list of fonts to display the text. The font tag supports the following attributes:
	`color`: Only hexadecimal color (#FFFFFF) values are supported.

Tag	Description
	`face`: Specifies the name of the font to use. You can specify a list of comma-delimited font names, in which case Flash Player selects the first available font. If the specified font isn't installed on the local computer system or isn't embedded in the SWF file, Flash Player selects a substitute font.
	`size`: Specifies the size of the font. You can use absolute pixel sizes, such as 16 or 18, or relative point sizes, such as +2 or -4.
Image tag	The `<img>` tag lets you embed external image files (JPEG, GIF, or PNG), SWF files, and movie clips inside text fields. Text automatically flows around images you embed in text fields. You must set the text field to be multiline to wrap text around an image.
	The `<img>` tag supports the following attributes:
	`src`: Specifies the URL to an image or SWF file, or the linkage identifier for a movie clip symbol in the library. This attribute is required; all other attributes are optional. External files (JPEG, GIF, PNG, and SWF files) do not show until they are downloaded completely.
	`width`: The width of the image, SWF file, or movie clip being inserted, in pixels.
	`height`: The height of the image, SWF file, or movie clip being inserted, in pixels.
	`align`: Specifies the horizontal alignment of the embedded image within the text field. Valid values are `left` and `right`. The default value is `left`.
	`hspace`: Specifies the amount of horizontal space that surrounds the image where no text appears. The default value is 8.
	`vspace`: Specifies the amount of vertical space that surrounds the image where no text appears. The default value is 8.
	`id`: Specifies the name for the movie clip instance (created by Flash Player) that contains the embedded image file, SWF file, or movie clip. This approach is used to control the embedded content with ActionScript.
	`checkPolicyFile`: Specifies that Flash Player checks for a URL policy file on the server associated with the image domain. If a policy file exists, SWF files in the domains listed in the file can access the data of the loaded image, for example, by calling the `Bitmap Data.draw()` method with this image as the `source` parameter. For more information, see *Essential ActionScript 3.0* by Colin Moock (O'Reilly).
	Flash displays media embedded in a text field at full size. To specify the dimensions of the media you're embedding, use the `<img>` tag's `height` and `width` attributes.
	In general, an image embedded in a text field appears on the line following the `<img>` tag. However, when the `<img>` tag is the first character in the text field, the image appears on the first line of the text field.
Italic tag	The `<i>` tag displays the tagged text in italic. An italic typeface must be available for the font used.
List item tag	The `<li>` tag places a bullet in front of the text that it encloses. Because Flash Player doesn't recognize ordered and unordered list tags (`<ol>` and `<ul>`), these tags don't modify how your list is rendered. All lists are unordered and all list items use bullets.

Tag	Description
Paragraph tag	The <p> tag creates a new paragraph. The text field must be set to be a multiline text field to use this tag. The <p> tag supports the following attributes:
	align: Specifies alignment of text within the paragraph. Valid values are left, right, justify, and center.
	class: Specifies a CSS style class defined by a flash.text.StyleSheet object.
Span tag	The <span> tag is available only for use with CSS text styles. It supports the following attribute:
	class: Specifies a CSS style class defined by a flash.text.StyleSheet object.
Text format tag	The <textformat> tag lets you use a subset of the paragraph formatting properties of the TextFormat class within text fields, including line leading, indentation, margins, and tab stops. You can combine <textformat> tags with the built-in HTML tags.
	The <textformat> tag has the following attributes:
	blockindent: Specifies the block indentation in points; corresponds to TextFormat.blockIndent.
	indent: Specifies the indentation from the left margin to the first character in the paragraph; corresponds to TextFormat.indent. Both positive and negative numbers are acceptable.
	leading: Specifies the amount of leading (vertical space) between lines; corresponds to TextFormat.leading. Both positive and negative numbers are acceptable.
	leftmargin: Specifies the left margin of the paragraph, in points; corresponds to TextFormat.leftMargin.
	rightmargin: Specifies the right margin of the paragraph, in points; corresponds to TextFormat.rightMargin.
	tabstops: Specifies custom tab stops as an array of non-negative integers; corresponds to TextFormat.tabStops.
Underline tag	The <u> tag underlines the tagged text.

a Table used courtesy of the Flash Help site.

> For more details on using HTML in ActionScript 3.0, see the TextField class in the ActionScript 3.0 Language and Components Reference in Flash Help.

You'll also need to understand what CSS is supported. Table 3-2 lists what CSS is supported in Flash Player 10 (again from Flash Help).

Table 3-2. CSS properties supported by Flash Player 10[a]

CSS property	Usage and supported values
color	Only hexadecimal color values are supported. Named colors (such as blue) are not supported. Colors are written in the following format: #FF0000.
display	Supported values are inline, block, and none.
font-family	A comma-separated list of fonts to use, in descending order of desirability. Any font family name can be used. If you specify a generic font name, it is converted to an appropriate device font. The following font conversions are available: mono is converted to _typewriter, sans-serif is converted to _sans, and serif is converted to _serif.
font-size	Only the numeric part of the value is used. Units (px, pt) are not parsed; pixels and points are equivalent.
font-style	Recognized values are normal and italic.
font-weight	Recognized values are normal and bold.
kerning	Recognized values are true and false. Kerning is supported for embedded fonts only. Certain fonts, such as Courier New, don't support kerning. The kerning property is supported only in SWF files created in Windows, not in SWF files created on the Macintosh. However, these SWF files can be played in non-Windows versions of Flash Player and the kerning still applies.
leading	The amount of space that is uniformly distributed between lines. The value specifies the number of pixels that are added after each line. A negative value condenses the space between lines. Only the numeric part of the value is used. Units (px, pt) are not parsed; pixels and points are equivalent.
letter-spacing	The amount of space that is uniformly distributed between characters. The value specifies the number of pixels that are added after each character. A negative value condenses the space between characters. Only the numeric part of the value is used. Units (px, pt) are not parsed; pixels and points are equivalent.
margin-left	Only the numeric part of the value is used. Units (px, pt) are not parsed; pixels and points are equivalent.
margin-right	Only the numeric part of the value is used. Units (px, pt) are not parsed; pixels and points are equivalent.
text-align	Recognized values are left, center, right, and justify.
text-decoration	Recognized values are none and underline.
text-indent	Only the numeric part of the value is used. Units (px, pt) are not parsed; pixels and points are equivalent.

[a] Table used courtesy of the Flash Help site.

For details about using CSS in ActionScript 3.0, see the StyleSheet class in the ActionScript 3.0 Language and Components Reference in Flash Help.

The ActionScript to load HTML and CSS into Flash will require you to be somewhat familiar with the language. Basically, you need to use the URLLoader class to load the external HTML and CSS files. Once you've loaded both files into Flash, you can parse the styles using an instance of the StyleSheet class, making it usable, by using the parseCSS method. From there, you connect the stylesheet object to a text field by using the text field's styleSheet property and then have the text field display the styled HTML data by using its htmlText property. That's it! Your code may look similar to this example:

```
var htmlReq:URLRequest = new URLRequest("html.txt");
var cssReq:URLRequest = new URLRequest("styles.css");
var loader:URLLoader = new URLLoader();
var sheet:StyleSheet = new StyleSheet();
var htmlData:String = "";

function fileLoaded(event:Event):void
{
    htmlData = loader.data;
    loader.removeEventListener(Event.COMPLETE, fileLoaded);
    loader.load(cssReq);
    loader.addEventListener(Event.COMPLETE, cssLoaded);
}

function cssLoaded(event:Event):void
{
    sheet.parseCSS(loader.data);
    html_txt.styleSheet = sheet;
    html_txt.htmlText = htmlData;
    html_txt.autoSize = TextFieldAutoSize.LEFT;
}

loader.load(htmlReq);
loader.addEventListener(Event.COMPLETE, fileLoaded);
```

 The entire workflow for HTML and CSS with ActionScript 3.0 appears in more detail in the exercises at the end of this chapter.

Solving the Link Dilemma

One basic advantage to using HTML over Flash for large applications or websites is the fact that HTML provides an easy, natural way to link to various states of the application because an application can be made into several linkable pages.

Earlier in this chapter, I mentioned that you can emulate this functionality in Flash to create a better user experience. In this section, we'll view three (some effective, some less effective) methods for linking in Flash.

Understanding named anchors

If you use frame labels in Flash, you may be familiar with named anchors. Named anchors are a way for you to communicate to your browser's back button to create a better user experience in your applications. Sadly, named anchor support extends only to Internet Explorer, and is unsupported in other web browsers. Though named anchors have little support, and thus aren't considered necessary, we'll still discuss the process of creating anchors in case you should choose to use them.

You can add named anchors to any keyframe in your Flash application via the Property Inspector. Simply select a keyframe, add the name of the anchor to the `Label` field in the Property Inspector, and choose "anchor" for the frame label type.

 Named anchors should not contain any spaces or special characters.

Creating multipage applications

Perhaps the easiest approach to optimizing a Flash application is simply to create multipage applications. So, instead of navigating the application asynchronously, users will be moved to different pages and will have to wait for the pages to load.

The great thing about this tactic is the easiness of it. Instead of using buttons in your site to trigger complex ActionScript or to navigate to frames or frame labels, you simply use URLs. This gives you a fast and easy method for linking to specific states of your application, and for SEO purposes it gives you an application similar to an HTML-based application.

Sadly, as easy as it is, creating multipage sites isn't necessarily the best way to optimize a Flash application. That's because one of the big reasons to use Flash is to easily create applications that run asynchronously—without multiple page loads. Waiting for a page load at every change in an application will make your application more similar to its HTML counterpart, which in some ways defeats the purpose of using Flash.

For practice creating multipage Flash applications, see the exercises at the end of this chapter.

Understanding deep links

Deep links are the best practice for linking in Flash SEO, because they allow you to link to any state of an application and they allow asynchronous navigation. Deep linking works by using pseudo anchors, which work similar to named anchors in HTML. You may or may not be familiar with named anchors, so here's a quick refresher—named anchors are what you use in HTML to navigate to a specific part of a page, and they don't require a page reload. The idea of deep linking is the same. The most popular tool for deep linking is SWFAddress, which is JavaScript-based and uses special addresses to communicate to Flash.

We'll cover how to implement SWFAddress in Chapter 4.

Exercises

Now that you're familiar with how to optimize applications in Flash, let's complete some exercises to practice the different techniques.

Exercise 3-1: Optimizing a Flash Application

In this exercise, you'll add static text, dynamic text, and metadata to a Flash application to optimize it for search engines.

Because this file was created for Flash Player 7, the code used is ActionScript 2.0.

File: *Optimizing.fla*

1. Open *Optimizing.fla* in the Chapter 3 folder.
2. Double click the INFO button at the bottom right of the Stage to enter the mcInfo timeline.

This timeline contains two frames. Both show the descriptive text, but one is off the Stage. This is because to auto-embed dynamic text field content into your published HTML file, the content must appear on the first frame.

3. Inside the mcInfo movie clip, move to frame 2 and note the descriptive text in the dynamic text field. This content will be embedded into your HTML file when you publish it.

4. Select the first keyframe of the actions layer and open the Actions panel (Window→Actions).

5. In the Actions panel, note the interactive code:

```
stop();

this.onRollOver = function():Void
{
    gotoAndStop(2);
}

this.onRollOut = function():Void
{
    gotoAndStop(1);
}
```

This code stops the playback of this movie clip, moves to frame 2 when the movie clip is rolled over, and moves back to frame 1 on rollout.

6. Return to the main timeline by clicking Scene 1 at the top of your screen.

7. On the main timeline, select the static text field, Target Time, at the top right of the Stage.

8. Because this text field is not useful for SEO, convert the text to vector shapes by choosing Modify→Break Apart twice.

 You need to run Break Apart twice because the first time it converts the letters in the text to individual text blocks. The second time it converts the text blocks into shapes.

9. Choose File→Info to add XMP metadata to the file.

10. In the metadata window, add some title and description information (see Figure 3-4), and then click OK when you're finished to accept the changes you've made.

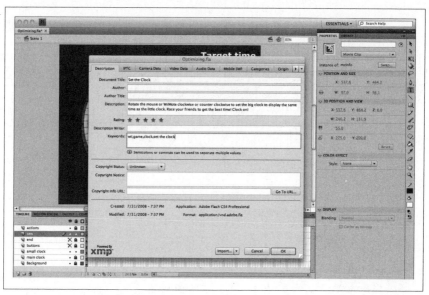

Figure 3-4. Entering XMP metadata to the file

11. Choose File→Publish Settings to open the Publish Settings window.

12. In the Publish Settings window, select the Flash tab and make sure the Include XMP Metadata checkbox is turned on.

13. Click Publish to publish the HTML and SWF files and then close the Publish Settings window by clicking OK.

14. Open the HTML file Flash just created for you in a web browser, and then choose View→Page Source to view the source code. In the source code, scroll to the bottom to view the descriptive text from Flash (see Figure 3-5).

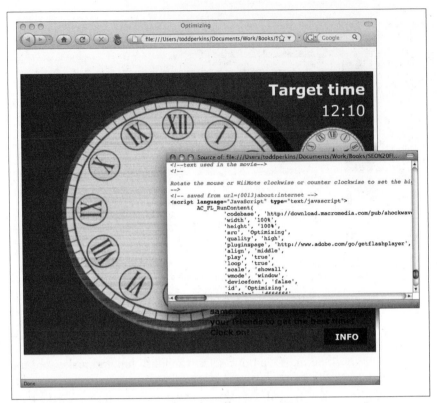

Figure 3-5. Viewing the auto-embedded HTML description in the source code

Exercise 2: Optimizing ActionScript-Driven Text in a Flash Application

When you're optimizing Flash applications, using HTML code can allow you to prioritize content, using links, headings, and other HTML tags. In this exercise, you'll look at the entire workflow of bringing external HTML into Flash, and how to style the HTML code using CSS.

1. First things first—you'll need some HTML code to import. In the exercise files for this book, you'll find *html.txt* in the folder for this chapter. Let's take a look at the HTML code in that file.

   File: *html.txt*

   ```
   <h1><a href="wii-games/xylophone-master.html">Xylophone Master</a></h1>
   <p>Learn to master playing the xylophone and simultaneously boost
   your memory!Listen to the computer play notes and simply play them back
   by moving your mouse or Wii remote up and down over the keys.</p>
   <h1><a href="wii-games/meteor-blaster.html">Meteor Blaster</a></h1>
   ```

```
<p>Shoot meteors with powerful laser cannons! Advance through levels
based on your score. Watch your energy meter! Those meteors are
relentless!</p>
<h1><a href="wii-games/fun-run.html">Fun Run</a></h1>
<p>Run a marathon as a giant man, completing up to 26.2 miles in
5 seconds! Move the mouse (or WiiMote) up and down to run.
Finish fast to get medals!</p>
<h1><a href="wii-games/set-the-clock.html">Set the Clock</a></h1>
<p>Rotate the mouse or WiiMote clockwise or counterclockwise to
set the big clock to display the same time as the little clock.
Race your friends to get the best time! Clock on!</p>
```

 This file is similar to the index page used in Chapter 2, but without images and DIV tags. For SEO, you can still use links and heading tags to optimize your content. When using HTML for Flash, it's typically best to stick to text content only, because you have little control over the layout of images.

2. Open *styles.css* in the folder for this chapter, and browse its contents.

   File: *styles.css*

```
p {
    font-family: Trebuchet MS, Arial, Helvetica, sans-serif;
    font-size: 14px;
    font-weight: normal;
    color: #FFFFFF;
}

h1 {
    color: #9FFF9F;
    font-size: 20px;
    font-weight: bold;
}

a {
    color: #9FFF9F;
    text-decoration: none;
}

a:hover {
    color: #C8FFC9;
    text-decoration: underline;
}
```

   Though CSS in Flash is limited, you can still style paragraphs, headings, and links.

3. Now we'll look at the ActionScript required. The file *HTML-CSS.fla* contains a simple layout with a dynamic text field that has an instance name of html_txt. The first keyframe of the actions layer in that file contains the following code.

File: *HTML-CSS.fla* (first keyframe of the actions layer)

```
var htmlReq:URLRequest = new URLRequest("html.txt");
var cssReq:URLRequest = new URLRequest("styles.css");
var loader:URLLoader = new URLLoader();
var sheet:StyleSheet = new StyleSheet();
var htmlData:String;

function fileLoaded(event:Event):void
{
    htmlData = loader.data;
    loader.removeEventListener(Event.COMPLETE, fileLoaded);
    loader.load(cssReq);
    loader.addEventListener(Event.COMPLETE, cssLoaded);
}

function cssLoaded(event:Event):void
{
    sheet.parseCSS(loader.data);
    html_txt.styleSheet = sheet;
    html_txt.htmlText = htmlData;
    html_txt.autoSize = TextFieldAutoSize.LEFT;
}

loader.addEventListener(Event.COMPLETE, fileLoaded);
loader.load(htmlReq);
```

Let's do a quick walkthrough of this code. The first five lines (the ones
that begin with "var") define the variables used. The variables represent
the URLs to the HTML and CSS files (htmlReq and cssReq), the object that
will load the data from the files (loader), the ActionScript version of the
stylesheet (called sheet), and the HTML data loaded from the external
TXT file:

```
var htmlReq:URLRequest = new URLRequest("html.txt");
var cssReq:URLRequest = new URLRequest("styles.css");
var loader:URLLoader = new URLLoader();
var sheet:StyleSheet = new StyleSheet();
var htmlData:String;
```

At the bottom of the code is where the application begins its work. The
loader object loads the URL for the HTML file (loader.load(htmlReq)),
and waits for the file to load (loader.addEventListener(Event.COMPLETE,
fileLoaded)), at which point the fileLoaded function will run:

```
loader.load(htmlReq);
loader.addEventListener(Event.COMPLETE, fileLoaded);
```

The fileLoaded function stores the HTML data within the htmlData variable, disassociates the loader from the fileLoaded function, loads the CSS
file, and sets the cssLoaded function to run once the CSS file is loaded:

```
function fileLoaded(event:Event):void
{
    htmlData = loader.data;
    loader.removeEventListener(Event.COMPLETE, fileLoaded);
    loader.load(cssReq);
    loader.addEventListener(Event.COMPLETE, cssLoaded);
}
```

The `cssLoaded` function parses the loaded CSS code, making it usable in
ActionScript, connects the text field on the stage (`html_txt`) to the stylesheet object, sets the text field to display the HTML text, and sets the text
field to `autosize`:

```
function cssLoaded(event:Event):void
{
    sheet.parseCSS(loader.data);
    html_txt.styleSheet = sheet;
    html_txt.htmlText = htmlData;
    html_txt.autoSize = TextFieldAutoSize.LEFT;
}
```

4. Once you're done viewing the ActionScript in this file, you can see the file
   in action by choosing Control→Test Movie (shown in Figure 3-6).

Figure 3-6. Viewing HTML text styled by CSS in Flash Player

If you click the HTML links in Flash Player, HTML pages will open. You can use HTML links like this to quickly and easily create a multipage Flash application.

Key Terms Used in This Chapter

Table 3-3 contains the terms that were introduced in this chapter and gives you their definitions.

Table 3-3. Key terms used in this chapter

Term	Definition
Deep links	Links that take a user to a specific state of your Flash application
XMP metadata	eXtensible Metadata Platform, a standards-based form of metadata used to embed information about a file into the file itself

CHAPTER 4

Using JavaScript with Flash for SEO

JavaScript can greatly enhance both the user experience and search engine optimization (SEO) for the Flash content in your websites. Using some third-party JavaScript, you can have an incredible amount of control over what users see when they visit your site without Flash, and you can even create deep links to your applications in any of their states. In this chapter, we'll look at how to use JavaScript in conjunction with Flash to add these enhancements.[*]

Prerequisite JavaScript Experience

You may be wondering how much JavaScript you'll need to know to make it through this chapter. Fortunately for those who aren't familiar with JavaScript, the code we're going to use is very simple to implement in a site, especially if you're already familiar with ActionScript.

JavaScript is an ECMAScript language, meaning it's compliant with certain standards (see *http://www.ecma-international.org/publications/standards/Ecma-262.htm*). ActionScript is also an ECMAScript language, so it has many similarities to JavaScript. Since ActionScript 3.0 is based on a different ECMAScript version than JavaScript, there are a few important differences between the two languages. The version of ActionScript that most resembles JavaScript is ActionScript 1.0, but if you're familiar with ActionScript 2.0 or ActionScript 3.0, JavaScript should be pretty easy for you to learn.

A detailed study of JavaScript is beyond the scope of this book. However, as with the other code we've used up to this point, we'll discuss all of the JavaScript code we write.

---

[*] The SWFAddress code referenced in this chapter is Copyright (c) 2006-2007 Rostislav Hristov, Asual DZZD and is used with permission. The SWFObject code referenced in this chapter is Copyright (c) 2007–2008 Geoff Stearns, Michael Williams, and Bobby van der Sluis and is used with permission.

Essential Flash SEO JavaScript

When using JavaScript for SEO, you'll need to become familiar with two essential code libraries: `SWFObject` and `SWFAddress`. Adding the capabilities of these libraries to your applications will dramatically increase the usability and SEO of your sites.

SWFObject

`SWFObject` is the generally accepted standard of using Flash content on the Web, for several reasons. Aside from it being standards-compliant, all major browsers (Firefox, Internet Explorer, Safari, Opera, etc.) support JavaScript, and therefore `SWFObject`, and it's extremely easy to use.

The latest version of `SWFObject`, which was originally developed by Geoff Stearns (*http://blog.deconcept.com/*), was created with help from other developers such as Michael Williams and Bobby Van Der Sluis (*http://www.bobby vandersluis.com/*).

Benefits of SWFObject

Using the `SWFObject` library for Flash SEO offers many benefits. Here are some of the most prominent benefits:

- Standards-compliant
- Supported by all major browsers on all major operating systems
- Easy to use
- Uses JavaScript to override "click to activate" messages in Internet Explorer
- No more worrying about browser-specific markup (`<object>` and `<embed>` tags) being interpreted differently by browsers
- SEO-friendly way to provide alternative content

Though Flash writes HTML with version detection for you with effectively one click (File→Publish), using `SWFObject` is worth the added effort. For SEO and usability, there are very few reasons *not* to use `SWFObject` (like when embedding Flash content on a social networking site, for example) for all of the Flash content you create.

> For full documentation of `SWFObject`, including a full list of features and benefits, see its section in Google Code at *http:// code.google.com/p/swfobject/wiki/documentation*.

Downloading SWFObject

The official site for `SWFObject` is at Google Code, *http://code.google.com/p/ swfobject/*. From there, you can download the necessary code files for the latest version of `SWFObject` from the Downloads page, at *http://code.google.com/p/ swfobject/downloads/list*, shown in Figure 4-1.

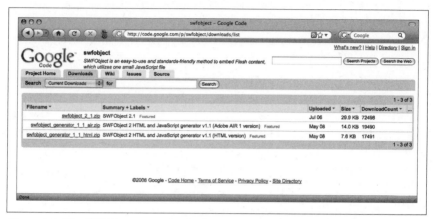

Figure 4-1. The SWFObject Downloads page

Once you've downloaded `SWFObject`, unzip the file and you'll find a folder called *swfobject*. The *swfobject* folder contains some demo files, source files, and the main file you'll need: *swfobject.js*. Whenever you use `SWFObject`, you'll need to copy *swfobject.js* into a directory that's accessible by the HTML file that'll house your Flash content.

Using SWFObject in a Flash application

You can publish `SWFObject` content via two methods: the static publishing method and the dynamic publishing method. The method you choose depends on your specific needs for a project.

Using the static publishing method

The static publishing method uses standards-compliant HTML markup to embed both Flash content and alternative content. Static publishing has two key advantages: standards-compliant markup, and JavaScript is not required to embed Flash content. In other words, even if someone viewing the page doesn't have JavaScript enabled, he can still see the Flash content if he has the appropriate Flash Player version.

Here's an example of using `SWFObject` (pasted from the `SWFObject` documentation page):

```
<!DOCTYPE html PUBLIC "-//W3C//DTD XHTML 1.0 Strict//EN"
"http://www.w3.org/TR/xhtml1/DTD/xhtml1-strict.dtd">
<html xmlns="http://www.w3.org/1999/xhtml" lang="en" xml:lang="en">
  <head>
    <title>SWFObject - step 3</title>
    <meta http-equiv="Content-Type" content="text/html; charset=
    iso-8859-1" />
    <script type="text/javascript" src="swfobject.js"></script>

    <script type="text/javascript">
    swfobject.registerObject("myId", "9.0.0", "expressInstall.swf");
    </script>

  </head>
  <body>
    <div>

      <object id="myId" classid="clsid:D27CDB6E-AE6D-11cf-96B8-444553540000"
width="780" height="420">

        <param name="movie" value="myContent.swf" />
        <!--[if !IE]>-->
        <object type="application/x-shockwave-flash" data="myContent.swf"
width="780" height="420">
          <!--<![endif]-->
            <p>Alternative content</p>
          <!--[if !IE]>-->
        </object>
        <!--<![endif]-->
      </object>
    </div>
  </body>
</html>
```

Let's walk through this code, starting with the outer <object> tag. Note its attributes: id, classid, width, and height. Also note the <param> element. This element and these attributes are necessary for using SWFObject. Here's what the values represent:

id

   The id attribute is the identifier for the <object> element, which JavaScript uses in SWFObject to reference this element.

classid

   The classid attribute corresponds to the type of content the <object> element will hold. For Flash content, this value will always be D27CDB6E-AE6D-11cf-96B8-444553540000.

width

   The width attribute refers to the pixel width of the Flash content.

weight

   The height attribute refers to the pixel height of the Flash content.

param

> The `<param>` element holds name and value pairs with information for the `<object>` element, including the location of the SWF file, as shown in the preceding code.

 Internet Explorer interprets the outer `<object>` element, and the other web browsers read the inner `<object>` element (as defined by the `!IE` conditional statement). There are two object elements because Internet Explorer reads `<object>` tags differently from other web browsers. Other browsers use the `type` attribute to tell the browser to expect Flash, whereas Internet Explorer uses the `clsid` attribute which, like the `type` attribute in the inner `<object>` element, will always have the same value for Flash content.

Within the outer `<object>` element, you'll notice some HTML conditional statements that look like the following code:

```
<!--[if !IE]>-->
<!--<![endif]-->
```

These statements are used to run blocks of HTML code that meet certain conditions, just like conditional statements in ActionScript. The code in this example will run the code within the two lines only if the browser is *not* Internet Explorer.

The inner `<object>` element contains syntax acceptable by non-Internet Explorer browsers. All four attributes in this element are required, and they correspond to the attributes and elements in the outer, Internet Explorer `<object>` element. The `width` and `height` attributes represent pixel values for width and height, just like the outer `<object>` tag. Here's what the other values represent:

type

> The `type` attribute refers to the type of content the `<object>` will display. For Flash content, the value will always be `application/x-shockwave-flash`.

data

> The `data` attribute refers to the SWF file.

All alternative content is contained within the inner `<object>` tag, and all browsers can read it. This is where you may want to place a title and description for your Flash content, as well as any other information about it that you'd like. This alternative content *is* indexed, so make sure to use your HTML SEO skills to properly communicate your Flash content to the search engines.

To use `SWFObject`, you'll need a link to *swfobject.js* in a `<script>` element, shown in the following code:

```
<script type="text/javascript" src="swfobject.js"></script>
```

Once you have a link to *swfobject.js*, you can create a separate script block in your HTML file and run the `swfobject.registerObject()` method to register your Flash content with `SWFObject`. The `swfobject.registerObject()` method accepts three string-valued parameters, the third of which is optional. First, the method accepts the `id` of the outer `<object>` element; second, the minimum version of Flash Player required to view the Flash content; and third, the file for a customized Flash Player Express Install version. Here's what the `swfobject.registerObject()` method looks like in code:

```
<script type="text/javascript">
    swfobject.registerObject("myId", "9.0.0", "expressInstall.swf");
</script>
```

You can find the version of Flash Player that you're publishing to in the Publish Settings window of Flash. In the Publish Settings window, click the HTML tab, and you'll see the Flash Player version under the Detect Flash Version checkbox (shown in Figure 4-2).

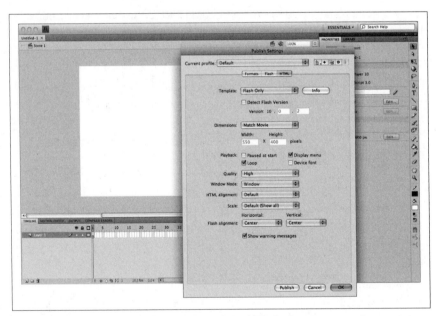

Figure 4-2. Viewing the Flash Player version in Publish Settings

Flash Player Express Install upgrades an installation of Flash Player if someone visiting your site has an earlier version of that which is required to view your

Flash content. You can find more information about Flash Player Express Install at *http://kb.adobe.com/selfservice/viewContent.do?externalId=6a253b75
&sliceId=1*.

 Static publishing should only be used when targeting devices
or browsers that have Flash but not JavaScript capability. For
SEO, dynamic publishing is the superior method for using
SWFObject.

Using the dynamic publishing method

The dynamic publishing method for SWFObject provides two key features: excellent integration with scripted applications, and removal of "click to activate" controls in Internet Explorer. Also, dynamic publishing uses less code
than static publishing.

Dynamic publishing is dependent on JavaScript to work properly. If someone
views your content in a browser that has poor JavaScript support (such as the
Sony PSP), she won't see the Flash content even if she has the appropriate Flash
Player version. Though most browsers have JavaScript support, and most
people browse the Web with JavaScript enabled, you may prefer to use static
publishing if you know some people will be viewing your content without
sufficient JavaScript power.

Dynamic publishing is primarily JavaScript-driven, and thus requires less
markup code to write. Here's an example of dynamic publishing (pasted from
SWFObject's documentation page):

```
<!DOCTYPE html PUBLIC "-//W3C//DTD XHTML 1.0 Strict//EN"
"http://www.w3.org/TR/xhtml1/DTD/xhtml1-strict.dtd">
<html xmlns="http://www.w3.org/1999/xhtml" lang="en" xml:lang="en">
  <head>
    <title>SWFObject dynamic embed - step 3</title>
    <meta http-equiv="Content-Type" content="text/html; charset=
iso-8859-1" />
    <script type="text/javascript" src="swfobject.js"></script>

    <script type="text/javascript">
    swfobject.embedSWF("myContent.swf", "myContent", "300", "120", "9.0.0");
    </script>

  </head>
  <body>
    <div id="myContent">
      <p>Alternative content</p>
    </div>
  </body>
</html>
```

First off, you'll notice that dynamic publishing requires significantly less markup code. This is because SWFObject does all the JavaScript work to replace your alternative content with the HTML necessary for Flash content, if the user has the appropriate version of Flash Player.

Let's review the code. Notice that the alternative content is placed inside a <div> element with an id value of myContent. With dynamic publishing, SWFObject writes all of the HTML <object> tag data.

Like the static publishing method, dynamic publishing requires that you link to the external file, *swfobject.js*. You then can place the code to use the dynamic publishing method in a script block, and it'll look similar to the following code:

```
<script type="text/javascript">
swfobject.embedSWF("myContent.swf", "myContent", "300", "120", "9.0.0");
</script>
```

The JavaScript method that uses dynamic publishing is called swfobject.embedSWF(), and it takes nine parameters, the last four of which are optional. Here are the parameter names, along with data types accepted, and descriptions (from the SWFObject documentation):

swfUrl *(String, required)*
> Specifies the URL of your SWF.

id *(String, required)*
> Specifies the id of the HTML element (containing your alternative content) that you'd like to have replaced by your Flash content.

width *(String, required)*
> Specifies the width of your SWF.

height *(String, required)*
> Specifies the height of your SWF.

version *(String, required)*
> Specifies the Flash Player version for which your SWF is published (the format is "major.minor.release").

expressInstallSwfurl *(String, optional)*
> Specifies the URL of your Express Install SWF and activates Adobe Express Install (*http://www.adobe.com/cfusion/knowledgebase/index.cfm?id=6a253b75*). Please note that Express Install will fire only once (the first time it's invoked), that it's supported only by Flash Player 6.0.65 and later on Windows or Mac platforms, and that it requires a minimal SWF size of 310x137 px.

flashvars *(Object, optional)*
> Specifies your flashvars with name/value pairs.

`params` *(Object, optional)*

Specifies your nested `object` element `params` with name/value pairs.

`attributes` *(Object, optional)*

Specifies your `object`'s attributes with name/value pairs.

It's also important to note that you can skip optional parameters as long as they're in the same order. Skipped parameters can take a value of `false` or `{}` (for `Object` data types such as `flashvars`).

 One of the methods for exchanging data between Flash and JavaScript is through the `flashvars` parameter, which we'll discuss in more detail later in this chapter.

Using the SWFObject generator

When using `SWFObject`, one of the options for writing the code is to use the `SWFObject` HTML and JavaScript generator at *http://www.bobbyvandersluis .com/swfobject/generator/index.html*. The generator (shown in Figure 4-3) creates the HTML and JavaScript for either the dynamic or the static publishing method automatically. Simply fill out the form, click Generate, and copy and paste the code given.

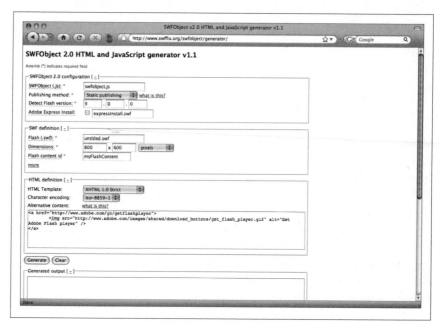

Figure 4-3. The SWFObject HTML and JavaScript generator

Here's an example of code that uses the static publishing method created by the generator:

```
<!DOCTYPE html PUBLIC "-//W3C//DTD XHTML 1.0 Strict//EN"
"http://www.w3.org/TR/xhtml1/DTD/xhtml1-strict.dtd">
<html xmlns="http://www.w3.org/1999/xhtml" lang="en" xml:lang="en">
    <head>
        <title></title>
        <meta http-equiv="Content-Type" content="text/html; charset=
iso-8859-1" />
        <script type="text/javascript" src="swfobject.js"></script>
        <script type="text/javascript">
            swfobject.registerObject("seoFlashContent", "10.0.0",
"expressInstall.swf");
        </script>
    </head>
    <body>
        <div>
            <object classid="clsid:D27CDB6E-AE6D-11cf-96B8-444553540000"
width="800" height="600" id="seoFlashContent">
                <param name="movie" value="seo.swf" />
                <!--[if !IE]>-->
                <object type="application/x-shockwave-flash" data="seo.swf"
width="800" height="600">
                <!--<![endif]-->
                    <a href="http://www.adobe.com/go/getflashplayer">
                        <img
src="http://www.adobe.com/images/shared/download_buttons/get_flash_player.gif"
alt="Get Adobe Flash player" />
                    </a>
                <!--[if !IE]>-->
                </object>
                <!--<![endif]-->
            </object>
        </div>
    </body>
</html>
```

If you're just dropping Flash content into an already created web page, you can copy the code you need from the generator and paste it in your page. There's no disadvantage to using the generator, so if you prefer code to be written for you, go for it!

SWFObject is an amazing tool for Flash and SEO, and it can greatly increase your control over how search engines index your Flash content by allowing you to provide fully searchable HTML content as an alternative to Flash content. In this alternative content, you can provide a title, description, or any other information in your Flash movie that should be searchable. Make sure to use it whenever you put Flash on the Web.

A comprehensive study of `SWFObject` is beyond the scope of this book. Go to *http://code.google.com/p/swfobject/wiki/documentation* to learn more about `SWFObject`.

SWFAddress

`SWFAddress` is an outstanding tool for Flash SEO. Using `SWFAddress`, you can deep-link to any state of your Flash application, and while navigating through your application you can update the browser window. This is great for SEO because it allows you to define links to any state of your application, and search engines index all of those links.

Benefits of SWFAddress

By using `SWFAddress`, you can get pages indexed that search engines wouldn't otherwise notice. Also, you can create *Rich Internet Applications* (RIA), robust, interactive web applications that have similar features to desktop applications, without having to completely compromise SEO. On top of that, `SWFAddress` allows you to interact with a browser's back and forward buttons. Like `SWFObject`, `SWFAddress` is invaluable when optimizing Flash on the Web.

`SWFAddress` was created for use with `SWFObject`, so you can take advantage of both tools seamlessly.

Limitations of SWFAddress

Though `SWFAddress` can provide excellent usability for your applications, it's important to understand that the SEO potential for `SWFAddress` ends with search engines indexing multiple pages for your applications. For example, your RIA may be on one HTML page, and using `SWFAddress` may get multiple URLs indexed for that page, but that doesn't mean the search engines will index different content for each URL. In other words, since the HTML page in each `SWFAddress` link for a one-page app is the same, search engines are basically indexing the same HTML content under different URLs. This is not to say you shouldn't use `SWFAddress`—just understand that `SWFAddress` is much better for usability than for SEO.

Downloading SWFAddress

You can download `SWFAddress` from *http://www.asual.com/swfaddress/*. It's open source, and free, but if you feel so inclined you can make a donation.

After downloading and unzipping SWFAddress, locate the ActionScript 3.0 classes SWFAddress and SWFAddressEvent, as well as the necessary JavaScript file, *swfaddress.js*.

Using SWFAddress in a Flash application

Before you use SWFAddress, you need to be aware that it'll work only on a server, or with additional configuration to your Flash Player. That means an ordinary Control→Test Movie command won't work. Because it's a best practice anyway to develop your site in a setting that best mimics a production environment, we're going to look at the server method here. Basically, you'll either have to upload the files to your web server for testing, or use a *testing server*, software you install on your computer that mimics a production server environment. If you use a testing server, I recommend downloading and installing WAMP on Windows and MAMP on Mac.

 See the exercises at the end of this chapter for more information about installing a testing server on your computer.

You don't need to use any JavaScript when using SWFAddress, other than a small addition of the id attribute in your call to the swfobject.embedSWF method, which we'll discuss soon. Start by linking to the file in your HTML code, which should look something like this:

```
<script type="text/javascript" src="swfaddress/swfaddress.js"></script>
```

To get SWFAddress to work properly with integrated back button functionality in the web browser, you'll need to add some code in your call to the swfobject.embedSWF method. All you need to do is assign a value for the id attribute of the object element that gets embedded when the Flash content is inserted. Here's what the line of code that makes a call to that method should look like:

```
swfobject.embedSWF(fileName.swf', 'altContentID', '1024', '660', '10.0.0',
'swfobject/expressinstall.swf', {}, {}, {id:'flashContent'});
```

The preceding code has three sets of curly braces ({}) for the last three parameter values. These are JavaScript objects used for defining values for FlashVars, parameters, and attributes, respectively. Here, the id attribute is assigned a value of flashContent.

Assigning some value to the `id` attribute in the `embedSWF` method is essential to make `SWFAddress` work properly in a web browser, and you'll lose much of the functionality of `SWFAddress` should you omit it.

When using `SWFAddress`, create navigation frame labels on the main timeline at the frames you want to navigate to. Name the frame labels beginning with a dollar sign ($), and use forward slashes (/) at the beginning and the end of the frame label name (shown in Figure 4-4). Other than that, you can set up your Flash application normally.

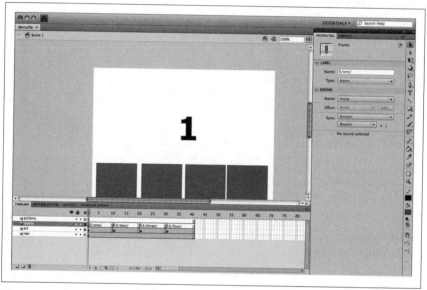

Figure 4-4. The FLA file prepared for use with SWFAddress

The ActionScript code for using `SWFAddress` is a little bit more complex than that for `SWFObject`, but it's fairly straightforward. Here's an example of using `SWFAddress` in a simple application.

File: *demo.fla* (frame 1 in the actions layer)

```
import SWFAddress;
import SWFAddressEvent;


function formatTitle(newTitle:String):String
{
    var updatedTitle:String = newTitle.replace("$","");
    updatedTitle = updatedTitle.replace("/","");
    updatedTitle = updatedTitle.replace("/","");
```

```
    updatedTitle = "SWFAddress Demo | " + updatedTitle;
    return updatedTitle;
}

function buttonClicked(event:MouseEvent):void
{
    var btnName:String = "/" + event.target.name + "/";
    SWFAddress.setValue(btnName);
}

function handleSWFAddress(event:SWFAddressEvent):void
{
    var link:String = event.value;
    if(link == "/")
    {
        link = currentLabels[0].name.replace("$","");
        SWFAddress.setValue(link);
        return;
    }
    gotoAndStop("$" + link);
    SWFAddress.setTitle(formatTitle(link));
}

SWFAddress.addEventListener(SWFAddressEvent.CHANGE, handleSWFAddress);
one.addEventListener(MouseEvent.CLICK, buttonClicked);
two.addEventListener(MouseEvent.CLICK, buttonClicked);
three.addEventListener(MouseEvent.CLICK, buttonClicked);
four.addEventListener(MouseEvent.CLICK, buttonClicked);
stop();
```

Now, we'll walk through this code. First, you'll need to import the
SWFAddress and **SWFAddressEvent** classes. Make sure to include them in the
same folder as your FLA file:

```
import SWFAddress;
import SWFAddressEvent;
```

Next, you will need to register an event listener with **SWFAddress** to listen for
the **SWFAddressEvent.CHANGE** event. This executes once JavaScript communication is established, and every time the **SWFAddress.setValue()** method is
called:

```
SWFAddress.addEventListener(SWFAddressEvent.CHANGE, handleSWFAddress);
```

The next four lines add event listeners to the four buttons on the stage, and
the line after that stops the movie:

```
one.addEventListener(MouseEvent.CLICK, buttonClicked);
two.addEventListener(MouseEvent.CLICK, buttonClicked);
three.addEventListener(MouseEvent.CLICK, buttonClicked);
four.addEventListener(MouseEvent.CLICK, buttonClicked);
stop();
```

The `buttonClicked` method is fairly simple. It adds forward slashes to the beginning and end of the instance name of the button that was clicked (`event.target.name`) and passes the string value to the `SWFAddress.set Value()` method, which triggers the `SWFAddressEvent.CHANGE` event, running the `handleSWFAddress()` function:

```
function buttonClicked(event:MouseEvent):void
{
    var btnName:String = "/" + event.target.name + "/";
    SWFAddress.setValue(btnName);
}
```

The `handleSWFAddress()` function defines what happens when the `SWFAddressEvent.CHANGE` event occurs. Through the event object, the property named *value* holds a value passed in via the `SWFAddress.setValue()` method. When the application initializes, the `SWFAddressEvent.CHANGE` event occurs, and the value of `event.value` is /. At that time, the value of the link is adjusted to be the first frame label in the application, without "$". Then `SWFAddress.set Value()` is called (mimicking a button click) and the `handleSWFAddress()` function stops executing (`return;`) and then runs again from the beginning (because `SWFAddress.setValue()` triggers the `SWFAddressEvent.CHANGE` event). After the first time `handleSWFAddress()` runs, it sends the playhead to the frame label that corresponds to the value of `$`, concatenated with `event.value`. The `SWFAddress.setTitle()` method is then called, passing in a formatted version of the value of `link`:

```
function handleSWFAddress(event:SWFAddressEvent):void
{
    var link:String = event.value;
    if(link == "/")
    {
        link = currentLabels[0].name.replace("$","");
        SWFAddress.setValue(link);
        return;
    }
    gotoAndStop("$" + link);
    SWFAddress.setTitle(formatTitle(link));
}
```

All the `formatTitle()` function does is adjust the `newTitle` string passed in, return a version with no spaces or dollar signs, and add that value to the end of the main title of the page ("SWFAddress Demo | "):

```
function formatTitle(newTitle:String):String
{
    var updatedTitle:String = newTitle.replace("$","");
    updatedTitle = updatedTitle.replace("/","");
    updatedTitle = updatedTitle.replace("/","");
    updatedTitle = "SWFAddress Demo | " + updatedTitle;
```

```
    return updatedTitle;
}
```

When you test the application in a web browser (using either a testing server or your web server), you can click through the application and watch the title in your browser update (shown in Figure 4-5), and even use your browser's back button. You can even type URLs directly to different states of your application.

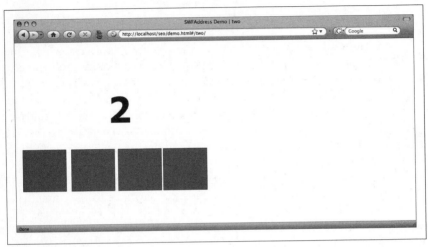

Figure 4-5. Testing SWFAddress using a testing server

For more details about SWFAddress, see its documentation and its official site at *http://www.asual.com/swfaddress/*.

Exchanging Data Between Flash and JavaScript

Earlier in this chapter, you used SWFAddress to communicate between Flash and JavaScript to update page titles and URLs in the browser window based on Flash instance names. SWFAddress uses the ExternalInterface class to exchange data between Flash and JavaScript. Other methods for sending data are also available, such as flashvars. When optimizing your site, you may want to exchange more data than what's done with SWFAddress, such as HTML code, between JavaScript and Flash. In this section, we'll look at using the ExternalInterface class, as well as flashvars to send data to and from Flash.

Understanding the ExternalInterface Class

The `ExternalInterface` class allows you to call JavaScript functions from Flash, and Flash functions from JavaScript. This way, you can easily exchange data that's uniquely available to JavaScript or to Flash. Like `SWFAddress`, you'll also need a web server or testing server (see the exercise in the next chapter) to see `ExternalInterface` in action.

> Flash Player version 8 and later support the `ExternalInter`
> `face` class, and for the supported versions it's the recommen-
> ded way to exchange JavaScript and ActionScript data. For
> earlier versions of Flash Player, use `flashvars`, which we'll
> discuss later in this section, or the built-in `FSCommand`
> functions.

Reasons to use ExternalInterface

Because nearly all browser information is unavailable to Flash directly and is readily available to JavaScript, it's often necessary to exchange data between the two. For example, you may want to get the URL of the page a SWF file is on, and use the data in Flash. Or you may want Flash to be notified when a JavaScript event occurs. As for SEO, you may want Flash to display text from its HTML container so that you have to write it only once, and you don't have to republish the SWF when the content is updated.

Using ExternalInterface to call JavaScript functions

The syntax for the `ExternalInterface` class is fairly straightforward. Use the `ExternalInterface.call()` method, and pass in the JavaScript function to call as a string and then the arguments to pass in, separated by commas. Arguments may be any ActionScript data types, and when sent to JavaScript they're converted to JavaScript data types. If you wanted to call a JavaScript function called `myFunction`, passing in a value of `some string`, the code would look like this:

```
ExternalInterface.call("myFunction", "some string");
```

Let's look at an example of `ExternalInterface` in action. The file *ExternalInterface.fla* contains the following code on frame 1 of the actions layer:

```
ExternalInterface.call("showAlert","Hello from Flash!");
```

Now we'll look at the HTML file. It's called *ExternalInterface.html*, and it was created using `SWFObject`'s dynamic publishing method.

```
<!DOCTYPE html PUBLIC "-//W3C//DTD XHTML 1.0 Strict//EN"
"http://www.w3.org/TR/xhtml1/DTD/xhtml1-strict.dtd">
<html xmlns="http://www.w3.org/1999/xhtml" lang="en" xml:lang="en">
    <head>
        <title>External Interface Test</title>
        <meta http-equiv="Content-Type" content="text/html; charset=
iso-8859-1" />
        <script type="text/javascript" src="swfobject/swfobject.js">
</script>
        <script type="text/javascript">
            swfobject.embedSWF("ExternalInterface.swf",
"myAlternativeContent", "550", "400", "10.0.0", false, {}, {},
{id:"flashContent"});
        </script>
        <script>
        function showAlert(a)
        {
            window.alert(a);
        }
        </script>
    </head>
    <body>
        <div id="myAlternativeContent">
            <p>This is just a test of ExternalInterface.</p>
        </div>
    </body>
</html>
```

Notice in the third <script> block, a function I created that matches the showAlert() function called from Flash that runs the JavaScript method window.alert(), passing in the value received from Flash. To see this in action, view this file using your testing server, making sure to include the *swfobject* folder containing *swfobject.js* and the *ExternalInterface.swf* file. When you view the file with your testing server, you should see the data passed in from Flash showing up as a JavaScript alert (shown in Figure 4-6).

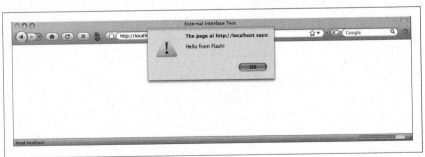

Figure 4-6. Viewing ExternalInterface in action on a testing server

Using returned JavaScript data

With `ExternalInterface`, you can not only send data from Flash to JavaScript, but also receive data returned from JavaScript in Flash. The method `ExternalInterface.call()`returns whatever data is returned from the Java-Script function called, and you can use that data however you like.

For an example, you can look at *ExternalInterfaceReturn.fla*. The file has a dynamic text field, `data_txt`, on the main timeline and the following code in the first keyframe of the actions layer:

```
if(ExternalInterface.call("getText"))
{
    data_txt.text = ExternalInterface.call("getText");
}
```

Here, the code checks to see whether the JavaScript `getText()` function returns a value. If so, that value is placed inside `data_txt`.

 It's not necessary here to check whether `getText()` returns a value before setting the text, but the code will return an error without it if you're just testing the movie from Flash. This is because unless you run this code on the Web or on a testing server, `ExternalInterface.call()` doesn't return anything (or rather, it returns null), which isn't an acceptable value for the `text` property of a text field.

The HTML and JavaScript code is contained in the file *ExternalInterfaceReturn.html*, and it is pretty straightforward:

```
<!DOCTYPE html PUBLIC "-//W3C//DTD XHTML 1.0 Strict//EN"
"http://www.w3.org/TR/xhtml1/DTD/xhtml1-strict.dtd">
<html xmlns="http://www.w3.org/1999/xhtml" lang="en" xml:lang="en">
    <head>
        <title>External Interface Return</title>
        <meta http-equiv="Content-Type" content="text/html; charset=
iso-8859-1" />
        <script type="text/javascript" src="swfobject/swfobject.js">
</script>
        <script type="text/javascript">
            swfobject.embedSWF("ExternalInterfaceReturn.swf",
"myAlternativeContent", "550", "400", "10.0.0", false, {}, {},
{id:'flashContent'});
        </script>
        <script>
        function getText()
        {
            return "Here's some text from JavaScript";
        }
        </script>
```

```
        </head>
        <body>
            <div id="myAlternativeContent">
                <p>This is just a test of ExternalInterface.</p>
            </div>
        </body>
    </html>
```

You'll notice that the getText() function within the third <script> block simply returns "Here's some text from JavaScript". If you test this file on your testing server, or on the Web, you should see the JavaScript text appear in Flash (see Figure 4-7).

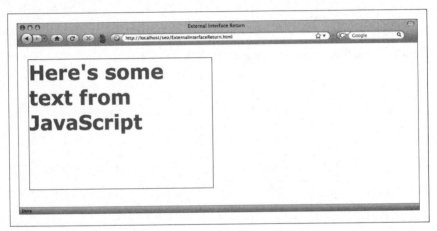

Figure 4-7. Viewing the data returned from JavaScript

Calling Flash functions from JavaScript

When you use ExternalInterface, you can also call Flash functions from Java-Script. To enable a Flash function to be called from JavaScript, you need to use the ExternalInterface.addCallback() method, passing in the name of the function JavaScript can use in the form of a string, and the ActionScript function that will be called in the form of a function. The general code looks like this:

```
ExternalInterface.addCallback("myFunction", myFunction);
```

 Although you can give different names for the JavaScript function and the Flash function, you may avoid some confusion by giving the functions the same name.

Here's an example from the first keyframe of the actions layer in the file *FromJavaScript.fla*, which contains a text field called data_txt:

```
ExternalInterface.addCallback("showText",showText);

function showText(msg:String):void
{
    data_txt.text = msg;
}
```

When the showText() function is called in JavaScript, the Flash version of showText() will run, accepting a message to show in the text field data_txt.

The JavaScript code required to send data to Flash is a little more complex than the examples we've looked at so far, but it's still relatively simple. Here's the HTML and JavaScript from *FromJavaScript.html*:

```
<!DOCTYPE html PUBLIC "-//W3C//DTD XHTML 1.0 Strict//EN"
"http://www.w3.org/TR/xhtml1/DTD/xhtml1-strict.dtd">
<html xmlns="http://www.w3.org/1999/xhtml" lang="en" xml:lang="en">
    <head>
        <title>From JavaScript</title>
        <meta http-equiv="Content-Type" content="text/html; charset=
iso-8859-1" />
        <script type="text/javascript" src="swfobject/swfobject.js"></script>
        <script type="text/javascript">
            var flashvars = {};
            var params = {};
            var attributes = {id:"fromJS",name:"fromJS"};
            swfobject.embedSWF("FromJavaScript.swf", "myAlternativeContent",
"550", "400", "10.0.0", false,flashvars,params,attributes);
            window.onload = windowLoaded;
            function windowLoaded()
            {
                document.getElementById("fromJS").showText("Hello from
JavaScript!");
            }
        </script>
    </head>
    <body>
        <div id="myAlternativeContent">
            <p>This is just a test of ExternalInterface.</p>
        </div>
    </body>
</html>
```

First, notice the three variables at the top of the second <script> block—flashvars, params, and attributes:

```
var flashvars = {};
var params = {};
var attributes = {id:"fromJS",name:"fromJS"};
```

These variables are object data types, written in shorthand notation, just like object shorthand notation in Flash. The `attributes` object is the only one that contains data, with `id` and `name` values of `"fromJS"`. These values will be added as attributes to the `<object>` element containing the loaded Flash content. By giving the element a name and ID, you have a method of communicating with the element through JavaScript to call the Flash function you're going to use.

Next, look at the `swfobject.embedSWF()` method:

```
swfobject.embedSWF("FromJavaScript.swf", "myAlternativeContent", "550",
"400", "10.0.0", false,flashvars,params,attributes);
```

Notice that the last three values passed in correspond to the variables created earlier: `flashvars`, `params`, and `attributes`. This is the order in which these parameters must be passed into `swfobject.embedSWF()`.

The rest of the code is connected. The `window.onload` event triggers the `windowLoaded()` function:

```
window.onload = windowLoaded;
function windowLoaded()
{
    document.getElementById("fromJS").showText("Hello from JavaScript!");
}
```

To communicate to the function within the Flash content, you need to wait until the Flash content is loaded and ready for communication. By the time the `window.onload` event occurs, the Flash content is available. The `windowLoaded()` function uses the *Document Object Model*, or *DOM*, to communicate to the Flash content. The `document.getElementById()` method returns the element with the name specified by the ID string passed in, which in this case is `"fromJS"`. From there, the Flash functions added using the `ExternalInterface.addCallback()` method are available. The `showText()` function you created in Flash is called and `"Hello from JavaScript!"` is passed in.

When you test this file using a testing server or web server, you should see the message from JavaScript appearing in the Flash text field (see Figure 4-8).

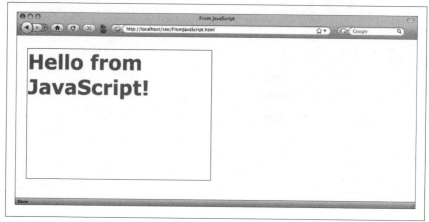

Figure 4-8. Viewing data sent from JavaScript to Flash

Using data returned from Flash with JavaScript

Just like using data returned from JavaScript in Flash, you can use data returned from Flash in JavaScript. To do that, all you have to do is make your Flash function return a value, and in JavaScript the data is usable as the returned value of the Flash function.

Here's the code from the actions layer in frame 1 in the file *FromJavaScriptReturn.fla*:

```
ExternalInterface.addCallback("getNewTitle",getNewTitle);

function getNewTitle():String
{
    data_txt.text = "Title updated";
    return "This is the new page title!";
}
```

This code adds a callback for the `getNewTitle()` function. When the function runs, `data_txt` will display notification of the updated title, and the new title name will be returned to JavaScript.

Here's the HTML and JavaScript code from *FromJavaScriptReturn.html*:

```
<!DOCTYPE html PUBLIC "-//W3C//DTD XHTML 1.0 Strict//EN"
"http://www.w3.org/TR/xhtml1/DTD/xhtml1-strict.dtd">
<html xmlns="http://www.w3.org/1999/xhtml" lang="en" xml:lang="en">
    <head>
        <title>From JavaScript Return</title>
        <meta http-equiv="Content-Type" content="text/html; charset=
iso-8859-1" />
        <script type="text/javascript" src="swfobject/swfobject.js"></script>
        <script type="text/javascript">
            var flashvars = {};
```

```
              var params = {};
              var attributes = {id:"fromJS",name:"fromJS"};
              swfobject.embedSWF("FromJavaScriptReturn.swf",
"myAlternativeContent", "550", "400", "10.0.0", false,flashvars,
params,attributes);
              window.onload = windowLoaded;
              function windowLoaded()
              {
                  document.title = document.getElementById("fromJS").
                  getNewTitle();
              }
          </script>
      </head>
      <body>
          <div id="myAlternativeContent">
              <p>This is just a test of ExternalInterface.</p>
          </div>
      </body>
  </html>
```

This code is pretty similar to what we looked at in the last example, except in the windowLoaded() function the value of document.title is being set to the returned value of the Flash function getNewTitle():

```
function windowLoaded()
{
    document.title = document.getElementById("fromJS").getNewTitle();
}
```

If you test this using your testing or web server, you should see the Flash text field update and the document title at the top of your browser window change (shown in Figure 4-9).

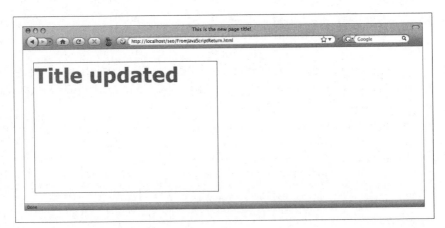

Figure 4-9. Viewing the updated Flash text and document title

---

Other features of the `ExternalInterface` class are beyond the scope of this book. For full documentation, see Flash Help.

Other Methods of Flash and JavaScript Communication

As I mentioned earlier in this chapter, the `ExternalInterface` class isn't the only method of working with data between JavaScript and Flash. You can exchange data in several ways, but the `ExternalInterface` class is the recommended method for Flash Player 8 and later. Before Flash Player 8, and even for later versions, another method of data exchange you can use is `flashvars`.

Some other methods for getting data in Flash Player 7 and earlier were the `getURL()` function and `fscommand()`. See Flash Help for more information about these methods.

Working with flashvars

`flashvars` are name/value pairs that you can use to send values from the HTML document into Flash. Without `SWFObject`, you add `flashvars` as the attribute value for `name` in a `<param>` element inside the `<object>` element. The value of the `flashvars` param is a URL-encoded string with name/value pairs separated by ampersands (&), which can be tedious to write and hard to read without some additional utilities and classes. With `SWFObject`, you can simply pass the property and value pairs into a JavaScript object and send that value into the `swfobject.embedSWF()` method, which is easy to both read and write.

Here's an example of some HTML and JavaScript code that uses `flashvars` in a file called *FlashVars.html*:

```
<!DOCTYPE html PUBLIC "-//W3C//DTD XHTML 1.0 Strict//EN"
"http://www.w3.org/TR/xhtml1/DTD/xhtml1-strict.dtd">
<html xmlns="http://www.w3.org/1999/xhtml" lang="en" xml:lang="en">
    <head>
        <title>FlashVars</title>
        <meta http-equiv="Content-Type" content="text/html; charset=
iso-8859-1" />
        <script type="text/javascript" src="swfobject/swfobject.js"></script>
        <script type="text/javascript">
            var flashvars = {title:document.title,anotherVar:"Some Value"};
            swfobject.embedSWF("FlashVars.swf", "myAlternativeContent",
"550", "400", "10.0.0", false,flashvars);
        </script>
    </head>
    <body>
        <div id="myAlternativeContent">
```

```
      <p>This is just a test of flashvars.</p>
    </div>
  </body>
</html>
```

All of the `flashvars` information is contained in the `flashvars` variable in the second `<script>` block, and is passed in after the Express Install URL, which in this case is `false`, in the `swfobject.embedSWF()` method:

```
<script type="text/javascript">
    var flashvars = {title:document.title,anotherVar:"Some Value"};
    swfobject.embedSWF("FlashVars.swf", "myAlternativeContent", "550",
"400", "10.0.0", false,flashvars);
</script>
```

Notice that the data type is `object`, and the names and values are written in shorthand, as in ActionScript. The values are `title`, which represents the title of the document, which in this case is "FlashVars," and `anotherVar` with a value of `"Some Value"`. You can add as many properties to the `flashvars` object as you'd like.

In ActionScript 3.0, you access the `flashvars` through the `parameters` property of the `loaderInfo` property of any display object on the stage, and the stage itself. The `parameters` property is an object data type (conveniently, just like the JavaScript version), which contains all of the name/value pairs you specified in HTML or JavaScript. You can access the name/value pairs just like any other object. Here's an example, from *FlashVars.fla*, that outputs all the flashvars using a `for..in` loop:

```
var parameters:Object = this.loaderInfo.parameters;
data_txt.text = "";
for(var p:String in parameters)
{
    data_txt.appendText(p + ":" + parameters[p] + "\n");
}
```

The `for..in` loop iterates through the properties of an object (in this case, `parameters` is the object). In this example, the names from `flashvars` (held in the `p` variable) are appended to the text field `data_txt`, along with a colon, the value of the `flashvars` parameter (`parameters[p]`), and a newline character (`\n`).

If you open the HTML file, *FlashVars.html*, in a web browser, you should see the data passed from `flashvars` into Flash. That will display the names and values of the `flashvars` in the text field, `data_txt` (shown in Figure 4-10).

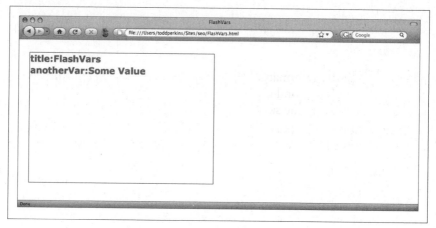

Figure 4-10. Viewing the data from flashvars in Flash

Exercises

Now that we've discussed the theory behind working with JavaScript and Flash, we'll go through some exercises to practice these techniques.

Exercise 4-1: Optimizing with SWFObject

In this exercise, you'll take a web page that was published using Flash and modify its HTML code to use SWFObject.

File: *xylophone-master.html*

1. Open the HTML file, *xylophone-master.html*, in a text editor to view the HTML code.

2. Save the file as *xylophone-master-swfobject.html* in the same folder.

3. In the <head> tag, find the line of code that links to *AC_RunActiveContent.js* and change the value of the src attribute to link to *swfobject.js* instead. After being modified, the code should look like this:

   ```
   <script src="swfobject.js" type="text/javascript"></script>
   ```

4. Right below the <script> block you just modified, create another <script> block.

   ```
   <script type="text/javascript">
   </script>
   ```

5. Inside the <script> block you just created, use the swfobject.embedSWF() method to embed the SWF file *xylophone-master.swf* using the dynamic publishing method. For the ID name, use altContent. Pass in 790 for width,

610 for height, 7.0.0 for minimum Flash Player version, and false for the URL value. When you're finished, the script block should match the following code:

```
<script type="text/javascript">
    swfobject.embedSWF("xylophone-master.swf", "altContent", "790",
"610", "7.0.0", false);
</script>
```

6. Next, you'll modify the HTML code created by Flash. Find the `<div>` element with an ID of game. The element should look like this:

```
<div id="game">
  <p>
    <script language="JavaScript" type="text/javascript">
    AC_FL_RunContent(
'codebase','http://download.macromedia.com/pub/shockwave/cabs/flash/
swflash.cab#version=7,0,0,0','width','790','height','610','id','Xylophone
Master','align','middle','src','xylophone-
master','quality','high','bgcolor','#000000','name','Xylophone
Master','allowscriptaccess','sameDomain','allowfullscreen','false',
'pluginspage',
'http://www.adobe.com/go/getflashplayer','movie','xylophone-master' );
//end AC code
    </script>
      <noscript>
        <object classid="clsid:d27cdb6e-ae6d-11cf-96b8-444553540000"
codebase="http://download.macromedia.com/pub/shockwave/cabs/flash/
swflash.cab#version=7,0,0,0" width="790" height="610" id="Xylophone Master"
align="middle">
            <param name="allowScriptAccess" value="sameDomain" />
            <param name="allowFullScreen" value="false" />
            <param name="movie" value="xylophone-master.swf" />
            <param name="quality" value="high" />
            <param name="bgcolor" value="#000000" />
            <embed src="xylophone-master.swf" quality="high" bgcolor="#000000"
width="790" height="610" name="Xylophone Master" align="middle"
allowScriptAccess="sameDomain" allowFullScreen="false" type="application
/x-shockwave-flash" pluginspage="http://www.adobe.com/go/getflashplayer"
  />
      </object>
      </noscript>
    </p>
  </div>
```

7. Delete all the content inside the `<div>` element so that it matches this code:

```
<div id="game">

</div>
```

8. Inside the `<div>` element, create another `<div>` element with an ID of altContent.

```
<div id="game">
<div id="altContent">

<div>
</div>
```

9. Within the altContent <div> element, write a title and description of the game. Your code should be similar to this:

```
<div id="game">
<div id="altContent">
<h1>Xylophone Master Game</h1>
<p>Move your mouse or WiiMote up and down to hit the keys on the
xylophone in thesame order that the xylophone master plays them.
Prove your coolness to your friends by getting to the highest
level!</p>
<div>
</div>
```

10. Save the file, and open it in a web browser to test it (see Figure 4-11).

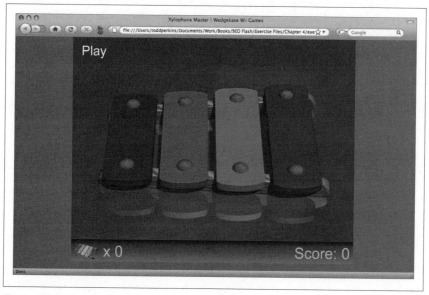

Figure 4-11. Viewing the finished exercise in a browser

Exercise 4-2: Deep Linking with SWFAddress

Now, you'll use SWFAddress to add deep linking to a previously created Flash application.

File: SWFAddress.fla

1. Open *SWFAddress.fla* in the *exercise 2* folder.

2. Notice the layout of the file—the frames, labels, and instance names of the buttons on the left side. Note that the instance names of the buttons correspond to the frame labels in the timeline. For example, the button Fun_Run will end up being connected to the label $/Fun_Run/ via ActionScript.

3. Select the first keyframe of the actions layer and open the Actions panel.

4. In the Actions panel, import the SWFAddress and SWFAddressEvent classes:

```
import SWFAddress;
import SWFAddressEvent;
```

5. Below the code you just wrote, add an event listener to SWFAddress to listen for the SWFAddressEvent.CHANGE event. Then, add event listeners to the three buttons on the stage, Meteor_Blaster, Set_the_Clock, and Fun_Run, to listen for MouseEvent.CLICK and react with a function called button Clicked(). Then stop the timeline.

```
SWFAddress.addEventListener(SWFAddressEvent.CHANGE, handleSWFAddress);
Meteor_Blaster.addEventListener(MouseEvent.CLICK, buttonClicked);
Set_the_Clock.addEventListener(MouseEvent.CLICK, buttonClicked);
Fun_Run.addEventListener(MouseEvent.CLICK, buttonClicked);
stop();
```

 The naming convention for the buttons is different here from what it was earlier in the chapter. The purpose of this is to make it easy to take an instance name and turn it into a string that you can place in the title bar, which you can do by simply removing the underscores.

6. Above the code you just wrote, and below the import statements, define the buttonClicked() function:

```
function buttonClicked(event:MouseEvent):void
{

}
```

7. In the buttonClicked() function, create a variable called newURL that has a value of the instance name of the button that was clicked, wrapped in forward slashes. Then, pass that value into the SWFAddress.setValue() method:

```
function buttonClicked(event:MouseEvent):void
{
    var newURL:String = "/" + event.target.name + "/";
    SWFAddress.setValue(newURL);
}
```

8. Next, define the handleSWFAddress() function:

```
function handleSWFAddress(event:SWFAddressEvent):void
{

}
```

9. Inside the `handleSWFAddress()` function, create a variable called `link` and assign it the value of the event object's `value` property. Then create a conditional statement that checks whether the value of `link` is only a forward slash. If so, set the value of `link` to be the first frame label without the dollar sign, and pass the new link value into the `SWFAddress.setValue()` method. Next, stop the function from running by using the `return` keyword:

```
function handleSWFAddress(event:SWFAddressEvent):void
{
    var link:String = event.value;
    if(link == "/")
    {
        link = currentLabels[0].name.replace("$","");
        SWFAddress.setValue(link);
        return;
    }
}
```

10. Below the conditional statement you just wrote, make the timeline `gotoAndStop()` at the appropriate frame label—a dollar sign and then the value of `link`. Then, call the `SWFAddress.setTitle()` method, passing in the returned value of a function called `formatTitle()` (defined in the next step), which itself should receive the value of `link`:

```
function handleSWFAddress(event:SWFAddressEvent):void
{
    var link:String = event.value;
    if(link == "/")
    {
        link = currentLabels[0].name.replace("$","");
        SWFAddress.setValue(link);
        return;
    }
    gotoAndStop("$" + link);
    SWFAddress.setTitle(formatTitle(link));
}
```

11. Next, define the `formatTitle()` function:

```
function formatTitle(newTitle:String):String
{

}
```

12. The `formatTitle()` function should take the value passed in, remove the dollar sign and forward slashes, and replace the underscores with spaces.

After that, append the text, " | Wedgekase Wii Games", to the updated title and return the value of the updated title. Your code should look like this:

```
function formatTitle(newTitle:String):String
{
    var updatedTitle:String = newTitle.replace("$","");
    updatedTitle = updatedTitle.replace(/\//g,"");
    updatedTitle = updatedTitle.replace(/_/g," ");
    updatedTitle += " | Wedgekase Wii Games";
    return updatedTitle;
}
```

 This function uses regular expressions—advanced tools for working with strings—to modify the title. If you're interested in learning more about regular expressions, see the section on working with regular expressions in Flash Help.

13. Test the movie (Control→Test Movie) to publish the SWF file.

14. Open the HTML file, *index.html*, to view its contents. Note that it's using SWFObject to embed the Flash content, and it contains a link to *swfaddress.js*:

```
<!DOCTYPE html PUBLIC "-//W3C//DTD XHTML 1.0 Strict//EN"
"http://www.w3.org/TR/xhtml1/DTD/xhtml1-strict.dtd">
<html xmlns="http://www.w3.org/1999/xhtml" lang="en" xml:lang="en">
    <head>
        <title>Wedgekase Wii Games</title>
        <meta http-equiv="Content-Type" content="text/html; charset=
utf-8" />
        <script type="text/javascript" src="swfobject/swfobject.js">
</script>
        <script type="text/javascript" src="swfaddress/swfaddress.js">
</script>
        <script type="text/javascript">
            swfobject.embedSWF('SWFAddress.swf', 'website', '1024',
'660', '10.0.0', 'swfobject/expressinstall.swf', {}, {},
{id:'flashContent'});
        </script>
    </head>
    <body>
        <div id="website">
            <p>In order to view this page you need Flash Player 10+
support!</p>
            <p><a href="http://www.adobe.com/go/getflashplayer"><img
src="http://www.adobe.com/images/shared/download_buttons/
get_flash_player.gif"
alt="Get Adobe Flash player" /></a></p>
        </div>
    </body>
</html>
```

15. Open this HTML file using your testing server or your web server (making sure to include all linked files), and click the buttons on the left side to watch the page title and addresses update (see Figure 4-12).

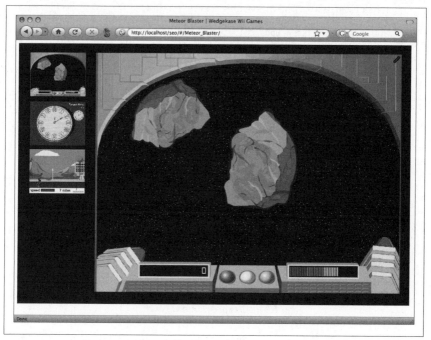

Figure 4-12. Viewing SWFAddress working on a testing server

Exercise 4-3: Flash/JavaScript Communication with ExternalInterface

In this exercise, you'll use the ExternalInterface class to send data to Java-Script. The application you'll be working with is made to capture mouse clicks, and to output that data to see what users are clicking in an application.

 Capturing user mouse-click input is a common web design tactic for finding what content people are viewing in a site. Using ExternalInterface, you can capture and save a Flash application's mouse-click data.

File: *ExternalInterface.fl*

1. Open the file *ExternalInterface.fla* in the *exercise 3* folder. Notice that its contents are identical to the file in Exercise 2, except for one line of code

added to the `handleClick()` function. The last line of code in the function calls a JavaScript function called `registerClick()`, passing in the name of the button instance that was clicked:

```
function buttonClicked(event:MouseEvent):void
{
    var newURL:String = "/" + event.target.name + "/";
    SWFAddress.setValue(newURL);
    ExternalInterface.call("registerClick",event.target.name);
}
```

2. Now we'll look at the JavaScript and HTML that control this application. Open *index.html* in the *exercise 3* folder and view its contents:

```
<!DOCTYPE html PUBLIC "-//W3C//DTD XHTML 1.0 Strict//EN"
"http://www.w3.org/TR/xhtml1/DTD/xhtml1-strict.dtd">
<html xmlns="http://www.w3.org/1999/xhtml" lang="en" xml:lang="en">
    <head>
        <title>Wedgekase Wii Games</title>
        <meta http-equiv="Content-Type" content="text/html; charset=
utf-8" />
        <script type="text/javascript" src="swfobject/swfobject.js">
</script>
        <script type="text/javascript" src="swfaddress/swfaddress.js">
</script>
        <script type="text/javascript">
            swfobject.embedSWF('SWFAddress.swf', 'website', '1024',
'660', '10.0.0',
                'swfobject/expressinstall.swf', {}, {},
{id:'flashContent'});
        </script>
        <script type="text/javascript">
        function registerClick(obj)
        {
            document.getElementById("clicks").innerHTML += obj + ", ";
        }
        </script>
    </head>
    <body>
        <div id="website">
            <p>In order to view this page you need Flash Player 10+
support!</p>
            <p><a href="http://www.adobe.com/go/getflashplayer"><img
src="http://www.adobe.com/images/shared/download_buttons/
get_flash_player.gif"
alt="Get Adobe Flash player" /></a></p>
        </div>
        <p id="clicks"></p>
    </body>
</html>
```

3. This file has some important changes from Exercise 2. First, notice the `<p>` element with the ID value of `clicks` toward the bottom of the code.

This is the element that JavaScript will write to in order to save the click data:

```
<p id="clicks"></p>
```

4. Next, notice the fourth `<script>` block. This block contains the `register Click()` function, which uses the DOM to reference the `<p>` element called `clicks`, and appends to the string value of its inner HTML. The value appended is whatever is passed in from Flash, plus a comma and a space to separate values:

```
<script type="text/javascript">
        function registerClick(obj)
        {
            document.getElementById("clicks").innerHTML += obj + ", ";
        }
</script>
```

5. Copy the swfobject, swfaddress, HTML, and SWF files to your testing or web server and browse to the HTML file there. Then, click the buttons in Flash and watch the instance name values appear in the text field below the Flash content (see Figure 4-13).

Set_the_Clock, Fun_Run, Set_the_Clock, Meteor_Blaster, Set_the_Clock, Fun_Run,

Figure 4-13. Viewing the data passed from Flash through ExternalInterface

Remember that you can pass more data from Flash than just instance names. You can include any information you like when sending data via ExternalInterface. Also, instead of showing the data in a text field, you could use a server-side language such as PHP to save all of the click data to a file, or a database.

Exercise 4-4A: Installing a Testing Server (Windows XP and Windows Vista)

To use some of the techniques in this chapter, including SWFAddress and ExternalInterface, you'll need to test your applications using a web server or a testing server. This exercise shows you how to set up a testing server if you're on a Windows computer.

1. Go to www.wampserver.com/en/download.php (*http://www.wampserver .com/en/download.php*) (see Figure 4-14) and click the download link to download the latest version of WAMP.

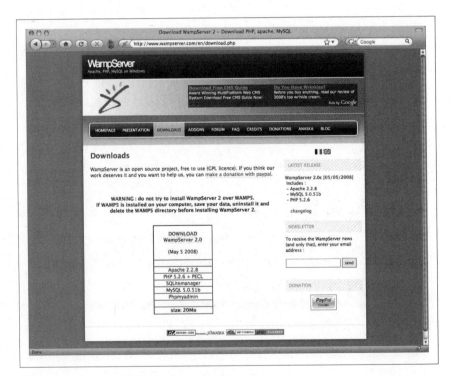

Figure 4-14. Viewing the WAMP download page

2. Once you've downloaded WAMP, launch its setup application to set up the software.

3. During WAMP setup, you can choose which features you'd like to install if you need customized features. Otherwise, the default install should be all you'll need for what we're doing.

4. After WAMP is installed, you can begin to run WAMP services through either the Windows task bar or the Program menu.

 You need to run WAMP to test Flash applications that need a testing server.

5. To make sure WAMP is working properly, browse to *http://localhost* in your web browser. You should see some text and an image telling you that WAMP is running properly. If you see an error message, check to make sure WAMP is running, and then reload the page.

6. Once WAMP is working, you can put the files you want to test in the *www* folder, or in a subdirectory of that folder.

 The *www* folder is inside the *wamp* folder, which by default installation should be in your computer's C drive folder. The full folder path should be *C:\\wamp\www*. This folder represents the root for your local website, and it corresponds directly to *http://localhost/*.

7. Now you'll do a simple test of the testing server. In your *www* directory, create a directory called *exint* (short for *ExternalInterface*).

8. Within the *exint* directory, copy the finished files from Exercise 4-3 in this chapter.

9. In your web browser, browse to the finished file at *http://localhost/exint/*. You should then see `ExternalInterface` working in your web browser.

Exercise 4-4B: Installing a Testing Server (Mac OS X)

This exercise shows you how to set up a testing server if you're on a Mac.

1. In System Preferences, under the Sharing category, make sure Web Sharing is turned off.

2. Visit www.mamp.info/en/download.html (*http://www.mamp.info/en/download.html*) (see Figure 4-15) to download MAMP.

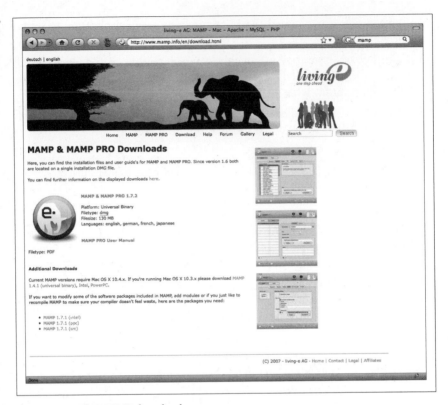

Figure 4-15. The MAMP download page

3. Open the MAMP installer file to begin installing MAMP.

4. For this exercise, you'll need only a default install, so you can go through the installer without changing anything (i.e., you won't need MAMP Pro). Feel free to customize any of the options if you need additional features.

5. Once MAMP is installed, launch MAMP, using your user credentials to log in (see Figure 4-16).

6. After MAMP launches, you should see that MAMP's services are running properly (see Figure 4-17), as indicated by green lights.

7. Click the Preferences button to open MAMP preferences, and then click the Ports tab.

8. In the Ports tab, click the "Set to default Apache and MySQL ports" button to make sure the ports are assigned to where you'll use them. Your screen should match Figure 4-18.

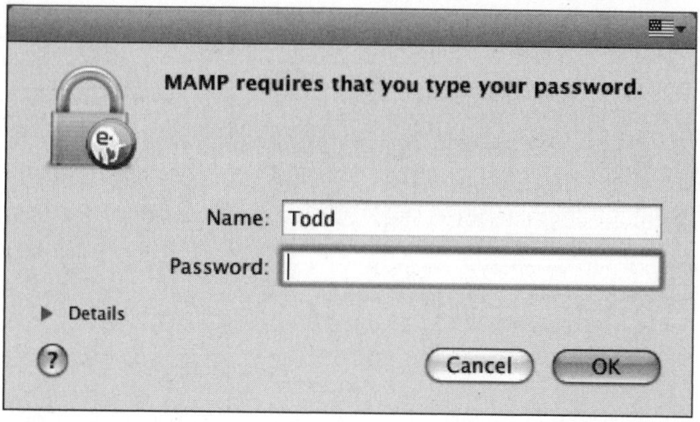

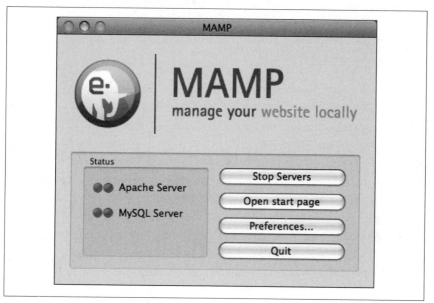

Figure 4-16. Logging in to MAMP

Figure 4-17. MAMP is running

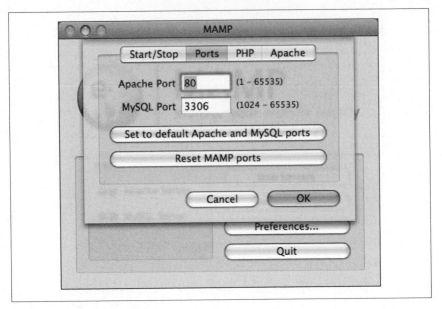

Figure 4-18. Setting default ports

9. Click the Apache button to go to Apache settings.

10. Make sure your document root folder is set to */Users/YOUR USERNAME/ Sites*, as shown in Figure 4-19. If not, click the Select button to set it correctly.

11. Click OK to accept the changes made to MAMP preferences. Authenticate using your username and password if necessary.

12. To make sure MAMP is working properly, browse to *http://localhost* in your web browser. You should see your computer's default web page in your */Users/<YOUR USERNAME>/Sites* folder.

13. Once MAMP is working, you can put the files you want to test in the *Sites* folder, or in a subdirectory of that folder.

 The *Sites* folder represents the root for your local website, and it corresponds directly to *http://localhost/*.

14. Now you'll conduct a simple test of the testing server. In your *Sites* directory, create a directory called *exint* (short for *ExternalInterface*).

15. Within the *exint* directory, copy the finished files from Exercise 4-3 in this chapter.

16. In your web browser, browse to the finished file at *http://localhost/exint/*.
You should then see `ExternalInterface` working in your web browser.

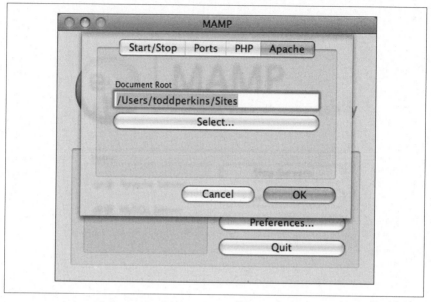

Figure 4-19. Setting the document root

Key Terms Used in This Chapter

Table 4-1 contains the terms that were introduced in this chapter and gives you their definitions.

Table 4-1. Key terms used in this chapter

Term	Definition
DOM	Document Object Model. Used to reference HTML elements using JavaScript.
ECMAScript	A vendor-neutral scripting language standard on which languages such as JavaScript and ActionScript are based.
ExternalInterface	An application programming interface that enables straightforward communication between ActionScript running inside the player and JavaScript on the page.
SWFAddress	A set of ActionScript and JavaScript tools that you can use to make search engines index states of a Flash application as different pages.
SWFObject	An SEO-friendly and syntax-effective way to embed Flash content in a web page. The standard for using Flash on the Web.
Testing server	Software installed on a computer that mimics a production server environment.

CHAPTER 5

Optimizing Dynamic Content

In the early days of the Web, most websites were based on static web pages. *Static web pages* are pages that do not use data that comes from a data source such as a database. Changes to a page's content required edits to the actual HTML code in that page.

Today, countless websites create pages dynamically. Blogs, social networking sites, online stores, and just about every type of website in between are typically powered by dynamic data. Because of the increasingly complex requirements for content delivery, visibility, and formatting, dynamically created content is necessary. But it can provide some SEO challenges. This chapter looks at the challenges that come with dynamic content, and the techniques you can use to overcome them.

Understanding Dynamic Content and Static Content

To understand dynamic content, it's important to have an idea of its opposite, static content. The term *static content* refers to web content that is generated without using a data source such as a database. Essentially, the site viewer sees exactly what is coded in the web page's HTML.

With dynamic pages, a site can display the same address for every visitor, and have totally unique content for each one to view. For example, when I visit the social networking site Facebook (facebook.com), I see *http://www.facebook .com/home.php* as the address in my web browser, but I see a unique page that's different from what anyone else sees if they view that page at the same time. The site shows information about my friends in my account, and different information for each person in his account, or for someone who has no account.

Not all dynamically generated content is unique to every viewer, but all dynamic content comes from a data source, whether it's a database or another source, such as an XML file. Dynamic content is not a problem at all for SEO by nature, but it can create issues when that content is accessible only through a web form, which this chapter discusses later.

Dynamic Content and SEO

SEO for dynamic content poses a few significant challenges. Luckily, you have ways to overcome these challenges to have a fully functional dynamic site that is optimized as much as a static site can be optimized. This section discusses the pitfalls of dynamic sites, and how to overcome them to create fully optimized dynamic sites.

Challenges for Optimizing Dynamic Content

Here are some common areas of dynamic sites that provide setbacks for humans as well as search engine spiders.

Dynamic URLs

A *Dynamic URL* is an address of a dynamic web page, as opposed to a *Static URL*, which is the address of a static web page. Dynamic URLs are typically fairly cryptic in their appearance. Here's an example from *http://www.amazon.com/* for a product called Kindle:

```
http://www.amazon.com/gp/product/B000FI73MA/ref=amb_link_7646122_1?pf_rd_
m=ATVPDKIKX0DER&pf_rd_s=center-
1&pf_rd_r=1FYB35NGH8MSMESECBX7&pf_rd_t=101&pf_rd_p=450995701&pf_rd_i=507846
```

Notice that the URL doesn't contain any information about the item's product type, or anything about the item's name. For a well-trusted site like Amazon, this is not a problem at all. But for a new site, or for a site that's gaining credibility and popularity, a better solution can help search results by showing a searcher some relevant keywords in the page's URL. Here's an example of something a little more effective:

```
http://www.site.com/products/electronics/kindle/
```

While search engines may not have problems indexing URLs with variables, it's important to note that highly descriptive URLs like the one just shown can get more clicks in searches than cryptic URLs. That's not to say that I'm promising that your pages will beat Amazon—you'll just have an edge over competitors if searchers can clearly see keywords that have to do with the content they're looking for in your page's URL.

Logins and other forms

Login forms can restrict access to pages not only to users, but also search engines. In some cases, you want pages behind logins made searchable. In those cases, you can place code in those pages that determines whether the person visiting has access to view that content, and determine what to do from there.

 This is discussed in more detail later in this chapter.

Other web forms, referring to content in <FORM> tags, can restrict access to pages as well. While Google has revealed that googlebot can go through simple HTML forms (see *http://googlewebmastercentral.blogspot.com/2008/04/crawl ing-through-html-forms.html*), not all search engines follow this same process, which means content hidden behind forms may or may not be indexed.

Cookies

Web cookies are small bits of data that are stored in a user's web browser. Cookies are used frequently on the Web for storing temporary data like shopping cart information or user preferences. Pages that require cookies can block spiders because spiders don't store cookies as web browsers do.

Session IDs

Session IDs are similar to cookies in that if you need them to view pages, then spiders don't index those pages.

"Hidden" pages

Sometimes, pages on a website are hidden from search engines because they're buried too deep in a site's architecture. For example, a page more than three clicks deep from the home page of a website may not be crawled without an XML sitemap. Other pages that may be hidden include pages only visible via a site search.

JavaScript

Search engines don't index content that requires full-featured JavaScript. Remember that spiders view content in much the same way as you would if you were using a browser with JavaScript disabled. Text that is created using

JavaScript, and therefore only accessible with JavaScript enabled, will not be indexed.

Ways to Optimize Dynamic Content

Dynamic content is often necessary in websites. In addition, content that is easily changed through an outside data source helps keep a site's content fresh and relevant. This increases its value to search engines. You don't need to worry that because your site is dynamic, your content won't be indexed. You just need to make sure you're following the appropriate guidelines when using dynamic content in order to keep your site optimized. Here are some things you can do to optimize your sites that contain dynamic content.

Creating static URLs

Dynamic URLs, especially dynamic URLs with vague names, can be a turnoff to searchers. In order to have friendly URLs, you want to rewrite your dynamic URLs as static URLs.

Blogs powered by Wordpress or Blogger make it easy to convert dynamic links to static links. Blogger automatically creates static URLs, and with Wordpress you need only a simple change in your settings. For Wordpress, log in to your administrator account, and then, under Settings, click the Permalink button. From there, you simply select a static URL publishing method or create a custom one and save the changes. Nice!

If your site isn't powered by a blogging application, you need to rewrite the URLs manually. The process is somewhat complex, and it requires modifying your *.htaccess* file. Because modifying your *.htaccess* file can cause permanent changes to your website, you want to either practice on a testing server or know exactly what you're doing before using these techniques on a production server. To test this process on a testing server, you can download and install a testing server (discussed in Chapter 4), and then download all or part of your website to your computer. That way, changes you make on your local computer don't affect your live site.

Optimizing content hidden by forms

The fact that web forms can hide content can be a good thing, but sometimes forms hide content you may not want hidden. Login forms (forms that require a user name and password) can potentially block search engines if a login form is the only way to access that information. Of course, sometimes this feature is intentional, like for protecting bank account information on a banking site. For non-login forms, assuming that search engines index content that's accessible only by filling out text fields or other form elements is dangerous.

Further, it's equally dangerous to assume that search engines don't index content that's accessible only via non-login forms. If you want your form's hidden content to be indexed, make sure to give access to it in ways other than through a form alone. If you don't want the content to be indexed, make sure to hide it from search engines via *robots.txt*, or some other method.

Typically, content that's viewable only after a user is logged into an account isn't necessary to index. If you have content that you want indexed hidden in a login-only area, consider taking that content out of the restricted area so it can be indexed.

 Don't give out people's personal information for the sake of SEO. Information that should be public and can be public without compromising security can help more of your content be searchable, while private information should always remain private.

Understanding AJAX

Asynchronous JavaScript and XML, known as *AJAX*, is another method (along with PHP and other server languages) for creating dynamic web content. AJAX is powered by JavaScript, and is used to update content on web pages without requiring a page refresh. One of the reasons for its popularity among web developers is that AJAX can be used to build powerful *RIAs* (Rich Internet Applications) without the need for the Flash Player or any other browser plug-in.

AJAX SEO Issues

Though AJAX is great because it doesn't require a plug-in and therefore can reach an extremely broad audience, it's not without its limitations as far as SEO is concerned. One of the major limitations of AJAX is that search engines generally don't execute JavaScript code, so anything that's revealed only through JavaScript isn't indexed. Further, fewer page refreshes mean fewer pages are indexed by search engines altogether.

Really, the only other SEO issues related to AJAX have to do with usability (and are thus indirectly related to SEO). First, AJAX applications don't necessarily communicate with a browser's Back button, though you can do this communication with some workarounds (just like Flash). Along those lines, AJAX applications are difficult to bookmark in a web browser unless the application updates the URL in the browser address bar. Finally, some screen readers have trouble reading the dynamic content generated by AJAX apps.

AJAX SEO Solutions

Like Flash, AJAX is still compatible with SEO, providing you set up your applications appropriately. This section discusses what you can do to optimize AJAX apps to make them more searchable.

Creating searchable AJAX applications

Since AJAX typically relies heavily on JavaScript, and search engines don't usually execute JavaScript, it's important to make sure your AJAX apps have searchable content. You have a few ways to achieve this.

One way you can make AJAX content searchable is by using unobtrusive Java-Script. That way, the behavior of the application is kept separate from its content. Look at a very simple application to compare obtrusive JavaScript to other scripting methods that separate content from behavior. Here's an example of obtrusive JavaScript in a simple grocery list creating application:

File: *Obtrusive.html*

```
<!DOCTYPE html PUBLIC "-//W3C//DTD XHTML 1.0 Transitional//EN"
"http://www.w3.org/TR/xhtml1/DTD/xhtml1-transitional.dtd">
<html xmlns="http://www.w3.org/1999/xhtml">
<head>
<meta http-equiv="Content-Type" content="text/html; charset=UTF-8" />
<title>Obtrusive JavaScript</title>
</head>
<body>
<p>Grocery List</p>
<form>
<input name="textinput" type="text" id="textinput"/>
<input name="add" type="submit" id="add" value="Add Item"
onclick="document.getElementById('list').innerHTML += '<li>'
+ textinput.value +
'</li>';textinput.value = '';"/>
</form>
<ul id="list">
</ul>
</body>
</html>
```

Though this is a somewhat exaggerated example of obtrusive JavaScript, the example is quite obvious. Look at the onclick attribute for the input tag named add. Here, the HTML markup and JavaScript code are inseparably connected, which not only leads to broken code when JavaScript isn't functioning in a user's browser, but also creates code that's extremely difficult to manage on a large scale. Again, SEO's goal is to separate content from behavior so that no searchable content is hidden from searchers. Here's an example of less obtrusive JavaScript in the same application:

File: *LessObtrusive.html*

```
<!DOCTYPE html PUBLIC "-//W3C//DTD XHTML 1.0 Transitional//EN"
"http://www.w3.org/TR/xhtml1/DTD/xhtml1-transitional.dtd">
<html xmlns="http://www.w3.org/1999/xhtml">
<head>
<meta http-equiv="Content-Type" content="text/html; charset=UTF-8" />
<title>Less Obtrusive JavaScript</title>
<script type="text/javascript">
<!-

function addText()
{
    var ul = document.getElementById("list");
    var input = document.getElementById("textinput");
    ul.innerHTML += "<li>" + input.value + "</li>";
    input.value = "";
}

-->
</script>
</head>
<body>
<p>Grocery List</p>
<input name="textinput" type="text" id="textinput"/>
<input name="add" type="submit" id="add" value="Add Item" onclick=
"addText()"/>
<ul id="list">
</ul>
</body>
</html>
```

In this example, the `onclick` attribute for the Add button contains a simple call to a JavaScript function held within the script block near the top of the code. The method is much easier to adjust, and keeps content more separated from structure, but an even better way exists. Here is some completely unobtrusive JavaScript using an HTML file as well as an external JavaScript file:

File: *Unobtrusive.html*

```
<!DOCTYPE html PUBLIC "-//W3C//DTD XHTML 1.0 Transitional//EN"
"http://www.w3.org/TR/xhtml1/DTD/xhtml1-transitional.dtd">
<html xmlns="http://www.w3.org/1999/xhtml">
<head>
<meta http-equiv="Content-Type" content="text/html; charset=UTF-8" />
<title>Unobtrusive JavaScript</title>
<script type="text/javascript" src="script.js"></script>
</head>
<body>

<p>Grocery List</p>
<input name="textinput" type="text" id="textinput"/>
<input name="add" type="submit" id="add" value="Add Item" />
<ul id="list">
```

```
    </ul>
  </body>
</html>
```

File: *script.js*

```javascript
window.onload = initialize;

function initialize()
{
    var addBtn = document.getElementById("add");
    addBtn.onclick = addText;
}

function addText()
{
    var ul = document.getElementById("list");
    var input = document.getElementById("textinput");
    ul.innerHTML += "<li>" + input.value + "</li>";
    input.value = "";
}
```

The unobtrusive JavaScript method completely separates content from structure. Using unobtrusive JavaScript, you can plainly see which content is searchable by looking at your HTML code. Anything that's revealed only through JavaScript, like the list items in the addText() function, isn't indexed because search engines don't run the JavaScript code.

In the grocery list application, data entered is unnecessary to index because it's unique each time a grocery list is made. Sometimes, your JavaScript code dynamically generates content that you *do* want to index, like data from an XML file. In those cases, you can provide searchable HTML in your markup via a noscript tag. The noscript tag defines what a user sees only if JavaScript (or another language in your application) is disabled. Your page has better usability because the content can reach a broader audience; plus, it will have better SEO because search engines index the content.

Here's a simple example of using the noscript block:

File: *NoScript.html*

```html
<!DOCTYPE html PUBLIC "-//W3C//DTD XHTML 1.0 Transitional//EN"
"http://www.w3.org/TR/xhtml1/DTD/xhtml1-transitional.dtd">
<html xmlns="http://www.w3.org/1999/xhtml">
<head>
<meta http-equiv="Content-Type" content="text/html; charset=UTF-8" />
<title>No Script</title>
<script type="text/javascript" src="noscript.js"></script>
</head>
<body>
<p id="content">
</p>
<noscript>
```

```
Content in a noscript block can be indexed! (JavaScript is OFF)
</noscript>
</body>
</html>
```

File: *noscript.js*

```
window.onload = viewText;

function viewText()
{
    var content = document.getElementById("content");
    content.innerHTML = "Content in a noscript block can be indexed!
(JavaScript is ON)";
}
```

This example shows the message Content in a noscript block can be indexed through JavaScript, which isn't searchable, and through a noscript block, which is searchable. Note that the content created dynamically with JavaScript indicates that JavaScript is enabled, and the content created in the noscript block indicates that JavaScript is disabled. To understand how this application works, in your web browser, open the file *NoScript.html*. If you have JavaScript enabled, then you should see something similar to Figure 5-1.

The Web Developer toolbar for Firefox has excellent tools for testing JavaScript in your web browser, along with some other useful web development tools.

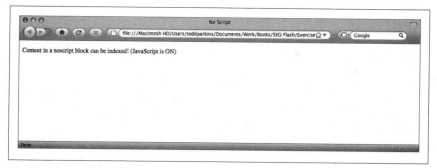

Figure 5-1. When JavaScript is enabled, you see the content created dynamically

You can typically disable JavaScript in your browser's Preferences menu. In Firefox, it's under Content (shown in Figure 5-2). After you disable JavaScript, you can see the noscript block's content in your browser.

Once JavaScript is enabled, refresh the page to see the searchable content in the noscript block. Note that it shows that JavaScript is off (Figure 5-3). If

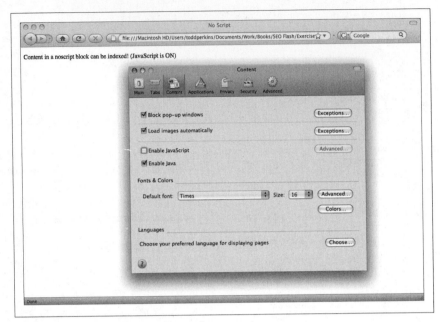

Figure 5-2. Disabling JavaScript in Firefox

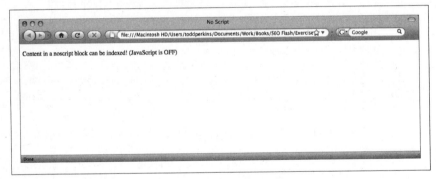

Figure 5-3. Viewing the content in the noscript block

you've disabled JavaScript and refreshed the page, but you still see that Java-Script is on, try closing and restarting your browser.

Using the <noscript> tag, you have complete control over what people and search engines see whether or not they have JavaScript enabled. Make sure that whenever you need to display alternate content for your dynamically created JavaScript/AJAX content, you provide that content in a noscript block.

For usability, you also can use a server-side scripting language like PHP or Perl along with the `<noscript>` tag to get similar interactivity to your JavaScript/AJAX applications when users have JavaScript disabled.

Exercise: Optimizing a Dynamic Application that Uses Flash

Now that you've seen the details of optimizing applications that use dynamic data as well as applications powered by JavaScript/AJAX technology, you'll look at an application that uses JavaScript and a dynamic server language, PHP, with Flash. The application utilizes XML data. In this exercise, you'll see how you can use these technologies together to create optimized applications that work whether or not the viewer has Flash or JavaScript.

You need a testing server to test the PHP code in this exercise. For information about installing a testing server, see Chapter 4.

File: *dynamic.fla*

1. Copy the exercise files from the Chapter 5 folder to your testing server.
2. In Flash, open the file *dynamic.fla*. Test the movie to preview the application (Figure 5-4), and then click the thumbnail images to navigate through the full-size pictures, and view the descriptions for each image. This application receives XML data from the file *data.xml*.
3. Open *data.xml* in a text editor to view its contents. Note that the root element is `gallery`, and the repeating element, `image`, represents each picture, and contains three child elements. The `file` element contains a reference to the main image file to load, the `thumb` element contains a reference to the thumbnail image, and the `description` element contains a description for the image:

```
<?xml version="1.0" encoding="UTF-8"?>
<gallery>
<image>
    <file>meteor-blaster.png</file>
    <thumb>meteor-blaster-thumb.jpg</thumb>
    <description>Shoot meteors with powerful laser cannons! Advance
through levels based on your score. Watch your energy meter!
Those meteors are relentless!</description>
</image>
<image>
```

```
<file>xylophone-master.png</file>
<thumb>xylophone-master-thumb.jpg</thumb>
<description>Learn to master playing the xylophone and
simultaneously boost your memory! Listen to the computer
play notes and simply play them back by moving your mouse
or Wii remote up and down over the keys.</description>
</image>
<image>
<file>fun-run.png</file>
<thumb>fun-run-thumb.png</thumb>
<description>Run a marathon as a giant man, completing up to
26.2 miles in 5 seconds! Move the mouse (or WiiMote) up and
down to run. Finish fast to get medals!</description>
</image>
<image>
<file>set-the-clock.png</file>
<thumb>set-the-clock-thumb.png</thumb>
<description>Rotate the mouse or WiiMote clockwise or counterclockwise
to set the big clock to display the same time as the little clock.
Race your friends to get the best time! Clock on!</description>
</image>
</gallery>
```

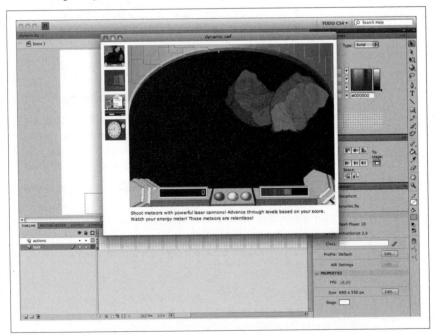

Figure 5-4. Testing the dynamic application

4. Return to *dynamic.fla* in Flash. Note the dynamic text field, desc_txt, on
   the stage. Select the first keyframe of the actions layer, and then open the
   Actions Panel to view the code:

```
        var req:URLRequest = new URLRequest("data.xml");
        var loader:URLLoader = new URLLoader();
        var xmlData:XML;
        var thumbHeight:int = 60;
        var mainLoader:Loader = new Loader();

        loader.addEventListener(Event.COMPLETE, fileLoaded);
        loader.load(req);
        mainLoader.x = 80;
        mainLoader.y = 10;
        addChild(mainLoader);

        function fileLoaded(event:Event):void
        {
            xmlData = new XML(loader.data);
            placeThumbs();
        }

        function placeThumbs():void
        {
            var thumbReq:URLRequest;
            var thumbLoader:Loader;

            for(var i:uint = 0; i < xmlData.image.length(); i++)
            {
                thumbReq = new URLRequest(xmlData.image[i].thumb);
                thumbLoader = new Loader();
                thumbLoader.load(thumbReq);
                thumbLoader.name = "thumb" + String(i);
                thumbLoader.x = 10;
                thumbLoader.y = (thumbHeight + 10) * i + 10;
                thumbLoader.addEventListener(MouseEvent.CLICK, thumbClicked);
                addChild(thumbLoader);
            }
            showMain(0);
        }

        function thumbClicked(event:MouseEvent):void
        {
            showMain(event.target.name.charAt(5));

        }

        function showMain(index:int = 0):void
        {
            var mainReq:URLRequest = new URLRequest(xmlData.image[index].file);
            mainLoader.load(mainReq);
            desc_txt.text = xmlData.image[index].description;
        }
```

5. The application uses a lot of code, but it's not too complex. First, the XML file loads:

```
var req:URLRequest = new URLRequest("data.xml");
var loader:URLLoader = new URLLoader();
var xmlData:XML;
var thumbHeight:int = 60;
var mainLoader:Loader = new Loader();

loader.addEventListener(Event.COMPLETE, fileLoaded);
loader.load(req);
mainLoader.x = 80;
mainLoader.y = 10;
addChild(mainLoader);
```

6. Once the XML loading is complete, the `placeThumbs()` function runs, placing all the thumbnail images on the stage, and connecting each with an index number and an event listener to load the appropriate main image when clicked:

```
function fileLoaded(event:Event):void
{
    xmlData = new XML(loader.data);
    placeThumbs();
}

function placeThumbs():void
{
    var thumbReq:URLRequest;
    var thumbLoader:Loader;

    for(var i:uint = 0; i < xmlData.image.length(); i++)
    {
        thumbReq = new URLRequest(xmlData.image[i].thumb);
        thumbLoader = new Loader();
        thumbLoader.load(thumbReq);
        thumbLoader.name = "thumb" + String(i);
        thumbLoader.x = 10;
        thumbLoader.y = (thumbHeight + 10) * i + 10;
        thumbLoader.addEventListener(MouseEvent.CLICK, thumbClicked);
        addChild(thumbLoader);
    }
    showMain(0);
}
```

7. Main images are loaded in the `showMain()` function:

```
function thumbClicked(event:MouseEvent):void
{
    showMain(event.target.name.charAt(5));

}

function showMain(index:int = 0):void
{
    var mainReq:URLRequest = new URLRequest(xmlData.image[index].file);
    mainLoader.load(mainReq);
```

```
            desc_txt.text = xmlData.image[index].description;
        }
```

8. Open the file *index.php* in a text editor to view its code:

```
<!DOCTYPE html PUBLIC "-//W3C//DTD XHTML 1.0 Transitional//EN"
"http://www.w3.org/TR/xhtml1/DTD/xhtml1-transitional.dtd"><html
xmlns="http://www.w3.org/1999/xhtml">
    <head>
        <title>Optimizing Dynamic Flash Content</title>
            <meta http-equiv="Content-Type" content="text/html; charset=
UTF-8" />
    <script type="text/javascript" src="swfobject.js"></script>
        <script type="text/javascript">
            swfobject.embedSWF("dynamic.swf", "xmlData", "690", "550",
"10.0.0", false);
        </script>
        <link href="styles.css" rel="stylesheet" type="text/css" />
    </head>
        <body>
        <div id="xmlData">
            <?php
            $xml = simplexml_load_file('data.xml');
            $num_of_elements = count($xml->image);
            for($i = 0; $i < $num_of_elements; $i++)
            {?>
            <p>
            <a href="<?php echo($xml->image[$i]->file);?>">
            <img src="<?php echo($xml->image[$i]->thumb);?>"/>
            </a>
            <?php echo($xml->image[$i]->description);?>
</p>

                            <div class="clearFloat"></div>
            <?php
            }?>
        </div>
        </body>
</html>
```

 For this example's sake, we have elements such as <p> tags, mixed in with php echo statements; in practice, however, it's best to separate logic from presentation.

9. Note that the file displays the Flash file *dynamic.swf* using SWFObject. SWFObject's dynamic publishing method is a powerful, unobtrusive way to use Flash content. Also note the alternate content is contained in the xmlData div, which is discussed in more detail later in this exercise:

```
<script type="text/javascript" src="swfobject.js"></script>
<script type="text/javascript">
            swfobject.embedSWF("dynamic.swf", "xmlData", "690", "550",
"10.0.0", false);
</script>
```

10. Test the file on your testing server, making sure your testing server is running and JavaScript is enabled in your web browser (Figure 5-5). You should then see the Flash version of the application. Return to *index.php* when you're done.

11. If the person viewing the content has JavaScript enabled and the Flash Player installed, then she sees the Flash application. If not, then the page uses PHP to make the same XML data that powers the Flash application display as HTML content. Here's the PHP code in the xmlData div:

```
<div id="xmlData">
        <?php

        $xml = simplexml_load_file('data.xml');
        $num_of_elements = count($xml->image);

        for($i = 0; $i < $num_of_elements; $i++)
        {?>

            <p>
            <a href="<?php echo($xml->image[$i]->file);?>">
            <img src="<?php echo($xml->image[$i]->thumb);?>"/>
            </a>
            <?php echo($xml->image[$i]->description);?>
            </p>
            <div class="clearFloat"></div>
        <?php
        }?>

</div>
```

12. This PHP code works using SimpleXML's PHP extension (*http://www.php .net/simplexml*). The file *data.xml* is loaded, the number of elements in the file is held in the $num_of_elements variable, and a loop displays a paragraph for each element. In the paragraph, the thumbnail is displayed, which is a link to the full-sized image. Along with each thumbnail is a description. The clearFloat div is necessary because the images are floating to the left as defined in the CSS file *styles.css*, where you can find more information about the layout of the application.

 The SimpleXML extension is a PHP5 toolset that can convert XML to an object. Once it's an object, the XML data can be accessed using PHP5's normal array iterators and property selectors.

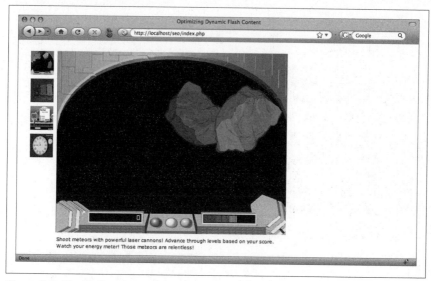

Figure 5-5. The Flash version of the application is running in a web browser

13. Test the file again in your web browser, this time with JavaScript disabled. You should then see the PHP-based version of the application (Figures 5-6 and 5-7), which contains the searchable version of the same data used by the Flash application.

14. As an optional step, you can update the XML file by adding or removing elements, and see the data updated in both the Flash and PHP versions of the app.

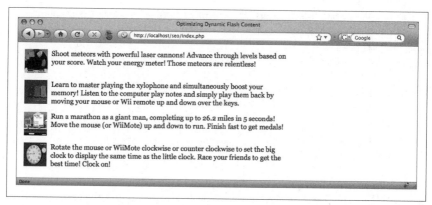

Figure 5-6. Viewing the thumbnails and descriptions

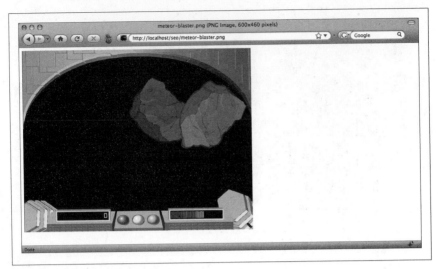

Figure 5-7. Viewing the full-size images

Key Terms Used in this Chapter

Table 5-1 contains the terms that were introduced in this chapter and gives you their definitions.

Table 5-1. Key terms used in this chapter

Term	Definition
Dynamic URL	URLs that contain variables and/or session IDs, like *http://www.example.com/index.php?id=28345987f987&product=234098*.
AJAX	Asynchronous JavaScript and XML. Web technology that allows for page updates without requiring a page refresh.
RIA	Rich Internet Application.

CHAPTER 6

SEO for Rich Internet Applications Using Flex

So far, you've optimized webpages that contain Flash. You can also create Flash applications by using Adobe Flex Builder. Using Flex, you can quickly create powerful and robust Rich Internet Applications, or RIAs. This chapter discusses how you can optimize your Flex applications to increase their visibility on the Web.

Getting to Know Flex

You may already be familiar with Flex. If not, you can read more about it at *http://www.adobe.com/products/flex/*. This section explains the Flex basics, including why you would want to use it, how Flex applications work, and a brief overview of the Flex interface.

 You can download a free trial of Adobe Flex Builder at *http://www.adobe.com/flex*. If you're a student or a teacher, you can get a full-featured free copy of the software at *https://freeria tools.adobe.com/*.

Reasons to Use Flex Instead of Flash

Understanding the missions of Flash and Flex is essential in choosing the right application for the job. Flex was created primarily to build RIAs, whereas Flash was originally created to build animations.

Flash is the best choice for animations or any applications that require a lot of drawing, because Flex doesn't have tools for creating art without using code. Also, Flash easily lets you connect custom created symbols to classes through the Library. Flash has a timeline where you can place code, so it works great for applications like games that contain both animations and interactivity.

Built on the Eclipse *Integrated Development Environment* (more commonly known as just Eclipse), an application used to make programming easier, Flex Builder is an amazing tool for writing code, and is far more advanced in terms of code hinting than Flash. Applications that make heavy use of classes or object-oriented programming (OOP) should be created in Flex Builder or another tool that has powerful ActionScript development tools, like FlashDevelop.

If your applications use a mix of interactivity and animations, consider using both applications. For example, you can use Flash to create animations, and Flex to write the interactive code. Also, you can create Flash components for use with Flex.

 Developing Flash components for use in Flex is beyond the scope of this book. For more information, see Flex Help or Adobe's Flash developer network at *http://www.adobe.com/ devnet/flash/*.

Understanding Flex Applications

Essentially, Flex applications are Flash applications once they're deployed. They typically use a container HTML file to house a Flash movie, and play the movie via a browser's Flash Player, just like applications published through Flash.

The main difference between Flash and Flex applications is that Flex applications use the Flex Framework of components. Similar to Flash components, components that leverage the Flex Framework are widgets that you can use to quickly architect Flex applications.

Further, while Flash applications use an FLA file as a working file, Flex uses an MXML file. MXML is, as its name implies, an XML-based markup language. Basically, an MXML file is a text file that contains layout information for a Flex application (MXML code) as well as the interactive code (ActionScript 3.0). Flex is like a Dreamweaver for building Flash applications, where MXML is to HTML as ActionScript is to JavaScript.

Becoming Familiar with Flex Builder

You use Flex Builder to write and lay out code for Flex applications. Like Dreamweaver, it has two views—Design view and Source view. Also like

---

Dreamweaver, it has a panel to organize all the files associated with individual projects—the Flex Navigator.

Design view

In Design view (Figure 6-1), the main working area is the stage, along with the Components panel and the Flex Properties panel. Note that the names of the panels and working areas are almost identical to those in Flash, and have similar functionality. This view is used to lay out a Flex application and to add limited interactivity. Using the Components panel, you can drag interactive widgets to the stage—just like components in Flash. Then, in the Flex Properties panel, you can set properties for them, like X and Y coordinates and colors.

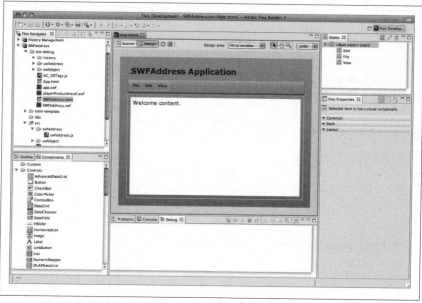

Figure 6-1. Flex Builder's Design view

Source view

Source view (Figure 6-2) is used to write code for a Flex application using ActionScript 3.0, MXML, and a variety of other supported languages. In Source view, the Outline panel shows the hierarchy of your Flex application.

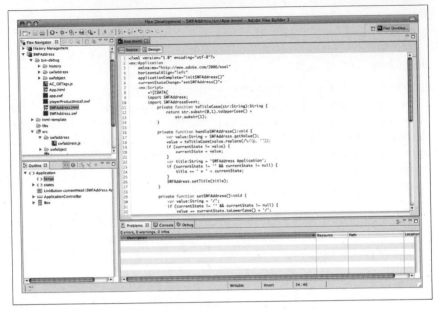

Figure 6-2. Flex Builder's Source view

The Flex Navigator

The Flex Navigator, comparable to the Files panel in Dreamweaver, stores your Flex Projects (similar to Dreamweaver websites) and gives you quick access to the files they use. Using the Flex Navigator, you can open any text file to make modifications as well as create new files of various types.

Creating a Flex Project

To create a new Flex Project, choose File→New→Flex Project. You see the New Flex Project window (Figure 6-3), where you can enter a name and location for your Flex Project. From there, click Finish to accept the project settings, and Flex creates the project and necessary files for you.

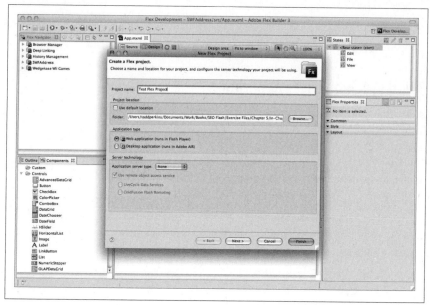

Figure 6-3. The New Flex Project window

A Flex Project is not a file or a folder; it's simply a reference to a folder that contains the necessary Flex Project working files and folders. If you're familiar with Dreamweaver, think of a Flex Project as a Dreamweaver site.

Here's a list of the folders Flex creates for you when you create a Flex Project:

bin-debug

The *bin-debug* folder is the output folder that contains all the files used in your application, including HTML, SWF, JavaScript, and all local files that are dynamically loaded rather than being embedded. To deploy a Flex application, simply place the contents of this folder on your web server.

html-template

The *html-template* folder contains the HTML template used to create the HTML file published to the *bin-debug* folder, as well as all of the JavaScript, CSS, and other files the template is connected to.

libs

The *libs* folder is made to store ActionScript classes and other similar files for use in your Flex application.

The *src* folder contains all of your source files, which by default is only your main working MXML file, *main.mxml*.

Building a Simple Flex Application

Now that you've had a top-level view of Flex, take a look at how to build applications. In this section, you'll create a simple interactive Flex application and then preview it in a web browser.

Adding components and modifying properties

To add components to a Flex application, just drag the components from the components panel onto the stage. Component properties are adjustable in Design view and Source view. Figure 6-4 shows a Button component on the stage along with a Label component.

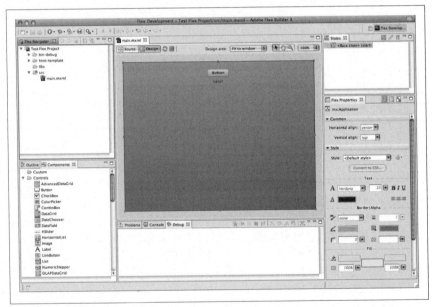

Figure 6-4. Viewing Button and Label components on the stage

In Design view, you can adjust properties for the current selected object using the Flex Properties panel. If you have the stage selected, you can adjust properties for the stage, like the background color of your application and application layout type. Flex has three layout types for applications, adjustable via the layout portion of the Flex Properties panel. The options are: vertical, horizontal, and absolute. Vertical applications organize elements vertically, horizontal applications organize them horizontally, and absolute applications let you place elements at any X and Y positions. The application shown in Figure 6-4 is created using a vertical layout.

When you want to use code to communicate to an object, to modify its properties for example, you need to give that object an ID (comparable to an instance name in Flash). You can assign ID values in Design view using the Flex Properties panel once an object is selected. Figure 6-5 shows an ID assignment of myLabel to the label component on the stage.

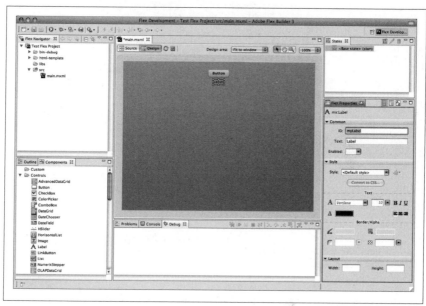

Figure 6-5. Assigning an ID of myLabel to the Label component

You can view and assign property values in Design view as well as in Source view. In Source view, you see the code behind the application you've created. The application shown in Figure 6-5 uses the following code:

```
<?xml version="1.0" encoding="utf-8"?>
<mx:Application xmlns:mx="http://www.adobe.com/2006/mxml" layout="vertical">
    <mx:Button label="Button"/>
    <mx:Label text="Label" id="myLabel"/>
</mx:Application>
```

Notice in the previous block of code that the Label component is represented by the MXML element, <mx:Label>, and the value of its id property is myLabel. You can modify properties exposed by the Label component or modify them here in Source View by adding or changing attribute values inside a particular element. For example, if you want to change the text in the Label

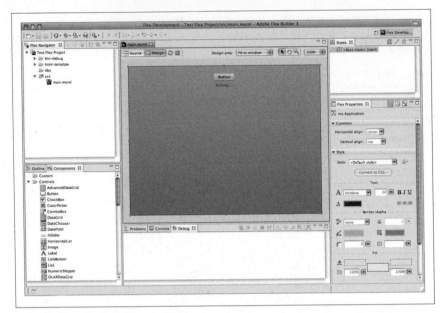

Figure 6-6. Viewing updates in Design view

to display `Waiting...`, you can modify its value for the attribute `text`, resulting in the following code:

```
<?xml version="1.0" encoding="utf-8"?>
<mx:Application xmlns:mx="http://www.adobe.com/2006/mxml" layout="vertical">
    <mx:Button label="Button"/>
    <mx:Label text="Waiting..." id="myLabel"/>
</mx:Application>
```

Changes in Source view are automatically updated when you change to Design view (Figure 6-6).

Adding simple interactivity

Now you'll look at how to add some simple interactivity to a Flex application using Design view. In Design view, you can add simple ActionScript code to a Button component by assigning a value to the `On click` property in the Flex Properties panel. Code assigned to this property executes when the button is clicked. For example, you can modify the text property of the Label component, `myLabel`, to display `Clicked!` using the following code in the `On click` field:

```
myLabel.text='Clicked!'
```

The previous code simply sets the value of myLabel's text property to Clicked!, just like a value would be assigned using an instance name in ActionScript—with dot syntax. Note the single quotes instead of double quotes; to add interactivity in this way, you must use single quotes. Double quotes are used in MXML to define property values, so you can't use them for property values. Just to make it extra clear, here it is again:

Make sure to use single quotes instead of double quotes when using an ActionScript String as a property value.

If you switch to Source again, you can view the concise code generated:

```
<?xml version="1.0" encoding="utf-8"?>
<mx:Application xmlns:mx="http://www.adobe.com/2006/mxml" layout="vertical">
    <mx:Button label="Button" click="myLabel.text='Clicked!'"/>
    <mx:Label text="Waiting..." id="myLabel"/>
</mx:Application>
```

Just like when setting a value for id with the Label component, the value set through the Flex Properties panel is transferred to the attribute value click for the Button component.

Testing the application

Once an application is ready for testing, you can preview the application in a web browser by clicking the Run button (green background play button icon) at the top left of your screen or by choosing Run→Run [your application name]. Your application then opens in a browser window (Figure 6-7).

Before you run your application, the application needs to be saved. If you attempt to run an application without saving, then Flex prompts you to save the file before continuing.

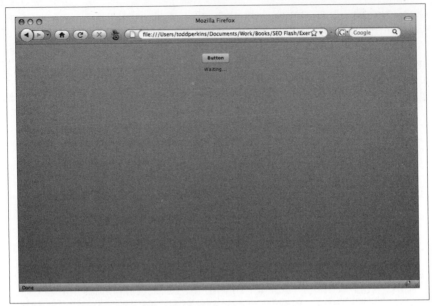

Figure 6-7. Viewing the Flex application in a browser window

The application in this example has simple interactivity that updates the label when the button is clicked (see Figure 6-8).

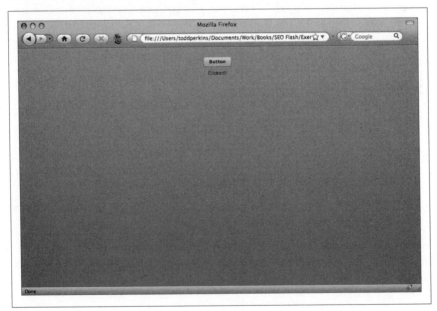

Figure 6-8. Viewing the result of clicking the button

Viewing the files created by Flex

Flex creates output files once you test an application. You can find these files in the Flex Navigator, in the *bin-debug* folder. Once your Flex application is complete, you can export the final release build using the Export Release Build button, shown in Figure 6-9.

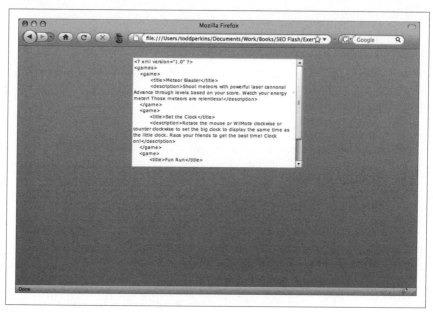

Figure 6-9. The Export Release Build button

More to learn

Covering every detail of Flex is beyond the scope of this book. For detailed information about Flex, you can find great Flex books from O'Reilly, and excellent video training at *http://www.lynda.com*.

Searchable Flex Content

Essentially, all content that's searchable in Flash is searchable in Flex, which makes sense because both applications are deployed to the Flash Player. This section discusses the specifics of which Flex components display data that's searchable according to the recent advancements in Flash content SEO (see Chapter 3 for details).

Static Text

Static text in Flex is a little different from that in Flash. Basically, static text in Flex means text displayed based on values set directly in Flex, or in other words, values that don't come from data that is based or external sources. These values are searchable in any text field components: Label, Text, TextArea, DataGrid, and so on.

Dynamic Text

Dynamic text includes all text content loaded into the various text components from external sources. External data sources can be XML files, plain-text files, database data, or any other textual data that appears in a Flex application.

 Currently, search engines do not index text from external sources like XML files. However, that content gets does indexed separately, so whether or not search engines index the dynamic content as part of the Flex application, using text from an XML or HTML file can get that text indexed one way or another.

Other Searchable Elements

Google and Yahoo!, according to Flash Player search advancements, can also index URLs in Flex applications. Since these advancements are relatively new at this point, not much public information exists concerning other searchable elements. However, other searchable elements may become public knowledge in the future.

Best Practices

Best practices in Flex match those in Flash. The new indexing of Flash content is great, but while the technology is maturing, people still consider it best to use HTML to show alternate content using a method like SWFObject. That way, you can ensure everything that needs to be indexed is spelled out plainly to search engines.

Essential Flex SEO Steps

Though it isn't Flex content, the HTML output of a Flex application is searchable just like any other HTML. When HTML content is created for output by Flex, some crucial SEO elements, like a page title for one, are left out. To solve these problems, you have to edit the HTML manually. One solution is to add

HTML to the output file created by Flex. Another solution is to adjust the template Flex uses to create the HTML output file. There are examples of both of these solutions later in this chapter.

Loading Text into Flex

Flex supports text data from any text file, just like Flash. In this section, you'll load XML-formatted textual data into a Flex application.

Understanding Data Loading

You have multiple ways of loading external text data into Flex. Since this book assumes you're familiar with Flash and ActionScript 3.0, you'll look at the ActionScript 3.0 method. Here's a look at the workflow for loading external data:

1. Create a URLRequest to reference the file you'll load.
2. Make an instance of the URLLoader class that'll load the file.
3. Have the URLLoader instance listen for the Event.COMPLETE event.
4. Call the URLLoader's load() method, passing in the URLRequest you created.
5. Data is then accessible as a String via the URLLoader's data property.

ActionScript 3.0 code blocks in Flex are placed in <mx:Script> elements, and encased in <![CDATA[]]> tags to tell Flex not to process the ActionScript code as XML data. This is what the Flex code looks like to perform the loading operation:

```
<?xml version="1.0" encoding="utf-8"?>
<mx:Application xmlns:mx="http://www.adobe.com/2006/mxml" layout="vertical"
creationComplete="initApp()">
<mx:Script>
    <![CDATA[
        private var req:URLRequest = new URLRequest("data.xml");
        private var loader:URLLoader = new URLLoader();

        private function initApp():void
        {
            loader.addEventListener(Event.COMPLETE,loadComplete);
            loader.load(req);
        }

        private function loadComplete(event:Event):void
        {
            myText.text = loader.data;
        }
    ]]>
</mx:Script>
```

```
    <mx:TextArea id="myText" height="250" width="400"/>
</mx:Application>
```

Notice the Application tag in the previous code has a value of `initApp()` for the `creationComplete` attribute:

```
<mx:Application xmlns:mx="http://www.adobe.com/2006/mxml" layout="vertical"
creationComplete="initApp()">
```

The `creationComplete` attribute defines what happens when the application has initialized, completed loading, and is ready to execute code. This place is the best one to run a function to initialize your application—one of the only ways to define code that runs immediately once your application is created.

Notice all variables and functions are scoped to the `private` access modifier.

```
private var req:URLRequest = new URLRequest("data.xml");
private var loader:URLLoader = new URLLoader();
```

The access modifier refers to where these functions and variables can be referenced outside of this file. For details about access modifiers in ActionScript 3.0, see *Essential ActionScript 3.0* by Colin Moock (O'Reilly).

In the `initApp()` function, the code that runs immediately upon creation of the application is placed, which listens for the `Event.COMPLETE` event and runs the `URLLoader.load()` method:

```
private function initApp():void
{
    loader.addEventListener(Event.COMPLETE,loadComplete);
    loader.load(req);
}
```

Once the external data is loaded, the `loadComplete()` function runs, which uses the `URLLoader`'s `data` property to place the text in the `TextArea` `myText`.

Upon testing the application, you'll see the externally loaded text in your browser window within a `TextArea` component (shown in Figure 6-10).

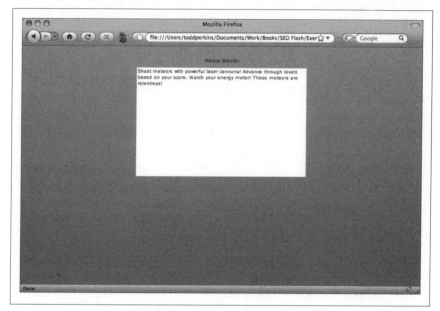

Figure 6-10. Viewing the external data in a TextArea component

Understanding E4X

E4X, EcmaScript for XML, is a standard for reading and writing XML data for EcmaScript-based languages like ActionScript 3.0. The great thing about E4X is that it lets you treat XML as a native data type, which means you can create, read, and update XML data using dot syntax.

Working with XML elements in ActionScript 3.0

To work with XML data using ActionScript 3.0, you first need to create a new instance of the XML class, passing in XML code as a string or as raw XML data to the constructor. Here's what the code looks like to create a new XML instance from a string:

```
var xml:XML = new XML("<games></games>");
```

Notice the XML data in the constructor is passed in as a string, and thus is wrapped in quotes. Here the code passing in XML data to the constructor:

```
var xml:XML = new XML(<games></games>);
```

You can also create XML objects without using the constructor as follows:

```
var xml:XML = <games></games>;
```

Once you have an XML instance, you can read and write elements using dot syntax. If you want to add a `<game>` element with a value of My Game to the games element in the previous code, you can use this ActionScript:

```
var xml:XML = new XML(<games></games>);
xml.game = "My Game";
```

The ActionScript code generates the following XML data, which can be captured using the XML class's `toXMLString()` method:

```
<games>
  <game>My Game</game>
</games>
```

Say you wanted to have the `<game>` element have two child elements, `<title>` and `<description>`, each having string values, without assigning a value to the `<game>` element itself as in the previous code. Here's the code:

```
var xml:XML = new XML(<games></games>);
xml.game.title = "My Game Title";
xml.game.description = "My Game Description";
```

Here's the XML code generated by the previous ActionScript:

```
<games>
  <game>
    <title>My Game Title</title>
    <description>My Game Description</description>
  </game>
</games>
```

Notice how quick and concise the ActionScript code is when using E4X. If you're familiar with XML in ActionScript 2.0, you may have used (and been frustrated by) the ambiguous properties to manipulate XML data. Using E4X, XML in ActionScript is a party!

Working with E4X attributes

E4X not only makes life easy when working with XML elements, it also has simple syntax for working with attributes. The syntax for working with attributes is @attributename. For example, if you're using the XML code you were looking at earlier in this section, and you want to create an attribute called id on the `<game>` element, with a value of game-001, you can add this line of ActionScript:

```
xml.game.@id = "game-001";
```

Here's what the ActionScript looks like in context:

```
var xml:XML = new XML(<games></games>);
xml.game.title = "My Game Title";
xml.game.description = "My Game Description";
xml.game.@id = "game-001";
```

And here is the XML code that is generated:

```
<games>
  <game id="game-001">
    <title>My Game Title</title>
    <description>My Game Description</description>
  </game>
</games>
```

> This is just a brief introduction to E4X syntax, as it applies to the projects you're working on in this chapter. For exhaustive coverage of E4X syntax in *ActionScript* 3.0, check out the ActionScript 3.0 definitive guide, O'Reilly's *Essential Action-Script 3.0* by Colin Moock.

Using XML Data in Flex

Now you'll look at using E4X to use XML data in Flex. First, review the XML data you looked at earlier in this section:

```
<? xml version="1.0" ?>
<games>
    <game>
        <title>Meteor Blaster</title>
        <description>Shoot meteors with powerful laser cannons! Advance
through levels based on your score. Watch your energy meter!
Those meteors are relentless!</description>
    </game>
    <game>
        <title>Set the Clock</title>
        <description>Rotate the mouse or WiiMote clockwise or counter-
clockwise to set the big clock to display the same time as the
little clock. Race your friends to get the best time!
Clock on!</description>
    </game>
    <game>
        <title>Fun Run</title>
        <description>Run a marathon as a giant man, completing up to 26.2
miles in 5 seconds! Move the mouse (or WiiMote) up and down to run.
Finish fast to get medals!</description>
    </game>
</games>
```

Here, you have a repeating element, `<game>`, that's used to hold each game's title and description. You want to display the data from any game in a Label and a TextArea component.

This is the MXML code you used earlier, along with an added Label component, to load the external XML file and display it as a string:

```
<?xml version="1.0" encoding="utf-8"?>
<mx:Application xmlns:mx="http://www.adobe.com/2006/mxml" layout="vertical"
creationComplete="initApp()">
<mx:Script>
    <![CDATA[
        private var req:URLRequest = new URLRequest("data.xml");
        private var loader:URLLoader = new URLLoader();

        private function initApp():void
        {
            loader.addEventListener(Event.COMPLETE,loadComplete);
            loader.load(req);
        }

        private function loadComplete(event:Event):void
        {
            myText.text = loader.data;
        }
    ]]>
</mx:Script>
    <mx:Label id="myLabel"/>
    <mx:TextArea id="myText" height="250" width="400"/>
</mx:Application>
```

To get the XML data into Flex, you first create a private member variable, connected to the Application object, to hold the XML. Here's the code alone:

```
private var xmlData:XML;
```

And here's the code in context (below the first two variables declared at the top of the script block):

```
<?xml version="1.0" encoding="utf-8"?>
<mx:Application xmlns:mx="http://www.adobe.com/2006/mxml" layout="vertical"
creationComplete="initApp()">
<mx:Script>
    <![CDATA[
        private var req:URLRequest = new URLRequest("data.xml");
        private var loader:URLLoader = new URLLoader();
        private var xmlData:XML;

        private function initApp():void
        {
            loader.addEventListener(Event.COMPLETE,loadComplete);
            loader.load(req);
        }
```

```
        private function loadComplete(event:Event):void
        {
            myText.text = loader.data;
        }
    ]]>
</mx:Script>
    <mx:Label id="myLabel"/>
    <mx:TextArea id="myText" height="250" width="400"/>
</mx:Application>
```

Next, you'll go to the loadComplete() function, and then pass the data that comes from the URLLoader's data property into the XML constructor to create the XML object:

```
private function loadComplete(event:Event):void
{
    xmlData = new XML(loader.data);
}
```

Now, you'll put the XML data for the first game into the Label and TextArea components. To reference an individual repeating element, like the `<game>` element in our XML file, you can use array operators. For example, the first `<game>` element can be accessed using the following code:

```
xmlData.game[0]
```

Note that the reason you use array operators is because in ActionScript 3.0 and E4X, repeating elements have a data type of XMLList, which is essentially an array of XML objects.

 For more information about the XMLList class, see Flex or Flash Help.

Once you've accessed a single element using the XMLList array access notation, you can read or write its properties using dot syntax. Here's the code to put the title and description for game zero into the Label and TextArea (viewing only the loadComplete() function):

```
private function loadComplete(event:Event):void
{
    xmlData = new XML(loader.data);
    myLabel.text = xmlData.game[0].title;
    myText.text = xmlData.game[0].description;
}
```

Here's all of the code in the application:

```
<?xml version="1.0" encoding="utf-8"?>
<mx:Application xmlns:mx="http://www.adobe.com/2006/mxml" layout="vertical"
creationComplete="initApp()">
```

```
<mx:Script>
    <![CDATA[
        private var req:URLRequest = new URLRequest("data.xml");
        private var loader:URLLoader = new URLLoader();
        private var xmlData:XML;

        private function initApp():void
        {
            loader.addEventListener(Event.COMPLETE,loadComplete);
            loader.load(req);
        }

        private function loadComplete(event:Event):void
        {
            xmlData = new XML(loader.data);
            myLabel.text = xmlData.game[0].title;
            myText.text = xmlData.game[0].description;
        }
    ]]>
</mx:Script>
    <mx:Label id="myLabel"/>
    <mx:TextArea id="myText" height="250" width="400"/>
</mx:Application>
```

If you save and test this application, then you can see the XML data displayed
in the Label and TextArea components in your web browser (Figure 6-11).

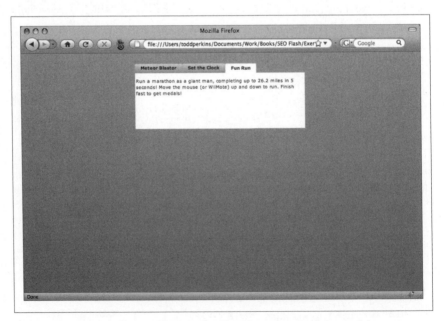

Figure 6-11. Viewing the XML data displayed in Flex components in a web browser

Understanding History Management

Using Flex, you can easily communicate application state changes to the web browser, letting users use the browser's Back and Forward buttons to navigate through your application. This feature of Flex is called History Management. In this section, we'll look at how to implement History Management, as well as its benefits and limitations.

Using History Management

You can very easily implement history management in an application. Simply set the `historyManagementEnabled` property of any navigation component in your application to true. Navigation components include the TabNavigator, Accordion, TabBar, and any other components in the Navigators section of the Components panel (or components that extend ViewStack if you're not working in Design view).

You can also set your entire application to use History Management. In the `<mx:Application>` tag, Flex will "remember" the states of your application by changing the URL of the page (using named anchors, like SWFAddress) each time your application's state changes.

Here's the XML based-application you looked at in the last section, modified to support History Management:

```
<?xml version="1.0" encoding="utf-8"?>
<mx:Application xmlns:mx="http://www.adobe.com/2006/mxml" layout="vertical"
creationComplete="initApp()" historyManagementEnabled="true">
<mx:Script>
    <![CDATA[
        import mx.controls.Text;
        import mx.containers.VBox;
        private var req:URLRequest = new URLRequest("data.xml");
        private var loader:URLLoader = new URLLoader();
        private var xmlData:XML;

        private function initApp():void
        {
            loader.addEventListener(Event.COMPLETE,loadComplete);
            loader.load(req);
        }

        private function loadComplete(event:Event):void
        {
            xmlData = new XML(loader.data);
            for each(var game:XML in xmlData.game)
            {
                var vbox:VBox = new VBox();
                var field:Text = new Text();
```

```
                 field.text = game.description;
                 vbox.label = game.title;
                 navigator.addChild(vbox);
                 vbox.addChild(field);
                 field.width = 375;
                 field.height = 100;
            }
        }
    ]]>
</mx:Script>
    <mx:TabNavigator id="navigator" width="400" height="150">
    </mx:TabNavigator>
</mx:Application>
```

Look at how this application works, starting from where you left off in the last section. First, note that `historyManagementEnabled` is set to `true` in the `<mx:Application>` tag:

```
<mx:Application xmlns:mx="http://www.adobe.com/2006/mxml" layout="vertical"
creationComplete="initApp()" historyManagementEnabled="true">
```

Next, notice the `TabNavigator` component is the only component in this application when it first renders:

```
<mx:TabNavigator id="navigator" width="400" height="150">
    </mx:TabNavigator>
```

The `loadComplete()` function has also been modified to use a loop to populate the TabNavigator with data:

```
private function loadComplete(event:Event):void
{
    xmlData = new XML(loader.data);
    for each(var game:XML in xmlData.game)
    {
        var vbox:VBox = new VBox();
        var field:Text = new Text();
        field.text = game.description;
        vbox.label = game.title;
        navigator.addChild(vbox);
        vbox.addChild(field);
        field.width = 375;
        field.height = 100;
    }
}
```

Notice the loop is a `for each in` loop, which can be used to loop through all of the XML elements in an XMLList, or repeating XML elements. In this example, the variable game is used to represent each `<game>` element repeated in the XML file.

Also notice that elements are created in the same way that they are in Flash when using ActionScript 3.0, using the new keyword. In this loop, the following code is executed for each `<game>` element:

1. A new VBox component is created:

```
var vbox:VBox = new VBox();
```

 A VBox component is a vertical layout container. Tab-Navigator components display tabs for every layout container held. The label on each tab comes from the label attribute value of the layout container contained in that tab. For example, the value of the `label` property of this VBox object determines the label in its tab.

2. A new Text component is created:

```
var field:Text = new Text();
```

3. The Text component's text property is set to display the description of the game:

```
field.text = game.description;
```

4. The VBox component displays the title of the game as its label:

```
vbox.label = game.title;
```

5. The VBox is added as a child element of the TabNavigator:

```
navigator.addChild(vbox);
```

6. The Text component is added as a child of the VBox:

```
vbox.addChild(field);
```

7. The Text component's width and height are set:

```
field.width = 375;
field.height = 100;
```

 In order to use the `Text` and `VBox` classes in ActionScript 3.0, you need to import those classes at the top of your `<mx:Script>` block.

If you test this application in a web browser, and click the tabs, then the URL in your browser window updates (Figure 6-12). This update lets you use the Back and Forward buttons in your browser to navigate through the application.

Benefits of History Management

The key benefits of History Management are its ease and simplicity. You can essentially turn on History Management with one small line of code. This

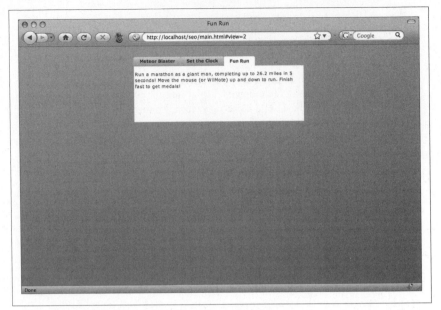

Figure 6-12. Viewing History Management in a web browser

feature is a good one to add to any application when you want to quickly add a great feature.

The feature also offers usability increase, another important benefit. History Management can greatly improve your RIA's usability by easing the navigation process, especially when navigation has traditionally been considered one of the weak points of RIAs.

Weaknesses of History Management

As great as History Management is, it does have some pretty significant weaknesses. First, the communication to your browser that updates the URL is only one-way. That means you can't update the URL properties and expect the application to update.

The other weakness is linked to the first. A lack of two-way communication between application and browser means you can't save or share URLs, a significant setback in SEO. For that reason, use History Management only when you want to add a quick simple feature to a low-profile application, and avoid it in favor of the other, more SEO-friendly methods of browser-RIA communication.

Understanding the BrowserManager Class and Deep Linking

One way you can enable two-way communication between the browser and your Flex applications is when you use the `BrowserManager` class. The `BrowserManager` class lets you capture and use *URL fragments*—name value pairs used as named anchors. This ability lets you update a Flex application based on its URL. It also lets you update URLs based on Flex input, so just like using SWFAddress in Flash, you can create two-way communication between your Flex application and the web browser.

BrowserManager Essentials

Before you begin using the `BrowserManager` class to control two-way communication between the browser and your Flex application, it's important to understand how the `BrowserManager` class works. This section explains the important parts of working with the `BrowserManager` class that you should be familiar with before implementing it in your applications.

Properties, methods, and events

Look at the BrowserManager properties, methods, and events you'll be working with for the BrowserManager example. Table 6-1 is a brief list of the `BrowserManager` class's features. For more features, see Flex Help.

Table 6-1. BrowserManager properties, methods, and events

Name	Type	Description
Fragment	Property	An object that holds the fragment portion of the current URL—data type is string
BrowserManager.getInstance()	Method (Static)	Returns an IBrowserManager instance
setTitle()	Method	Sets the browser's title
setFragment()	Method	Sets the fragment of the current URL
BrowserChangeEvent.BROWSER_URL_CHANGE	Event	Triggered when the browser's URL is changed

Using the URLUtil class

Since the BrowserManager uses strings only as a data type for getting and setting URL fragments, in order to access the fragment values of the string, you need to do some processing. For example, a fragment string may be `view=1,` and in order to use the data you have to separate the property (view) from the value (1).

That's where the URLUtil class comes in. Using the URLUtil class helps you skip the step of processing strings, and gives you easy object access to fragment properties and values. It converts strings to objects for processing fragments using its stringToObject() method, and converts objects to strings for sending fragments using its objectToString() method. That way, you can use an object to represent the fragment and access its property names and values using object notation. For example, you can get the value of the view fragment through your fragment's view property, so the code would be fragment.view.

Creating a Deep Linking Application

Now you'll look at using the BrowserManager class to build an application that uses two-way deep linking. Here's a complete application that uses this technique:

```
<?xml version="1.0" encoding="utf-8"?>
<mx:Application xmlns:mx="http://www.adobe.com/2006/mxml" layout="vertical"
creationComplete="initApp()">
<mx:Script>
    <![CDATA[
        import mx.managers.IBrowserManager;
        import mx.managers.BrowserManager;
        import mx.events.BrowserChangeEvent;
        import mx.utils.URLUtil;

        import mx.controls.Text;
        import mx.containers.VBox;

        private var req:URLRequest = new URLRequest("data.xml");
        private var loader:URLLoader = new URLLoader();
        private var xmlData:XML;

        private var manager:IBrowserManager;

        private function initApp():void
        {
            manager = BrowserManager.getInstance();
            manager.addEventListener(BrowserChangeEvent.BROWSER_URL_CHANGE,
parseURL);
            manager.init("","Wedgekase Wii Games");
            loader.addEventListener(Event.COMPLETE,loadComplete);
            loader.load(req);
        }

        private function loadComplete(event:Event):void
        {
            xmlData = new XML(loader.data);
            for each(var game:XML in xmlData.game)
            {
                var vbox:VBox = new VBox();
                var field:Text = new Text();
```

```
                        field.text = game.description;
                        vbox.label = game.title;
                        navigator.addChild(vbox);
                        vbox.addChild(field);
                        field.width = 375;
                        field.height = 100;
                    }
                }

                private function parseURL(event:BrowserChangeEvent):void
                {
                    var fragment:Object = URLUtil.stringToObject(manager.fragment);
                    if(fragment.view == undefined)
                    {
                        fragment.view = 0;
                    }
                    navigator.selectedIndex = fragment.view;
                    manager.setTitle(xmlData.game[navigator.selectedIndex].title);
                }

                private function updateURL():void
                {
                    var newFragment:Object = {};
                    var fragmentStr:String = "";
                    newFragment.view = navigator.selectedIndex;
                    fragmentStr = URLUtil.objectToString(newFragment);
                        manager.setFragment(fragmentStr);
                        manager.setTitle(xmlData.game[navigator.selectedIndex].title);
                }
            ]]>
        </mx:Script>
            <mx:TabNavigator id="navigator" width="400" height="150" change=
    "updateURL()">
            </mx:TabNavigator>
    </mx:Application>
```

Take a look at how this application uses the BrowserManager class. First, note that it's the same application you used in the last section, with a few updates. The first update is the extra import statements:

```
import mx.managers.IBrowserManager;
import mx.managers.BrowserManager;
import mx.events.BrowserChangeEvent;
import mx.utils.URLUtil;
```

These statements import the necessary classes for working with the Browser-Manager class. Note the IBrowserManager class is imported, because an instance of IBrowserManager will be used to work with the BrowserManager because the BrowserManager class is a type of class that never gets instantiated.

The only new variable is manager, which is data typed to be an instance of any class that implements the IBrowserManager interface:

```
private var manager:IBrowserManager;
```

An interface is a list of methods. Any class that implements an interface must contain all the methods in that interface. See *Essential ActionScript 3.0* by Colin Moock for more details.

Next, look at the `initApp()` function:

```
private function initApp():void
{
    manager = BrowserManager.getInstance();
    manager.addEventListener
    (BrowserChangeEvent.BROWSER_URL_CHANGE, parseURL);
    manager.init("","Wedgekase Wii Games");
    loader.addEventListener(Event.COMPLETE,loadComplete);
    loader.load(req);
}
```

The `initApp()` function has three new lines of code. First, the manager variable is set to `BrowserManager.getInstance()`, which returns an instance that implements IBrowserManager. Next, an event listener is added to the manager instance, listening for the browser's URL to change. Upon changing, the `parseURL()` function runs. Finally, the BrowserManager is initialized using its `init()` method. The first parameter represents the initial URL fragment, which is left blank here. The second represents the initial browser title.

Now you'll discuss the `parseURL()` function:

```
private function parseURL(event:BrowserChangeEvent):void
{
    var fragment:Object = URLUtil.stringToObject(manager.fragment);
    if(fragment.view == undefined)
    {
        fragment.view = 0;
    }
    navigator.selectedIndex = fragment.view;
    manager.setTitle(xmlData.game[navigator.selectedIndex].title);
}
```

This function gets triggered when the browser's URL changes. First, the `fragment` object uses the URLUtil to convert the `manager`'s `fragment` from a string to an object. Then, if the `view` property of the `fragment` is undefined, it is set to 0. Then, the `navigator`'s selected index is set to whatever value is in the `fragment`'s `view` property, which updates the TabNavigator according to the current URL fragment. Finally, the page's title is updated using the `manager`'s `setTitle()` method. The title is set to the value of the game title that corresponds to the current selected index of the `TabNavigator` component (which was previously received from the URL fragment).

So far you've looked at what happens when the URL is updated, but not at what makes a change in the URL. The first thing that initiates the change is the change event of the TabNavigator, which is set to run the `updateURL()` function:

```
<mx:TabNavigator id="navigator" width="400" height="150" change="updateURL()">
</mx:TabNavigator>
```

The `updateURL()` function looks like this:

```
private function updateURL():void
{
    var newFragment:Object = {};
    var fragmentStr:String
    newFragment.view = navigator.selectedIndex;
    fragmentStr = URLUtil.objectToString(newFragment);
    manager.setFragment(fragmentStr);
    manager.setTitle(xmlData.game[navigator.selectedIndex].title);
}
```

First, this function creates a new empty object to represent the new fragment that will appear in the URL (`newFragment`) and a new empty string that will represent the string version of `newFragment` (`fragmentStr`). Next, the `newFragment` object's `view` property is set to the selected index of the TabNavigator (i.e. the index number of whatever tab was clicked to initiate the change event). Then, a string version of the `newFragment` object is held in `fragmentStr`, and set as the current fragment using the BrowserManager's `setFragment()` method. Finally, the page's title is set to the current game's title from the XML file.

You need a server to test this application's two-way communication. The files in the history folder created by Flex Builder should also be copied to your server, since they're the supporting files that control communication between the browser and the Flex application. When testing this file on your server, click through the tabs to watch the URLs update (Figure 6-13), and change the view number in the URL to watch the application update.

BrowserManager Limitations

Though the BrowserManager class is a powerful tool for two-way communication between the browser and the application, it's lacking an important SEO feature. The problem with the BrowserManager class as you've used it here is that in order to navigate to an application state, the application must first be initialized. That means, if you pass in a fragmented URL to your application, desiring to start on view 2, the application would start at view 0. Once at view 0, the application can then be moved to view 2 via a URL change. Even though this feature allows two-way communication, and with an extra step allows for saving URLs, you're still better off going with a system like SWFAddress for deep linking.

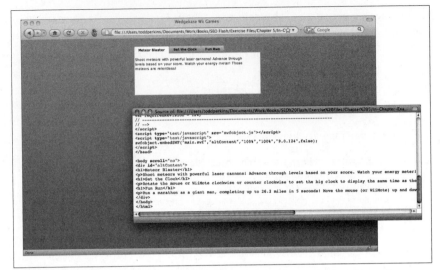

Figure 6-13. Viewing the BrowserManager class in two-way communication action.

 Deep linking in Flex is possible without using SWFAddress or any third party code, but it's more complex than the example shown here. For information about deep linking in Flex that supports fragment URLs when an application is first initialized, in Flex Help, see Deep Linking.

The `BrowserManager` class doesn't work in every web browser. Currently, the BrowserManager class is not supported by Safari, Chrome, or Opera. This doesn't harm how spiders index your site, but it can decrease traffic on your site for anyone using those browsers, so it's best to use SWFAddress or another method that's more broadly supported.

Implementing SWFObject in a Flex Application

SWFObject is the commonly accepted method for using Flash published content in an HTML page, and works well with Flex, too. This section looks at implementing SWFObject in a Flex application.

Using SWFObject with Flex

As mentioned earlier in this chapter, Flex places all of its output files in the *bin-debug* folder. In that folder, you find the HTML and SWF files used in your application. You can implement SWFObject in a Flex application by modifying the output HTML file in the same way you do for using SWFObject with Flash.

To modify the HTML file, simply open the file *main.html* (or the main HTML file for your application) from the *bin-debug* folder in a text editor, and then make the necessary changes. Here's an example of the HTML that is created by Flex:

```html
<!-- saved from url=(0014)about:internet -->
<html lang="en">

<!--
Smart developers always View Source.

This application was built using Adobe Flex, an open source framework
for building rich Internet applications that get delivered via the
Flash Player or to desktops via Adobe AIR.

Learn more about Flex at http://flex.org
// -->

<head>
<meta http-equiv="Content-Type" content="text/html; charset=utf-8" />

<!-- BEGIN Browser History required section -->
<link rel="stylesheet" type="text/css" href="history/history.css" />
<!-- END Browser History required section -->

<title>Wedgekase Wii Games</title>
<script src="AC_OETags.js" language="javascript"></script>

<!-- BEGIN Browser History required section -->
<script src="history/history.js" language="javascript"></script>
<!-- END Browser History required section -->

<style>
body { margin: 0px; overflow:hidden }
</style>
<script language="JavaScript" type="text/javascript">
<!--
// -----------------------------------------------------------------------
// Globals
// Major version of Flash required
var requiredMajorVersion = 9;
// Minor version of Flash required
var requiredMinorVersion = 0;
// Minor version of Flash required
var requiredRevision = 124;
// -----------------------------------------------------------------------
// -->
</script>
</head>

<body scroll="no">
<script language="JavaScript" type="text/javascript">
<!--
```

```
// Version check for the Flash Player that has the ability to start
Player Product Install (6.0r65)
var hasProductInstall = DetectFlashVer(6, 0, 65);

// Version check based upon the values defined in globals
var hasRequestedVersion = DetectFlashVer(requiredMajorVersion,
requiredMinorVersion, requiredRevision);

if ( hasProductInstall && !hasRequestedVersion ) {
    // DO NOT MODIFY THE FOLLOWING FOUR LINES
    // Location visited after installation is complete if installation is
required
    var MMPlayerType = (isIE == true) ? "ActiveX" : "PlugIn";
    var MMredirectURL = window.location;
    document.title = document.title.slice(0, 47) + " -
Flash Player Installation";
    var MMdoctitle = document.title;

    AC_FL_RunContent(
        "src", "playerProductInstall",
        "FlashVars",
"MMredirectURL="+MMredirectURL+'&MMplayerType='+MMPlayerType+'
&MMdoctitle='+MMdoctitle+"",
        "width", "100%",
        "height", "100%",
        "align", "middle",
        "id", "main",
        "quality", "high",
        "bgcolor", "#869ca7",
        "name", "main",
        "allowScriptAccess","sameDomain",
        "type", "application/x-shockwave-flash",
        "pluginspage", "http://www.adobe.com/go/getflashplayer"
    );
} else if (hasRequestedVersion) {
    // if we've detected an acceptable version
    // embed the Flash Content SWF when all tests are passed
    AC_FL_RunContent(
            "src", "main",
            "width", "100%",
            "height", "100%",
            "align", "middle",
            "id", "main",
            "quality", "high",
            "bgcolor", "#869ca7",
            "name", "main",
            "allowScriptAccess","sameDomain",
            "type", "application/x-shockwave-flash",
            "pluginspage", "http://www.adobe.com/go/getflashplayer"
    );
} else {  // flash is too old or we can't detect the plugin
    var alternateContent = 'Alternate HTML content should be placed here. '
        + 'This content requires the Adobe Flash Player. '
        + '<a href=http://www.adobe.com/go/getflash/>Get Flash</a>';
```

```
        document.write(alternateContent);  // insert non-flash content
    }
// -->
</script>
<noscript>
        <object classid="clsid:D27CDB6E-AE6D-11cf-96B8-444553540000"
            id="main" width="100%" height="100%"

codebase="http://fpdownload.macromedia.com/get/flashplayer/current
/swflash.cab">
                <param name="movie" value="main.swf" />
                <param name="quality" value="high" />
                <param name="bgcolor" value="#869ca7" />
                <param name="allowScriptAccess" value="sameDomain" />
                <embed src="main.swf" quality="high" bgcolor="#869ca7"
                    width="100%" height="100%" name="main" align="middle"
                    play="true"
                    loop="false"
                    quality="high"
                    allowScriptAccess="sameDomain"
                    type="application/x-shockwave-flash"
                    pluginspage="http://www.adobe.com/go/getflashplayer">
                </embed>
        </object>
</noscript>
</body>
</html>
```

Even though this application sets the document's title via
JavaScript, it's still important for the application to have a
value for the <title> tag. That's because search engines don't
record the JavaScript updates to the <title> tag—only the
<title> tag in the HTML before JavaScript is executed.

Notice the large amounts of JavaScript code used in the file, as well as the large
amount of HTML content. The first thing you'll do is delete all code within
the <body> tag so the body tag looks like this:

```
<body scroll="no">

</body>
```

When you modify this code, you may get a warning message
telling you that this file is derived from a template. In this case,
you can click OK to confirm that you know what you're doing.

Next, create a <div> element with an id value of altContent and place some
alternate content inside it. Here's an example of the entire <body> tag after the

changes using the data from the XML file you've been working with formatted as HTML:

```
<body scroll="no">
<div id="altContent">
<h1>Wedgekase Wii Games</h1>
Here are some free games playable on your computer or your Wii!
<h2>Meteor Blaster</h2>
<p>Shoot meteors with powerful laser cannons! Advance through levels based
on your score. Watch your energy meter! Those meteors are relentless!</p>
<h2>Set the Clock</h2>
<p>Rotate the mouse or WiiMote clockwise or counter clockwise to set the
big clock to display the same time as the little clock. Race your
friends to get the best time! Clock on!</p>
<h2>Fun Run</h2>
<p>Run a marathon as a giant man, completing up to 26.2 miles in 5 seconds!
Move the mouse (or WiiMote) up and down to run. Finish fast to get
medals!</p>
</div>
</body>
```

Now that you have some alternate content, you'll create two <script> blocks in the <head> tag to use SWFObject. The first one should be a link to swfobject.js (which should be copied to the *bin-debug* directory), and the second should use SWFObject's dynamic publishing method to embed the SWF. After that, make sure to delete any references to the file that you won't be using, *AC_OETags.js*. Here's what the entire <head> tag looks like:

```
<head>
<meta http-equiv="Content-Type" content="text/html; charset=utf-8" />

<!-- BEGIN Browser History required section -->
<link rel="stylesheet" type="text/css" href="history/history.css" />
<!-- END Browser History required section -->

<title>Wedgekase Wii Games</title>

<!-- BEGIN Browser History required section -->
<script src="history/history.js" language="javascript"></script>
<!-- END Browser History required section -->

<style>
body { margin: 0px; overflow:hidden }
</style>
<script type="text/javascript" src="swfobject.js"></script>
<script type="text/javascript">
swfobject.embedSWF("main.swf","altContent","100%","100%","9.0.124",false);
</script>
</head>
```

After making the changes, you can test the application in a web browser to make sure it works. You can also the see the alternate content in the code from your web browser's View > Source command (Figure 6-14).

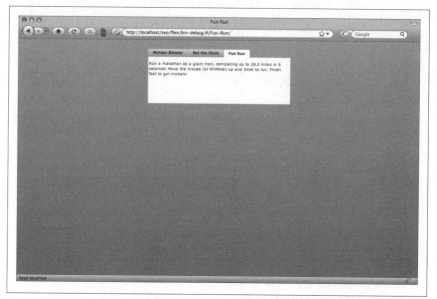

Figure 6-14. Viewing the source code to see the alternate content in the HTML

Any changes made to the *bin-debug* HTML file should either be made once your application is ready for deployment, or during development by adjusting the project's run/debug settings in Project Properties (see Flex help for more info). If you test your app again in Flex after modifying the HTML file, then Flex may overwrite the HTML file using its HTML template. To be able to continue to test your application with custom HTML, you can modify the HTML template Flex uses. You can find information about that process in Flex Help.

Using SWFAddress with Flex

SWFAddress is not only a great deep linking solution with applications created in Flash, it also works incredibly well for deep linking in Flex. It's an excellent solution because along with easily implementing in an application, you can use SWFAddress to display any state of an application when it initializes. This section demonstrates how to use SWFAddress in a Flex application.

Implementing SWFAddress in Flex

You begin with a few small steps when implementing SWFAddress in a Flex app. First, you need to have the right files in the right places. The

SWFAddress.as and *SWFAddressEvent.as* files need to be in the *src* folder for your application, and the JavaScript folder *swfaddress* containing *swfaddress.js* needs to be in your output folder, *bin-debug.* You can create a Flex project using the *SWFAddress* folder as your main folder, and by setting *App.mxml* as your main application file.

After the files are in the appropriate places, you can write the code for your application to implement SWFAddress. Start by making sure your output HTML file links to *swfaddress.js* using the following code:

```
<script type="text/javascript" src="swfaddress/swfaddress.js"></script>
```

Your HTML code should also be using SWFObject, which was discussed earlier in this chapter. Next, you're ready to write the MXML code. Here's an example of code that utilizes SWFAddress:

```
<?xml version="1.0" encoding="utf-8"?>
<mx:Application xmlns:mx="http://www.adobe.com/2006/mxml"
creationComplete="initApp()">
    <mx:Script>
        <![CDATA[
        import mx.containers.VBox;
        import flash.events.Event;
        import flash.net.URLLoader;
        import flash.net.URLRequest;
        import mx.controls.Text;
        import SWFAddress;

        private var req:URLRequest = new URLRequest("data.xml");
        private var loader:URLLoader = new URLLoader();
        private var xmlData:XML;

        private var urls:Array = new Array();

        private function initApp():void
        {
            loader.addEventListener(Event.COMPLETE,loadComplete);
            loader.load(req);
            SWFAddress.onChange = handleSWFAddress;
        }

        private function loadComplete(event:Event):void
        {
            xmlData = new XML(loader.data);
            for each(var game:XML in xmlData.game)
            {
                var vbox:VBox = new VBox();
                var field:Text = new Text();
                field.text = game.description;
                vbox.label = game.title;
                navigator.addChild(vbox);
                vbox.addChild(field);
                field.width = 375;
```

```
                        field.height = 100;
                        urls.push(formatAsURL(game.title));
                    }
                }

                private function handleSWFAddress():void
                {
                    var value:String = SWFAddress.getValue();
                    value = value.replace(/\//g, "");
                    navigator.selectedIndex = urls.indexOf(value);
                    SWFAddress.setTitle(formatAsTitle(value));
                }

                private function setSWFAddress():void
                {
                    SWFAddress.setValue("/" + urls[navigator.selectedIndex] + "/");
                }

                private function formatAsURL(t:String):String
                {
                    var formatted:String = t;
                    return formatted.replace(/ /g,"-");
                }

                private function formatAsTitle(t:String):String
                {
                    var formatted:String = t;
                    return formatted.replace(/-/g," ");
                }
            ]]>
        </mx:Script>
        <mx:TabNavigator id="navigator" width="400" height="150"
    change="setSWFAddress()">
        </mx:TabNavigator>
    </mx:Application>
```

Now walk through how this application works. Much of the app is the same
application you looked at earlier in this chapter. For example, in the
`<mx:Application>` tag, the `creationComplete` event is set to trigger `initApp()`,
which initiated the loading of the XML file. Here's the `<mx:Application>` tag:

```
<mx:Application xmlns:mx="http://www.adobe.com/2006/mxml"
creationComplete="initApp()">
```

And here's the `initApp()` function:

```
private function initApp():void
{

    loader.addEventListener(Event.COMPLETE,loadComplete);
    loader.load(req);
    SWFAddress.onChange = handleSWFAddress;
}
```

Notice the `initApp()` function has only one new line of code:

```
SWFAddress.onChange = handleSWFAddress;
```

This line of code runs the `handleSWFAddress()` function whenever the `SWFAddressEvent.CHANGE` event occurs. This way is a shorthand way of using `addEventListener()` to connect an event handler function to an event. You'll look at what `handleSWFAddress()` does later in this section.

The application has one new variable, `urls`:

```
private var urls:Array = new Array();
```

This variable holds the URL formatted versions of all URLs, as stated in the bottom of the loop at the end of the `loadComplete()` function:

```
private function loadComplete(event:Event):void
{
    xmlData = new XML(loader.data);
    for each(var game:XML in xmlData.game)
    {
        var vbox:VBox = new VBox();
        var field:Text = new Text();
        field.text = game.description;
        vbox.label = game.title;
        navigator.addChild(vbox);
        vbox.addChild(field);
        field.width = 375;
        field.height = 100;
        urls.push(formatAsURL(game.title));
    }
}
```

The URLs are formatted using the `formatAsURL()` function to format each game title. The returned URL is then stored in the `urls` array. Here's the `formatAsURL()` function:

```
private function formatAsURL(t:String):String
{
    var formatted:String = t;
    return formatted.replace(/ /g,"-");
}
```

This function simply holds a duplicate of the string passed in within the formatted variable, and then uses the string's replace method to replace all spaces with hyphens. The code `/ /g` is a *Regular Expression*—powerful string referencing code, that identifies all spaces using the global g operator.

 For more information about Regular Expressions, see Flex Help.

Address changes for SWFAddress are initiated with the TabNavigator's change event, which triggers the `setSWFAddress()` function:

```
<mx:TabNavigator id="navigator" width="400" height="150" change=
"setSWFAddress()">
```

Look at the `setSWFAddress()` function:

```
private function setSWFAddress():void
{
    SWFAddress.setValue("/" + urls[navigator.selectedIndex] + "/");
}
```

This function simply calls SWFAddress' `setValue()` method to update the address in the browser's URL. The updated address is the URL formatted game title that corresponds to the `selectedIndex` of the TabNavigator, wrapped in forward slashes (/). SWFAddress also begins all updates to URLs with a hash character (#).

SWFAddress' `setValue()` method triggers the `SWFAddressEvent.CHANGE` event, which runs the `handleSWFAddress()` function. Here's that function:

```
private function handleSWFAddress():void
{
    var value:String = SWFAddress.getValue();
    value = value.replace(/\//g, "");
    navigator.selectedIndex = urls.indexOf(value);
    SWFAddress.setTitle(formatAsTitle(value));
}
```

The `handleSWFAddress()` function begins by capturing SWFAddress' value—the fragment portion of the URL, using its `getValue()` method. Then, the forward slashes in the value are stripped using the `String.replace()` method and a Regular Expression. Next, the TabNavigator's `selectedIndex` is set to whatever index corresponds to the current value of `SWFAddress`, which is retrieved using the `urls` Array's `indexOf()` method. Finally, the title in the browser window is updated using SWFAddress' `setTitle()` method. The value passed in is the value returned from the `formatAsTitle()` function.

Let's look at `formatAsTitle()`:

```
private function formatAsTitle(t:String):String
{
    var formatted:String = t;
    return formatted.replace(/-/g," ");
}
```

Where the `formatAsURL()` function accepts a game title and returns a URL, this function does the opposite. It accepts a game's URL, and then returns its title.

In order to work properly, the application should be tested using a testing server. When you do test this in a testing server, you see the URLs and page titles update when you click the different tabs (Figure 6-15). Further, if you attempt to initialize the application with a URL that contains a fragment, then the application initializes to show its correct state.

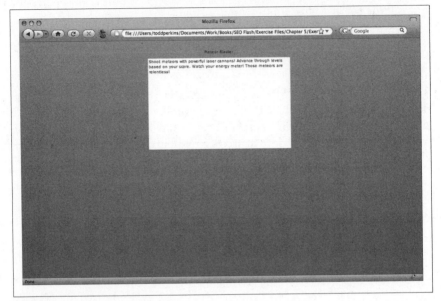

Figure 6-15. Viewing SWFAddress working in a Flex application

Deep Linking with URLKit

You can create deep links in Flex applications in many ways. So far, we've looked at the BrowserManager and SWFAddress. Another excellent and popular method of deep linking is URLKit. In this section, we'll explore URLKit, its advantages, and how to use it in a Flex application.

Benefits of URLKit

URLKit essentially does the same thing that SWFAddress does. It allows you to create deep links in your Flex applications using URL fragments. As with SWFAddress, these links can be used to create bookmarks and can even be indexed by search engines. Using URLKit, you get a lot of control in deciding how your deep links work. With this control, you can generate multi-fragment URLs based on property values of multiple UI elements. In addition to giving you a great control over deep links, URLKit is quite easy to use, even in a preexisting application.

Implementing URLKit in a Flex Application

To implement URLKit in your applications, you'll first need to download the necessary files at the URLKit website, *http://code.google.com/p/urlkit/*. Once you have the files, you just need to add an *.swc* file to your project's build path; then you can add the URLKit code to add deep linking to your Flex application.

Adding urlkitFlex3.swc to your project's build path

Adding a file to your project's build path is simple. Start by opening your project's Properties window by right-clicking or Control-clicking your folder in the Flex Navigator and choosing Properties (Figure 6-16). Then, in the Properties window (Figure 6-17), click the Flex Build Path option on the left. In the Flex Build Path area, click Library, and click the Add SWC... button on the right side of the window (Figure 6-18). From there, browse for the file *urlkit/bin/urlkitFlex3.swc* and choose that file to add to your Flex Build Path. Then click OK to close the Properties window.

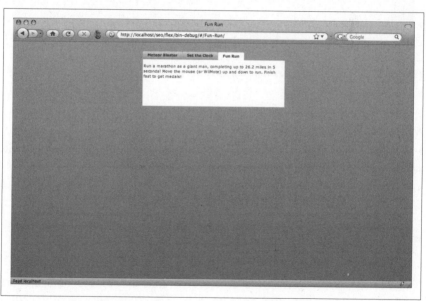

Figure 6-16. Choosing Project Properties

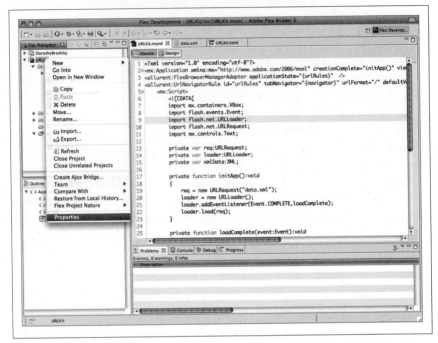

Figure 6-17. The Project Properties window

Adding the URLKit code

Once you've added the URLKit file to your project's build path, you're ready to start using URLKit in your code. Basically, it's set up in such a way that you can use virtually any navigation component (ViewStack, TabNavigator, etc.) and URLKit will write the URL fragments for you.

To implement URLKit in your Flex application, you first need to create a FlexBrowserManagerAdapter component using the allurent namespace:

```
<allurent:FlexBrowserManagerAdapter />
```

The FlexBrowserManagerAdapter component connects to the built-in Flex BrowserManager, which uses some JavaScript code to handle communication between the browser and the Flash Player.

Next, you will need to use a URL rule component to control how URLKit creates the URL fragments you'll be working with. Your URL rule needs to be connected to the FlexBrowserManagerAdapter component using the FlexBrowserManagerAdapter component's applicationState property. The following is an example of connecting the FlexBrowserManagerAdapter component to the URL rule component UrlValueRule.

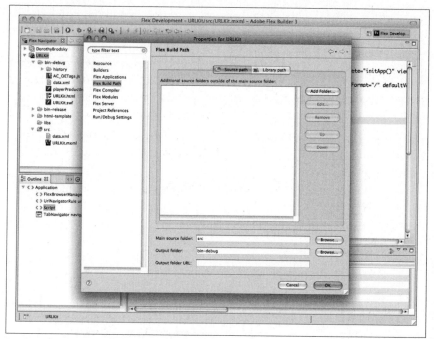

Figure 6-18. The Add SWC window

```
<allurent:FlexBrowserManagerAdapter applicationState="{allRules}" />
<allurent:UrlValueRule id="allRules"/>
```

 There are four different URL rules, but for the sake of this example, we're going to look at the UrlValueRule and how to use it multiple times in one URL. For information about the other rules, see the note at the end of this section.

The UrlValueRule requires three more properties to function properly. The urlFormat property defines how to format the URL fragment created, the sourceValue property defines what component property to follow to get the data for the fragment, and the defaultValue property allows you to set a default value for the property used to create the URL fragment. Here's an example of this implemented in code, connecting the UrlValueRule to a TabNavigator component with an id value of navigator:

```
<allurent:FlexBrowserManagerAdapter applicationState="{allRules}" />
<allurent:UrlValueRule id="allRules" urlFormat=";selectedIndex=*"
    sourceValue="navigator.selectedIndex" defaultValue="0" />
```

In the previous code, the value for urlFormat is ;selectedIndex=*. Remember, this is the value after the hash symbol (#) that defines the URL fragment. It starts with a semicolon to allow for easy separation of multiple values in the fragment. Then, an identifier name, selectedIndex, is given to the fragment, and the value is set to an asterisk (*). The asterisk character is a placeholder, and when URLKit processes the URL fragment, the asterisk will be replaced with the value of the property being followed, which in this case is navigator.selectedIndex. For example, when the selectedIndex of the TabNavigator is 1, the URL fragment will be #;selectedIndex=1.

The last step to this working properly is assigning a selectedIndex value that matches the defaultValue property of the UrlValueRule (which is 0) to the TabNavigator component:

```
<mx:TabNavigator id="navigator" width="400" height="150" selectedIndex="0">
</mx:TabNavigator>
```

Here's what the entire application looks like:

File: *URLKit.mxml*

```
<?xml version="1.0" encoding="utf-8"?>
<mx:Application xmlns:mx="http://www.adobe.com/2006/mxml"
creationComplete="initApp()" viewSourceURL="srcview/index.html"
xmlns:allurent="http://www.allurent.com/2006/urlkit">
<allurent:FlexBrowserManagerAdapter applicationState="{allRules}" />
<allurent:UrlValueRule id="allRules" urlFormat=";selectedIndex=*"
    sourceValue="navigator.selectedIndex" defaultValue="0" />
<mx:Script>
        <![CDATA[
        import mx.containers.VBox;
        import flash.events.Event;
        import flash.net.URLLoader;
        import flash.net.URLRequest;
        import mx.controls.Text;

        private var req:URLRequest;
        private var loader:URLLoader;
        private var xmlData:XML;

        private function initApp():void
        {
            req = new URLRequest("data.xml");
            loader = new URLLoader();
            loader.addEventListener(Event.COMPLETE,loadComplete);
            loader.load(req);
        }

        private function loadComplete(event:Event):void
        {

            xmlData = new XML(loader.data);
            for each(var game:XML in xmlData.game)
            {
                var vbox:VBox = new VBox();
```

```
                  var field:Text = new Text();
                  field.text = game.description;
                  vbox.label = game.title;
                  navigator.addChild(vbox);
                  vbox.addChild(field);
                  field.width = 375;
                  field.height = 100;
              }

          }
          ]]>
      </mx:Script>
      <mx:TabNavigator id="navigator" width="400" height="150" selectedIndex=
"0">
      </mx:TabNavigator>
</mx:Application>
```

If you test this application in a web browser (see Figure 6-19), you'll find that
it works as you'd expect it to, and pretty similar to SWFAddress. You can use
the browser's Back button, bookmark any application view, and return to it
later to watch the application launch in that view.

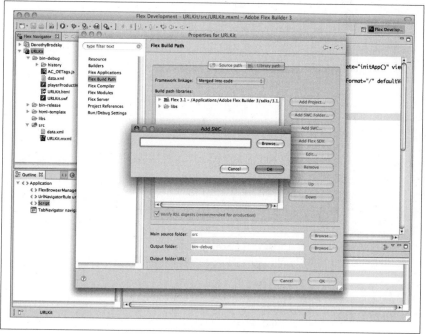

Figure 6-19. URLKit working in Firefox

Earlier in this section, I mentioned that you could easily implement multi-
fragment URLs using URLKit. To do that, all you have to do is wrap multiple

rules in an `UrlRuleSet` component, giving the `UrlRuleSet` an `id` value that matches that of the `applicationState` value for the `FlexBrowserManagerAdap` ter component. Here's an example of the application we just looked at, with the addition of a `CheckBox` component:

File: *URLKitCheckbox.mxml*

```
<?xml version="1.0" encoding="utf-8"?>
<mx:Application xmlns:mx="http://www.adobe.com/2006/mxml"
creationComplete="initApp()" viewSourceURL="srcview/index.html"
xmlns:allurent="http://www.allurent.com/2006/urlkit">
<allurent:FlexBrowserManagerAdapter applicationState="{allRules}" />
<allurent:UrlRuleSet id="allRules">
<allurent:UrlValueRule urlFormat=";checked=*"
    sourceValue="box.selected" defaultValue="false" />
<allurent:UrlValueRule urlFormat=";selectedIndex=*"
    sourceValue="navigator.selectedIndex" defaultValue="0" />
</allurent:UrlRuleSet>
    <mx:Script>
        <![CDATA[
        import mx.containers.VBox;
        import flash.events.Event;
        import flash.net.URLLoader;
        import flash.net.URLRequest;
        import mx.controls.Text;

        private var req:URLRequest;
        private var loader:URLLoader;
        private var xmlData:XML;

        private function initApp():void
        {
            req = new URLRequest("data.xml");
            loader = new URLLoader();
            loader.addEventListener(Event.COMPLETE,loadComplete);
            loader.load(req);
        }

        private function loadComplete(event:Event):void
        {

            xmlData = new XML(loader.data);
            for each(var game:XML in xmlData.game)
            {
                var vbox:VBox = new VBox();
                var field:Text = new Text();
                field.text = game.description;
                vbox.label = game.title;
                navigator.addChild(vbox);
                vbox.addChild(field);
                field.width = 375;
                field.height = 100;
            }
```

```
            }
        ]]>
    </mx:Script>
    <mx:TabNavigator id="navigator" width="400" height="150" selectedIndex=
"0">
    </mx:TabNavigator>
    <mx:CheckBox label="Checkbox" id="box" selected="false"/>
</mx:Application>
```

The previous code follows the `CheckBox` component's `selected` property. If you test the application in a web browser, you'll find that both the `selectedIndex` of the `TabNavigator` and the selected value of the `CheckBox` are reflected in the URL fragment. (See Figure 6-20.)

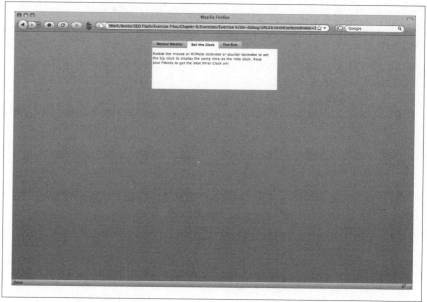

Figure 6-20. Viewing multiple fragments in the address bar created with URLKit

 Though exhaustive coverage of URLKit is beyond the scope of this book, there are other places where you can learn as many details as you'd like. David Tucker (RIA guru) wrote a great article about implementing URLKit in your Flex applications, which you can find at *http://www.insideria.com/2008/09/advanced-flex-deep-linking-wit-1.html*. Further, documentation for URLKit is available at *http://www.davidtucker.net/docs/urlkit/*.

Exercises

Now that you've covered all the theory for optimizing Flex applications for search engines, you'll get some practice building those applications in the following exercises.

Exercise 6-1: Loading XML-Based Text

Search engines can index any text that appears in a Flex application, and one of the most common ways you get text in a Flex application is by using XML data. Data in XML files can be indexed by search engines, so by using that XML data in your Flex application, you ensure that at least the data retrieved from the XML file is searchable. In this exercise, you'll look at loading some external XML data into Flex. You'll also display that data in an application.

1. Create a new Flex Project, setting the main folder to be the Exercise 6-1 folder.

2. View the XML data in the file `data.xml` in the `src` folder:

```
<? xml version="1.0" ?>
<games>
    <game>
        <title>Meteor Blaster</title>
        <description>Shoot meteors with powerful laser cannons! Advance
through levels based on your score. Watch your energy meter! Those
meteors are relentless!</description>
    </game>
    <game>
        <title>Set the Clock</title>
        <description>Rotate the mouse or WiiMote clockwise or
counterclockwise to set the big clock to display the same
time as the little clock. Race your friends to get the
best time! Clock on!</description>
    </game>
    <game>
        <title>Fun Run</title>
        <description>Run a marathon as a giant man, completing up to 26.2
miles in 5 seconds! Move the mouse (or WiiMote) up and down to run.
Finish fast to get medals!</description>
    </game>
</games>
```

3. Look at the code within `main.mxml`. Notice the app runs `initApp()` once the application is done being created. Also notice a Label with an `id` of `myLabel` and a TextArea with an `id` of `myText`:

```
<?xml version="1.0" encoding="utf-8"?>
<mx:Application xmlns:mx="http://www.adobe.com/2006/mxml" layout=
"vertical"
```

```
      creationComplete="initApp()">
      <mx:Script>
          <![CDATA[
              private function initApp():void
              {

              }
          ]]>
      </mx:Script>
          <mx:Label id="myLabel"/>
          <mx:TextArea id="myText" height="250" width="400"/>
      </mx:Application>
```

4. Above the `initApp()` function, create three private variables. Name the first variable **req**, with a data type of `URLRequest`. Set its value to a new instance of the `URLRequest` class, passing in the value **data.xml**. Call the next variable **loader**, data type it to `URLLoader`, and then create a new instance of the `URLLoader` class. Finally, call the third variable **xmlData**, and data type it to the `XML` class, but don't instantiate it just yet:

```
private var req:URLRequest = new URLRequest("data.xml");
private var loader:URLLoader = new URLLoader();
private var xmlData:XML;
```

5. In the `initApp()` function, have the `URLLoader` instance listen for the `Event.COMPLETE` event, and set the event handler to be a function called `loadComplete`. Next, have the `URLLoader` instance load the `URLRequest`:

```
private function initApp():void
{
    loader.addEventListener(Event.COMPLETE,loadComplete);
    loader.load(req);
}
```

6. Define the `loadComplete()` function:

```
private function loadComplete(event:Event):void
{

}
```

7. In the `loadComplete()` function, instantiate the `xmlData` variable by creating a new instance of the XML class and passing in the URLLoader's data property. Then, set the Label to display the title of the first game in the XML file. Finally, set the TextArea to display the first game's description:

```
private function loadComplete(event:Event):void
{
    xmlData = new XML(loader.data);
    myLabel.text = xmlData.game[0].title;
    myText.text = xmlData.game[0].description;
}
```

8. Run the application in a web browser to view the XML data displayed in your Flex application (Figure 6-21). If you have any problems, you can check your code against *main_final.mxml*.

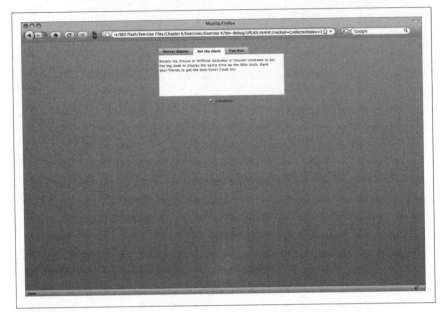

Figure 6-21. Viewing the finished application's XML data

Exercise 6-2: Using SWFObject with a Flex Application

SWFObject can greatly optimize your Flex applications by letting you easily add alternate HTML content. In this exercise, you'll update an application to use SWFObject:

1. Open the file *bin-debug/main.html* from the Exercise 6-2 folder in Flex to view its HTML code. Note that *swfobject.js* is included in the *bin-debug* folder.

2. Copy the file, and then rename the copy *index.html*.

3. Delete all the code within *index.html*.

4. Add the following code to *index.html* to make the file utilize SWFObject:

```
<!DOCTYPE html PUBLIC "-//W3C//DTD XHTML 1.0 Strict//EN"
"http://www.w3.org/TR/xhtml1/DTD/xhtml1-strict.dtd">
<html xmlns="http://www.w3.org/1999/xhtml" lang="en" xml:lang="en">
    <head>
        <title>Exercise 2</title>
        <meta http-equiv="Content-Type" content="text/html; charset=
```

```
            iso-8859-1" />
            <script type="text/javascript" src="swfobject.js"></script>
            <script type="text/javascript">
                swfobject.embedSWF("main.swf", "altContent", "100%", "100%",
        "9.0.124",false);
            </script>
            <style>
            body { margin: 0px; overflow:hidden }
            </style>
        </head>
        <body scroll="no">
            <div id="altContent">
                <p>Alt content goes here!</p>
            </div>
        </body>
    </html>
```

5. View the application in a web browser to see SWFObject working. Check the application's source code by choosing View→Source from your browser's menu.

Exercise 6-3: Deep Linking Using SWFAddress

Using SWFAddress, you can easily implement deep linking in your site. This exercise gives you practice using SWFAddress with Flex.

1. Open the output file, *index.html* in the *bin-debug* folder for Exercise 6-3 in Flex and notice it links to *swfaddress/swfaddress.js*.

2. In the *src* folder, open the file *App.mxml*, and then, in Flex, view its code.

3. Notice the file's <mx:Application> has a value of initApp() for its creationComplete property.

4. In the initApp() function, notice that SWFAddress's change event executes the handleSWFAddress() function.

5. Look at the TabNavigator's change property. Notice that runs the setSWFAddress() function.

6. Notice the utility and XML loading and displaying functions that are already written.

7. In the setSWFAddress() function, add the code to update the page's URL using SWFAddress's setValue() method:

    SWFAddress.setValue("/" + urls[navigator.selectedIndex] + "/");

8. Remember, the SWFAddress.setValue() method triggers the SWFAddressEvent.CHANGE event, which causes handleSWFAddress() to run. In the handleSWFAddress() function, write the code to get SWFAddress' value, remove the forward slashes, set the appropriate selected index of the TabNavigator based on SWFAddress' value, and then use the format-

ted version of the value to set the title in the browser window using `SWFAddress.setTitle()`. The finished version of `handleSWFAddress()` should look like this:

```
private function handleSWFAddress():void
{
    var value:String = SWFAddress.getValue();
    value = value.replace(/\//g, "");
    navigator.selectedIndex = urls.indexOf(value);
    SWFAddress.setTitle(formatAsTitle(value));
}
```

9. Save the file, and then, from the *bin-debug* folder in your web browser, open *index.html* using your testing server to view SWFAddress working when you click through the tabs. Nice!

Exercise 6-4: Deep Linking with URLKit

In this exercise, we'll add deep linking to a pre-built application using URLKit.

1. Choose File→Import→Flex Project, and import the Exercise 6-4 folder into your Flex workspace.
2. Open the file *URLKit.mxml* in the *src* folder to view its contents.

File: *URLKit.mxml*

```
<?xml version="1.0" encoding="utf-8"?>
<mx:Application xmlns:mx="http://www.adobe.com/2006/mxml"
creationComplete="initApp()" viewSourceURL="srcview/index.html">
    <mx:Script>
        <![CDATA[
        import mx.containers.VBox;
        import flash.events.Event;
        import flash.net.URLLoader;
        import flash.net.URLRequest;
        import mx.controls.Text;

        private var req:URLRequest;
        private var loader:URLLoader;
        private var xmlData:XML;

        private function initApp():void
        {
            req = new URLRequest("data.xml");
            loader = new URLLoader();
            loader.addEventListener(Event.COMPLETE,loadComplete);
            loader.load(req);
        }

        private function loadComplete(event:Event):void
        {
```

```
                    xmlData = new XML(loader.data);
                    for each(var game:XML in xmlData.game)
                    {
                        var vbox:VBox = new VBox();
                        var field:Text = new Text();
                        field.text = game.description;
                        vbox.label = game.title;
                        navigator.addChild(vbox);
                        vbox.addChild(field);
                        field.width = 375;
                        field.height = 100;
                    }


                }
            ]]>
        </mx:Script>
        <mx:TabNavigator id="navigator" width="400" height="150"
    selectedIndex="0">
        </mx:TabNavigator>
        <mx:CheckBox label="Checkbox" id="box" selected="false"/>
    </mx:Application>
```

3. Note that the setup of the application is similar to other files we've worked with throughout this chapter, in that it uses data from an XML file to populate a `TabNavigator` component.

4. Next, add the file *urlkitFlex3.swc* to your Flex project's build path. Start by opening the Project Properties window. Do this by right-clicking (or Control-clicking) your Flex project in the Flex navigator and choosing Properties.

5. In the Project Properties window, select the Flex Build Path option on the left side of the window.

6. Select the Library Path option in the center of the window.

7. Click the Add SWC button on the right side of the window, which opens the Add SWC window.

8. Click the Browse button and find the file *urlkitFlex3.swc*, which is located in the *urlkit-0.92/urlkit/bin* directory.

9. Click OK to accept the changes you've made and to close the Project Properties window.

10. In the file *URLKit.mxml*, add the following code below the `<mx:Application>` tag:

    ```
    <allurent:FlexBrowserManagerAdapter applicationState="{allRules}" />
    ```

11. Below the code that you just wrote, create an `UrlRuleSet` component with an id of `allRules`:

```
<allurent:FlexBrowserManagerAdapter applicationState="{allRules}" />
<allurent:UrlRuleSet id="allRules">
</allurent:UrlRuleSet>
```

12. Inside of the `UrlRuleSet`, create an `UrlValueRule` component connected to the `selected` property of the `CheckBox` component. The `CheckBox` component has an `id` of `box`:

```
<allurent:FlexBrowserManagerAdapter applicationState="{allRules}" />
<allurent:UrlRuleSet id="allRules">
<allurent:UrlValueRule urlFormat=";checked=*"
    sourceValue="box.selected" defaultValue="false" />
</allurent:UrlRuleSet>
```

13. Below the code you wrote in the last step, create an `UrlValueRule` connected to the `selectedIndex` property of the `TabNavigator` component, which is named `navigator`:

```
<allurent:FlexBrowserManagerAdapter applicationState="{allRules}" />
<allurent:UrlRuleSet id="allRules">
<allurent:UrlValueRule urlFormat=";checked=*"
    sourceValue="box.selected" defaultValue="false" />
<allurent:UrlValueRule urlFormat=";selectedIndex=*"
    sourceValue="navigator.selectedIndex" defaultValue="0" />
</allurent:UrlRuleSet>
```

14. Review your code for errors. Here's what the finished application should look like:

```
<?xml version="1.0" encoding="utf-8"?>
<mx:Application xmlns:mx="http://www.adobe.com/2006/mxml"
creationComplete="initApp()" viewSourceURL="srcview/index.html"
xmlns:allurent="http://www.allurent.com/2006/urlkit">
<allurent:FlexBrowserManagerAdapter applicationState="{allRules}" />
<allurent:UrlRuleSet id="allRules">
<allurent:UrlValueRule urlFormat=";checked=*"
    sourceValue="box.selected" defaultValue="false" />
<allurent:UrlValueRule urlFormat=";selectedIndex=*"
    sourceValue="navigator.selectedIndex" defaultValue="0" />
</allurent:UrlRuleSet>
    <mx:Script>
        <![CDATA[
        import mx.containers.VBox;
        import flash.events.Event;
        import flash.net.URLLoader;
        import flash.net.URLRequest;
        import mx.controls.Text;

        private var req:URLRequest;
        private var loader:URLLoader;
        private var xmlData:XML;

        private function initApp():void
        {
            req = new URLRequest("data.xml");
```

```
        loader = new URLLoader();
        loader.addEventListener(Event.COMPLETE,loadComplete);
        loader.load(req);
    }

    private function loadComplete(event:Event):void
    {

        xmlData = new XML(loader.data);
        for each(var game:XML in xmlData.game)
        {
            var vbox:VBox = new VBox();
            var field:Text = new Text();
            field.text = game.description;
            vbox.label = game.title;
            navigator.addChild(vbox);
            vbox.addChild(field);
            field.width = 375;
            field.height = 100;
        }

    }
    ]]>
    </mx:Script>
    <mx:TabNavigator id="navigator" width="400" height="150"
selectedIndex="0">
    </mx:TabNavigator>
    <mx:CheckBox label="Checkbox" id="box" selected="false"/>
</mx:Application>
```

15. Test the application, and notice the browser address updating as you click the different tabs and the checkbox.

Key Terms Used in This Chapter

Table 6-2 contains the terms that were introduced in this chapter and gives you their definitions.

Table 6-2. Key terms used in this chapter

Term	Definition
E4X	EcmaScript for XML—a way to communicate with XML data using dot syntax
Regular Expressions	Powerful string identifying tools, commonly used to find and replace parts of strings
URL Fragments	URL information stored after a #, used with SWFAddress and other deep linking tools

CHAPTER 7

Optimizing Your Site

Now that you have all the tools and techniques you need to optimize Flash content, you're ready to find out how to apply those concepts in the real world. In this chapter, you'll look at some examples of sites with Flash content and evaluate them from a Search Engine Optimizer's perspective. Then you'll find out how to improve an existing site that contains Flash content that is poorly optimized.

Looking at Your Site As a Search Engine Optimizer

Before you started reading this book, you likely had one or more websites with Flash content that were not fully optimized. At this point, you're probably planning to apply what you've learned in this book to an already existing site and are wondering where to start. In order to fully optimize a prebuilt website for search engines, you have to look at your site through the eyes of an SEO. Since you may have sites that vary in optimization effectiveness, I'm going to show you some examples of different sites so you can examine the level of optimization for each one. To prepare for that, I begin this section with a brief review of the essential Flash SEO tactics.

Reviewing Flash SEO Techniques

Knowing the main Flash SEO techniques is crucial to evaluating the optimization of your site as well as other sites. Ideally, each Flash or Flex application should have the following associated with it in this order of priority: searchable text, deep links, and a shared data source with the rendered HTML.

Creating searchable text

Above all, Flash SEO demands that there be fully searchable HTML text to describe your Flash/Flex content and to act as alternate content when the person viewing your site doesn't have the Flash Player installed. You can accomplish both objectives by using SWFObject, which is discussed in detail in Chapter 4. Using SWFObject, you have complete control over which content is indexed when you use Flash. You can use fully searchable HTML to define headings, paragraphs, lists, and other tags to communicate your Flash content to search engines.

Implementing SWFObject requires three things: a link to the *swfobject.js* file, using the `swfobject.embedSWF()` method (when using dynamic publishing), and defined alternate content:

```
<script type="text/javascript" src="swfobject/swfobject.js"></script>
<script type="text/javascript">
    swfobject.embedSWF('swfFileToLoad.swf', 'alternateContent', '800',
'600', '9.0.45', false);
</script>
<div id="alternateContent">

            <p>In order to view this page you need Flash Player 9+
support!</p>

        <p>

            <a href="http://www.adobe.com/go/getflashplayer">

                <img
src="http://www.adobe.com/images/shared/download_buttons/
get_flash_player.gif"
alt="Get Adobe Flash player" />

            </a>

        </p>

</div>
```

 You can view documentation for SWFObject, download SWFObject, and download SWFObject code generators from *http://code.google.com/p/swfobject/*.

Adding deep links

Using deep links, discussed in Chapter 6, you can greatly optimize your Flash/Flex applications by adding the capability to generate multiple URLs for one application. These deep link URLs serve two powerful purposes. First, deep linking is excellent for people. With deep links, a person can bookmark any deep-linked states of your application, as well as share links to states in an application, and if applicable, the application will initialize to that state. Deep linking also makes your site more search-engine friendly because search engines can access and index deep links in your application.

Several different methods are available for deep linking. SWFAddress is an ActionScript 2.0 and ActionScript 3.0 method that works in Flash and Flex, whereas URLKit works only in Flex, but is powerful and easy to use.

To use SWFAddress in Flash, you need to set up your timeline using frame labels, as shown in Figure 7-1.

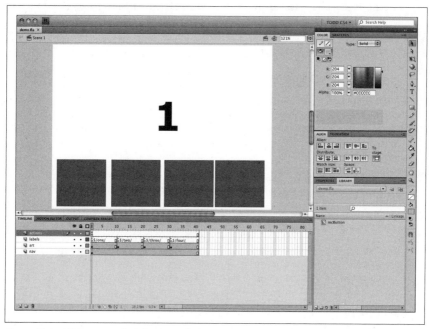

Figure 7-1. All Frame Labels begin with $/

In ActionScript 3.0, you need to import the SWFAddress and SWFAddress event classes:

```
import SWFAddress;
import SWFAddressEvent;
```

Listen for the SWFAddressEvent.CHANGE event:

```
SWFAddress.addEventListener(SWFAddressEvent.CHANGE, handleSWFAddress);
```

Handle the event, using SWFAddress.setValue() to format the URL and SWFAddress.setTitle() to control the page's title:

```
function handleSWFAddress(event:SWFAddressEvent):void
{
    var link:String = event.value;
    if(link == "/")
    {
        link = currentLabels[0].name.replace("$","");
        SWFAddress.setValue(link);
        return;
    }
    gotoAndStop("$" + link);
    SWFAddress.setTitle(link);
}
```

Then you need to import the *swfaddress.js* file into your HTML file:

```
<script type="text/javascript" src="swfaddress/swfaddress.js"></script>
```

And be sure to assign an `id` attribute to your Flash content using SWFObject:

```
<script type="text/javascript">

            swfobject.embedSWF('c.swf?path=website.swf', 'website', '100%',
'100%', '9.0.45',

            'swfobject/expressinstall.swf', {}, {bgcolor: '#CCCCCC',
menu: 'false'}, {id: 'website'});

</script>
```

When using URLKit, you must add the allurent XML namespace to three areas: Application tag, elements that control deep linking, and URL rules:

```
<mx:Application xmlns:mx="http://www.adobe.com/2006/mxml"
creationComplete="initApp()" viewSourceURL="srcview/index.html"
xmlns:allurent="http://www.allurent.com/2006/urlkit">
<mx:TabNavigator id="navigator" width="400" height="150" selectedIndex="0">
</mx:TabNavigator>
<mx:CheckBox label="Checkbox" id="box" selected="false"/>
<allurent:UrlRuleSet id="allRules">
<allurent:UrlValueRule urlFormat=";checked=*"
    sourceValue="box.selected" defaultValue="false" />
<allurent:UrlValueRule urlFormat=";selectedIndex=*"
    sourceValue="navigator.selectedIndex" defaultValue="0" />
</allurent:UrlRuleSet>
```

 You can find information about SWFAddress, including documentation and downloads at *http://www.asual.com/swfaddress/*. The website for URLKit is *http://code.google.com/p/urlkit/*, and documentation can be found at *http://www.davidtucker.net/docs/urlkit/*.

Optimizing development time with reusable XML data

XML data is an excellent choice for optimizing Flash applications. With it you can use the same data source for your Flash or Flex application that you use for its alternate content using a tool like SWFObject. That said, using a shared data source doesn't have a direct effect on search engine indexing, but it does ensure that the data in your Flash or Flex application is the same as its alternate content. So, rather than optimizing your site for search engines, this technique optimizes it for the site's developer because sharing data can save development time. In Chapter 5, you look at using XML data and PHP to achieve this purpose since the process is pretty straightforward, but you could definitely use a different data source, like a database, and/or another server-side language to get the same result.

> The Google Webspam team has been known to do visuals on sites. They do this to make sure that the content displayed on the screen matches the content in the HTML source. This is the equivalent of an IRS audit, and you want make sure your site would pass if this happens.

To reuse XML data, you need an XML data source similar to this one:

```
<?xml version="1.0" encoding="UTF-8"?>
<gallery>
<image>
    <file>meteor-blaster.png</file>
    <thumb>meteor-blaster-thumb.jpg</thumb>
    <description>Shoot meteors with powerful laser cannons!
Advance through levels based on your score. Watch your
energy meter! Those meteors are relentless!</description>
</image>
<image>
    <file>xylophone-master.png</file>
    <thumb>xylophone-master-thumb.jpg</thumb>
    <description>Learn to master playing the xylophone and
simultaneously boost your memory! Listen to the computer
play notes and simply play them back by moving your mouse
or Wii remote up and down over the keys.</description>
</image>
<image>
    <file>fun-run.png</file>
    <thumb>fun-run-thumb.png</thumb>
    <description>Run a marathon as a giant man, completing
up to 26.2 miles in 5 seconds! Move the mouse (or WiiMote)
up and down to run. Finish fast to get medals!</description>
</image>
<image>
    <file>set-the-clock.png</file>
    <thumb>set-the-clock-thumb.png</thumb>
```

```
    <description>Rotate the mouse or WiiMote clockwise or
counterclockwise to set the big clock to display the same
time as the little clock. Race your friends to get
the best time! Clock on!</description>
</image>
</gallery>
```

You then need to access and use that data with ActionScript in your Flash application:

```
var req:URLRequest = new URLRequest("data.xml");
var loader:URLLoader = new URLLoader();
var xmlData:XML;

loader.addEventListener(Event.COMPLETE, fileLoaded);
loader.load(req);

function fileLoaded(event:Event):void
{
    xmlData = new XML(loader.data);
    // code to use loaded xml data (not shown here)
}
```

And to use the same XML data in PHP, you can utilize PHP5's SimpleXML extension:

```
<div id="xmlData">
        <?php

            $xml = simplexml_load_file('data.xml');
            $num_of_elements = count($xml->image);

            for($i = 0; $i < $num_of_elements; $i++)
            {?>

                <p>
                <a href="<?php echo($xml->image[$i]->file);?>">
                <img src="<?php echo($xml->image[$i]->thumb);?>"/>
                </a>
                <?php echo($xml->image[$i]->description);?>
                </p>
                }

</div>
```

Case Studies: Two Flash-Based Websites

Many sites that contain Flash content are not optimized. To optimize a preexisting Flash-based site, you need to know how to find what can be improved. In this section, you start practicing by looking at two websites: *http://www .andrewthorn.com/* and *http://www.chrisorwig.com/*. You'll evaluate the optimization of the sites and learn where they can be improved. Later in this chapter, you'll adjust the code in the sites to optimize them so they can properly portray their content to searchers and search engines.

> The sites discussed in this section and their search results may have been changed since the writing of this book. For that reason, we'll look at the sites as they were at the time of the writing of this book.

ChrisOrwig.com

Chris Orwig is a well-known photographer, speaker, and author, who uses his site to advertise his work. The title and description of this site in search results should display that information; so we'll evaluate the site based on how well the search results describe the site's content. Before you look at the site, look at Google search results for `site:chrisorwig.com`. Direct your attention to the first result (Figure 7-2), noting both the title and description.

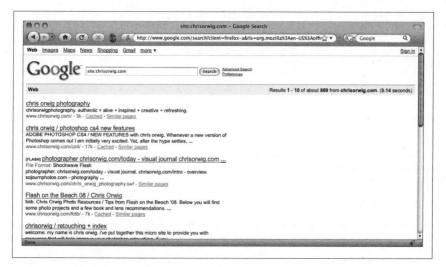

Figure 7-2. Google search results for site:chrisorwig.com

> If you search for `site:sitename.com` in the major search engines (Google, Yahoo!, and MSN), you will find all the pages indexed for a particular site. Yahoo!'s results are a little different from those in Google and MSN, because Yahoo! omits the site's description text in a site search. Google has other tools like this that you can use for searches in its webmaster tools.

Notice that the first result has an appropriate title (`chris orwig photography`), but the description is not so normal. It's `chrisorwigphotography. authentic + alive + inspired + creative + refreshing`. Now, look at the results of the same search in MSN (shown in Figure 7-3) and the results of the search for `chris orwig` in Yahoo! (shown in Figure 7-4), and then compare these results with what you saw in Google.

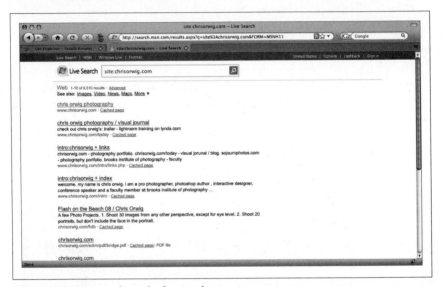

Figure 7-3. MSN search results for site:chrisorwig.com

What's the difference among Google, MSN, and Yahoo!'s results? Neither MSN nor Yahoo! has a description for the site, and Google's description seems a little strange. Where is this weird description coming from, and why isn't it showing up in Yahoo! or MSN?

To find where the different description is coming from, look at what is currently shown at *http://www.chrisorwig.com/*. Before the full site opens, you see a pre-loader (Figure 7-5).

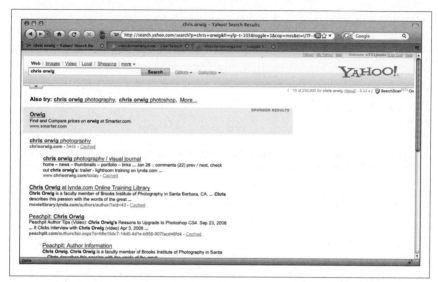

Figure 7-4. Yahoo! search results for chris orwig

Figure 7-5. The chrisorwig.com preloader

Does any of the text look familiar? Google indexed that Flash content and displayed it in the search results. Since Yahoo! and MSN don't index Flash in the same way Google does, or at least don't display the content in search results in the same way, you see a Flash description in Google and no description at all in the other search engines.

Now that you've looked at this site, it's time for a few questions. First, is the site optimized? If not, what is the problem? How can this site be improved? We know for sure that the site has no searchable content, other than Flash content that's only searchable by Google and doesn't give much control. The site also doesn't have deep links. Here's what the source code looks like:

File: *chrisorwig-source-code.html*

```
<html xmlns="http://www.w3.org/1999/xhtml" xml:lang="en" lang="en">
<head>
<meta http-equiv="Content-Type" content="text/html; charset=ISO-8859-1" />
<title>chris orwig photography</title>

<script language="javascript">AC_FL_RunContent = 0;</script>
<script src="AC_RunActiveContent.js" language="javascript"></script>
<style type="text/css">
<!--
body {
    margin-left: 0px;
    margin-top: 0px;
    margin-right: 0px;
    margin-bottom: 0px;
}
-->
</style></head>
<body bgcolor="#000000">
<script language="javascript">
    if (AC_FL_RunContent == 0) {
        alert("This page requires AC_RunActiveContent.js.");
    } else {
        AC_FL_RunContent(
'codebase','http://download.macromedia.com/pub/shockwave /cabs/flash/
swflash.cab#version=9,0,0,0','width','100%','height','100%','id',
'portfolio_final','align','middle', 'src','chris_orwig_photography',
'quality','high','scale','noscale','bgcolor','#000000','name',
'portfolio_final','allowscriptaccess','sameDomain','allowfullscreen','
false','pluginspage','http://www.macromedia.com/go/getflashplayer',
'movie','chris_orwig_photography' ); //end AC code
    }
</script>
<noscript>
    <object classid="clsid:d27cdb6e-ae6d-11cf-96b8-444553540000"
codebase="http://download.macromedia.com/pub/shockwave/cabs/flash/
swflash.cab#version=9,0,0,0" width="100%" height="100%" id=
"portfolio_final" align="middle">
    <param name="allowScriptAccess" value="sameDomain" />
    <param name="allowFullScreen" value="false" />
    <param name="movie" value="chris_orwig_photography.swf" />
<param name="quality"
value="high" /><param name="scale" value="noscale" /><param name=
"bgcolor" value="#000000" />
    <embed src="chris_orwig_photography.swf" quality="high"
scale="noscale" bgcolor="#000000" width="100%" height=
```

```
"100%" name="portfolio_final"
align="middle" allowScriptAccess="sameDomain" allowFullScreen=
"false"
type="application/x-shockwave-flash"
pluginspage="http://www.macromedia.com/go/getflashplayer" />
    </object>

</noscript>

        <script type="text/javascript">
var gaJsHost = (("https:" == document.location.protocol) ? "https://ssl." :
"http://www.");
document.write(unescape("%3Cscript src='" + gaJsHost +
"google-analytics.com/ga.js'
type='text/javascript'%3E%3C/script%3E"));
</script>
<script type="text/javascript">
try {
var pageTracker = _gat._getTracker("UA-4066807-2");
pageTracker._trackPageview();
} catch(err) {}</script>
</body>
</html>
```

Even with a quick glance at the site and its source code, you can easily spot several things that can be improved to greatly enhance the site's optimization. Later in this chapter, we'll come back to this site to fix the SEO issues.

AndrewThorn.com

Andrew Thorn trains businesses and individuals to be more productive. His site shows testimonials from his clients and has his contact information. When the site comes up in the SERPs, you should see testimonials and contact information information in its title and description.

Start by viewing the results for site:andrewthorn.com in Google (Figure 7-6) and MSN (Figure 7-7). The results differ a little because, again, Google is getting some of its information from the site's Flash content.

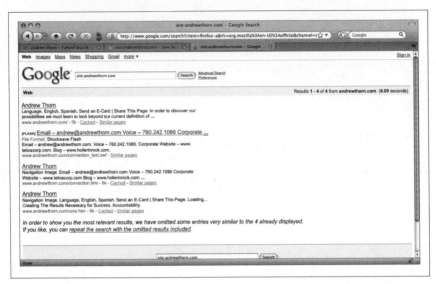

Figure 7-6. Searching for site:andrewthorn.com in Google

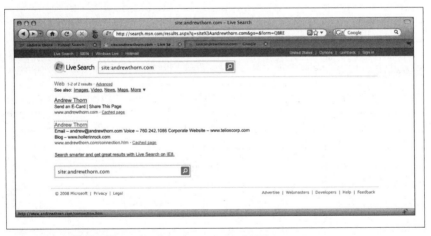

Figure 7-7. Searching for site:andrewthorn.com in MSN

Finally, look at the Yahoo! results (Figure 7-8) for andrew thorn. His site shows up first, which is good, but the description doesn't reveal what the site is about.

Now, look at the current state of the site itself (*http://www.andrewthorn.com*) and view its content (Figure 7-9). Based on the site's content, think about what might be a better description for the site. That description could come from the site's content, or it could be a general description of what's inside the Flash movie.

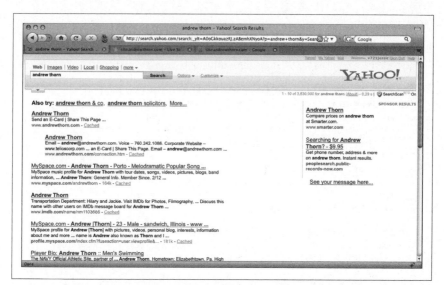

Figure 7-8. Searching for andrew thorn in Yahoo!

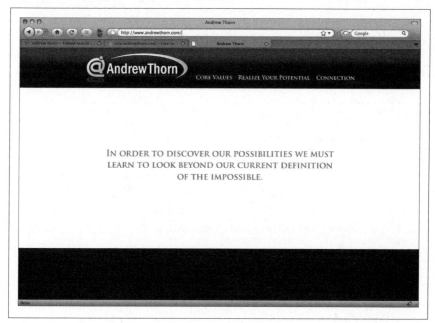

Figure 7-9. Opening quote for andrewthorn.com

Now, check the source code for any obvious issues.

File: *andrewthorn-source-code.html*

```html
<!DOCTYPE html PUBLIC "-//W3C//DTD XHTML 1.0 Transitional//EN"
"http://www.w3.org/TR/xhtml1/DTD/xhtml1-transitional.dtd">
<html xmlns="http://www.w3.org/1999/xhtml"><!-- InstanceBegin
template="/Templates/main.dwt" codeOutsideHTMLIsLocked="false" -->
<head>
<meta http-equiv="Content-Type" content="text/html; charset=utf-8" />
<!-- InstanceBeginEditable name="doctitle" -->
<title>Andrew Thorn</title>
<!-- InstanceEndEditable -->
<script src="Scripts/AC_RunActiveContent.js" type="text/javascript">
</script>
<script type="text/javascript">
<!--
function MM_jumpMenu(targ,selObj,restore){ //v3.0
  eval(targ+".location='"+selObj.options[selObj.selectedIndex].value+"'");
  if (restore) selObj.selectedIndex=0;
}
function MM_preloadImages() { //v3.0
  var d=document; if(d.images){ if(!d.MM_p) d.MM_p=new Array();
    var i,j=d.MM_p.length,a=MM_preloadImages.arguments; for(i=0;
i<a.length; i++)
    if (a[i].indexOf("#")!=0){ d.MM_p[j]=new Image; d.MM_p[j++].src=a[i];}}
}

function MM_swapImgRestore() { //v3.0
  var i,x,a=document.MM_sr; for(i=0;a&&i<a.length&&(x=a[i])&&x.oSrc;i++)
x.src=x.oSrc;
}

function MM_findObj(n, d) { //v4.01
  var p,i,x;  if(!d) d=document; if((p=n.indexOf("?"))
>0&&parent.frames.length) {
    d=parent.frames[n.substring(p+1)].document; n=n.substring(0,p);}
  if(!(x=d[n])&&d.all) x=d.all[n]; for (i=0;!x&&i<d.forms.length;i++)
x=d.forms[i]
[n];
  for(i=0;!x&&d.layers&&i<d.layers.length;i++)
x=MM_findObj(n,d.layers[i].document);
  if(!x && d.getElementById) x=d.getElementById(n); return x;
}

function MM_swapImage() { //v3.0
  var i,j=0,x,a=MM_swapImage.arguments; document.MM_sr=new Array;
for(i=0;i<(a.length-2);i+=3)
    if ((x=MM_findObj(a[i]))!=null){document.MM_sr[j++]=x; if(!x.oSrc)
x.oSrc=x.src; x.src=a[i+2];}
}
//-->
</script>
<link href="styles/main.css" rel="stylesheet" type="text/css"
```

```
media="screen" />
<!-- InstanceBeginEditable name="head" --><!-- InstanceEndEditable -->
</head>

<body
onload="MM_preloadImages('images/coreVal.gif','images/realize.gif',
'images/connections.gif')">

<div id="header">
  <div id="logo"><a href="index.htm"><img src="images/AT_LOGO.png" name=
"Image1"
width="303" height="85" id="Image1" /></a></div>
  <div id="topNav">
    <div align="right"><img src="images/header.gif" alt="Navigation Image"
name="nav" width="475" height="22" border="0" usemap="#NavigationMap"
id="nav" />
        <map name="NavigationMap" id="NavigationMap">
          <area shape="rect" coords="0,0,111,17" href="core.htm"
alt="Core Values Link" onmouseover="MM_swapImage('nav','',
'images/coreVal.gif',1)"onmouseout="MM_swapImgRestore()" />
          <area shape="rect" coords="126,0,343,21" href="index.htm"
alt="Realize Your Potential Link" onmouseover="MM_swapImage('nav','',
'images/realize.gif',1)"
onmouseout="MM_swapImgRestore()" />
          <area shape="rect" coords="358,0,475,19" href="connection.htm"
alt="Connection Link"
onmouseover="MM_swapImage('nav','','images/connections.gif',1)"
onmouseout="MM_swapImgRestore()" />
        </map>
    </div>
  </div>
</div>
<div id="mainBG">
  <div id="mainFlash"><!-- InstanceBeginEditable name="content" -->
    <div id="htmlContent">
      <p>Email - <a href="mailto:andrew@andrewthorn.com"
target="_blank">andrew@andrewthorn.com</a><br />
        <br />
        Voice - 760.242.1086<br />

        <br />
        Corporate   Website - <a href="http://www.telioscorp.com"
target="_blank">www.telioscorp.com</a><br />
        <br />
        Blog - <a href="http://www.hollerinrock.com"
target="_blank">www.hollerinrock.com</a></p>
    </div>
    <div id="flashLinks">
      <script type="text/javascript">
AC_FL_RunContent(
'codebase','http://download.macromedia.com/pub/shockwave/cabs/flash/
swflash.cab#version=9,0,28,0','width','381','height','157','title',
'Connection Text (Flash)','src','connection_text','quality','high',
'pluginspage','http://www.adobe.com/shockwave/download/download.
```

```
cgi?P1_Prod_Version=ShockwaveFlash','movie','connect
ion_text' ); //end AC code

</script><noscript><object classid=
"clsid:D27CDB6E-AE6D-11cf-96B8-444553540000"
codebase="http://download.macromedia.com/pub/shockwave/cabs/flash/
swflash.cab#version=9,0,28,0" width="381" height="157" title=
"Connection Text (Flash)">
        <param name="movie" value="connection_text.swf" />
        <param name="quality" value="high" />
        <embed src="connection_text.swf" quality="high"
pluginspage="http://www.adobe.com/shockwave/download/download.cgi?P1_
Prod_Version=ShockwaveFlash" type="application/x-shockwave-flash"
width="381" height="157"></embed>
      </object>
    </noscript></div>
  <!-- InstanceEndEditable -->  </div>
</div>
<div id="footer">

  <div id="jumpBottom">
    <form name="form" id="form"><select name="language" id="language"
onchange="MM_jumpMenu('parent',this,1)">
        <option value="#">Language</option>
        <option value="#">English</option>

        <option value="#">Spanish</option>
      </select>
    </form>
  </div>
  <div id="footLinks"><a href="#">Send an E-Card</a>  |  <a
href="#">Share This Page</a></div>
</div>
</body>
<!-- InstanceEnd --></html>
```

This page has many HTML comments. These particular comments show that
a Dreamweaver template was used to create the page, which is most obvious
right after the opening <html> tag:

```
<!-- InstanceBegin template="/Templates/main.dwt" codeOutsideHTMLIsLocked=
"false" - ->
```

The page has a few obvious SEO issues. Although there is some searchable
HTML, much of it appears to be hidden using CSS. The footer in particular
seems to have a lot of unused content. The page has some poorly structured
links, missing name attributes, ineffective link text, and so on. Later in this
chapter, we'll go through these issues one by one, and fix them to optimize
this page.

Top SEO Hazards

Your sites may not be set up like the two examples we looked at earlier in this chapter. For that reason, you need to know the two main things to look for in a Flash application. In this section, I discuss the most important Flash SEO issues that you'll face when optimizing your sites.

Searchable text

Flash content without searchable text, as you've seen in two examples, is the most important thing to look for when optimizing Flash-heavy sites. Without searchable HTML text, you're telling Yahoo! and MSN that it's not necessary to index any content in your site, and you're allowing Google to pick whatever it wants out of the text in your site to provide the site's description. This way of doing things was a problem for SEO in both of the earlier examples.

When finding what to optimize in your websites, start by performing searches for your site to see what the search engines have indexed. In Google and MSN, you can search for site:*yoursite*.com to see all the pages in your site that are indexed by those search engines. In Yahoo!, you can perform the same search to see which pages are indexed, but in order to see the descriptions for your pages, you'll need to perform a regular web search where your pages come up.

Once you've seen what search engines are indexing for your pages, determine whether the titles' descriptions accurately describe the content on your site. If not, make the necessary changes by adjusting your pages' titles, <meta> tags, headings, main HTML content, or Flash alternate content using SWFObject. After you've made the appropriate changes to your site, check your search results often to make sure the search results are accurately representing your site's content.

 Some search engines choose content from your pages that is relevant to a search to display in search results, rather than just displaying your <meta> description. This process can be great, since the same page can have many descriptions, and searchers seeing exactly what they want in a description will bring more visitors to that site. You can prevent search engines from picking what displays in your site's description by using <meta> tags (see Chapter 2).

Deep links

As I discuss throughout this book, deep links can add valuable functionality to your Flash applications; they allow for bookmarking and indexing of multiple states of an application.

When using deep links, note that every click in a Flash application doesn't need to be connected to a unique URL. When adding deep links, make sure that each deep link has value, either to search engines or to people. Deep links have value for search engines when your application contains different states that have content that is different enough that an HTML version of your application warrants a new page. Deep links have value when your application has states people may visit often and may want to bookmark or states that contain content that might be shared with others. Well-considered deep linking will simultaneously create a better experience and get multiple pages indexed from your application.

Though deep linking can enhance many Flash applications, it isn't necessary for every Flash movie. Simple Flash animations or games, for example, don't require deep links unless they have content that people might want to bookmark or share or that should be indexed as a separate page.

Think of the Andrew Thorn site you looked at previously. Each link at the top takes you to a different HTML page, and each HTML page has Flash content. The Flash content is generally a set of images and quotes that are animated. For that site, it's unnecessary to create deep links because the Flash content only contains animations or still images. In other words, adding deep linking doesn't benefit search engines or users.

Improving High and Low Priority Areas

After you've identified the optimization of your site, you may be overwhelmed at the work required to fix it, and you may not have the time or resources to optimize every aspect of your site. Here, you find out what is essential to improve in your site and what can wait.

 With enough time and resources, you would ideally optimize all the Flash content in your site. This section is mainly for getting the best results in the least amount of time.

Identifying higher priority areas

Above all, your Flash applications need searchable HTML text. Since you may not be able to add searchable text to all the Flash content in your sites, start by finding the Flash content that contains the most textual data and work from there. Starting with Flash content that uses XML data may be easier because then you can quickly use a server language like PHP to use the same data for its alternate content.

You should also think about whether all of the Flash content should contain a searchable counterpart. If I had very little time to optimize the Chris Orwig site that we looked at earlier,and the Flash content wasn't using XML data for its images, I wouldn't bother creating HTML descriptions for the images or the links to those images.. Instead, I'd go through the application looking for the text with the most value as a description for the content and copy and paste that text from the FLA file into its HTML alternate content. That way, I would get the best return on my time investment.

Recognizing lower priority areas

Lower optimization areas are pretty easy to spot. You're mainly looking for animations or content that is primarily graphical. Pure animation is unlikely to need much searchable content. You might want to incorporate SWFObject to use JavaScript to give a simple description to the Flash content, but you don't need to do much more than that.

Exercises

Now that you've seen how to optimize an existing site, it's time for some practice exercises. These exercises will optimize the sites you looked at earlier in this chapter—*http://www.andrewthorn.com/* and *http://www.chrisorwig.com/*.

Exercise 1: Optimizing a Site's HTML Code to Adjust Its Description in the SERPs

Earlier in this chapter, you looked at the website www.andrewthorn.com (*http://www.andrewthorn.com*) as an example of a site that could use some improvement in terms of SEO. The site's description showed some of its Flash content (Google only) and some of its HTML content that was hidden using CSS. In this exercise, you will optimize the page's HTML code so a more accurate description of its content will show up in the SERPs.

 We won't be using SWFObject to add alternate content in this exercise, since the exercise is focused on using HTML only to control a page's description in search results.

1. Open *index.html* in Dreamweaver or in a text editor and view its contents:

```
<!DOCTYPE html PUBLIC "-//W3C//DTD XHTML 1.0 Transitional//EN"
"http://www.w3.org/TR/xhtml1/DTD/xhtml1-transitional.dtd">
<html xmlns="http://www.w3.org/1999/xhtml"><!-- InstanceBegin
```

```
template="/Templates/main.dwt" codeOutsideHTMLIsLocked="false" -->
<head>
<meta http-equiv="Content-Type" content="text/html; charset=utf-8" />
<!-- InstanceBeginEditable name="doctitle" -->
<title>Andrew Thorn</title>
<!-- InstanceEndEditable -->
<script src="Scripts/AC_RunActiveContent.js" type="text/javascript">
</script>
<script type="text/javascript">
<!--
function MM_jumpMenu(targ,selObj,restore){ //v3.0
  eval(targ+".location='"+selObj.options[selObj.selectedIndex].value+"'");
  if (restore) selObj.selectedIndex=0;
}
function MM_preloadImages() { //v3.0
  var d=document; if(d.images){ if(!d.MM_p) d.MM_p=new Array();
    var i,j=d.MM_p.length,a=MM_preloadImages.arguments; for(i=0;
i<a.length; i++)
    if (a[i].indexOf("#")!=0){ d.MM_p[j]=new Image; d.MM_p[j++].src=a[i];}}
}

function MM_swapImgRestore() { //v3.0
  var i,x,a=document.MM_sr; for(i=0;a&&i<a.length&&(x=a[i])&&x.oSrc;i++)
x.src=x.oSrc;
}

function MM_findObj(n, d) { //v4.01
  var p,i,x; if(!d) d=document; if((p=n.indexOf("?"))>
0&&parent.frames.length) {
    d=parent.frames[n.substring(p+1)].document; n=n.substring(0,p);}
  if(!(x=d[n])&&d.all) x=d.all[n]; for (i=0;!x&&i<d.forms.length;i++)
x=d.forms[i][n];
  for(i=0;!x&&d.layers&&i<d.layers.length;i++)
x=MM_findObj(n,d.layers[i].document);
  if(!x && d.getElementById) x=d.getElementById(n); return x;
}

function MM_swapImage() { //v3.0
  var i,j=0,x,a=MM_swapImage.arguments; document.MM_sr=new Array;
for(i=0;i<(a.length-2);i+=3)
    if ((x=MM_findObj(a[i]))!=null){document.MM_sr[j++]=x; if(!x.oSrc)
x.oSrc=x.src; x.src=a[i+2];}
}
//-->
</script>
<link href="styles/main.css" rel="stylesheet" type="text/css"
media="screen" />
<!-- InstanceBeginEditable name="head" --><!--
InstanceEndEditable -->
</head>

<body
onload="MM_preloadImages('images/coreVal.gif','images/realize.gif','
images/connections.gif')">
```

```html
<div id="header">
  <div id="logo"><a href="index.htm"><img src="images/AT_LOGO.png"
name="Image1" width="303" height="85" id="Image1" /></a></div>
  <div id="topNav">
    <div align="right"><img src="images/header.gif" alt="Navigation
Image" name="nav" width="475" height="22" border="0" usemap=
"#NavigationMap" id="nav" />
        <map name="NavigationMap" id="NavigationMap">
          <area shape="rect" coords="0,0,111,17" href="core.htm"
alt="Core Values Link" onmouseover="MM_swapImage('nav','',
'images/coreVal.gif',1)" onmouseout="MM_swapImgRestore()" />
          <area shape="rect" coords="126,0,343,21" href="index.htm"
alt="Realize Your Potential Link" onmouseover="MM_swapImage('nav',
'','images/realize.gif',1)"
onmouseout="MM_swapImgRestore()" />
          <area shape="rect" coords="358,0,475,19" href="connection.htm"
alt="Connection Link"
onmouseover="MM_swapImage('nav','','images/connections.gif',1)"
onmouseout="MM_swapImgRestore()" />
        </map>

    </div>
  </div>
</div>
<div id="mainBG">
  <div id="mainFlash"><!-- InstanceBeginEditable name="content" -->
    <div id="htmlContent">
      <p>Email - <a href="mailto:andrew@andrewthorn.com"
target="_blank">andrew@andrewthorn.com</a><br />
        <br />
        Voice - 760.242.1086<br />
        <br />
        Corporate   Website - <a href="http://www.telioscorp.com"
target="_blank">www.telioscorp.com</a><br />
        <br />
        Blog - <a href="http://www.hollerinrock.com"
target="_blank">www.hollerinrock.com</a></p>
    </div>
    <div id="flashLinks">
      <script type="text/javascript">
AC_FL_RunContent(
'codebase','http://download.macromedia.com/pub/shockwave/cabs/flash/
swflash.cab#version=9,0,28,0','width','381','height','157','title',
'Connection Text (Flash)','src','connection_text','quality','high',
'pluginspage','http://www.adobe.com/shockwave/download/download.cgi?
P1_Prod_Version=ShockwaveFlash','movie','connection_text' );
//end AC code

</script><noscript><object classid=
"clsid:D27CDB6E-AE6D-11cf-96B8-444553540000"
codebase="http://download.macromedia.com/pub/shockwave/cabs/flash/
swflash.cab#version=9,0,28,0" width="381" height="157" title=
"Connection Text (Flash)">
```

```
        <param name="movie" value="connection_text.swf" />
        <param name="quality" value="high" />
        <embed src="connection_text.swf" quality="high"
pluginspage="http://www.adobe.com/shockwave/download/download.cgi?P1_
Prod_Version=ShockwaveFlash" type="application/x-shockwave-flash"
width="381" height="157"></embed>
        </object>
      </noscript></div>
    <!-- InstanceEndEditable -->  </div>
  </div>
  <div id="footer">

    <div id="jumpBottom">
      <form name="form" id="form"><select name="language" id=
    "language"
onchange="MM_jumpMenu('parent',this,1)">
          <option value="#">Language</option>
          <option value="#">English</option>

          <option value="#">Spanish</option>
      </select>
    </form>
  </div>
  <div id="footLinks"><a href="#">Send an E-Card</a> 
|  <a href="#">Share This Page</a></div>
</div>

</body>
<!-- InstanceEnd --></html>
```

2. Earlier in this chapter, I mentioned that a Dreamweaver template was used
   to create this site. In order to edit the template in Dreamweaver, you will
   need to detach this file from the template with the command
   Modify→Templates→Detach From Template.

 If you're not working in Dreamweaver, you can ignore
step 2.

If you are using Dreamweaver, know that we are detach-
ing this file from the original template because we don't
have the original template file. With the original template
file, you could modify the template to accept these
changes.

3. Recall that when you looked at the site previously, all of the footer information was hidden using CSS. Since the information is hidden from people
   and has no use to search engines (all links are set to #, suggesting that the
   links are placeholders), I suggest removing the content from the HTML
   page and putting it back when it has more use. In a real world scenario,
   you would cut and paste this code into another file. Since you won't be

using the code later, delete the entire footer `<div>` tag. Here's the code you should delete:

```
<div id="footer">

  <div id="jumpBottom">
    <form name="form" id="form"><select name="language" id="language"
onchange="MM_jumpMenu('parent',this,1)">
        <option value="#">Language</option>
        <option value="#">English</option>

        <option value="#">Spanish</option>
      </select>
    </form>
  </div>
  <div id="footLinks"><a href="#">Send an E-Card</a>  |  <a
href="#">Share This Page</a></div>
</div>
```

4. Next, find the section with the image map. It's in a `<div>` tag called topNav, which looks like this:

```
<div id="topNav">
    <div align="right"><img src="images/header.gif" alt="Navigation
Image" name="nav" width="475" height="22" border="0" usemap=
"#NavigationMap" id="nav" />
      <map name="NavigationMap" id="NavigationMap">
        <area shape="rect" coords="0,0,111,17" href="core.htm" alt=
"Core Values Link" onmouseover="MM_swapImage('nav','',
'images/coreVal.gif',1)" onmouseout="MM_swapImgRestore()" />
        <area shape="rect" coords="126,0,343,21" href="index.htm"
alt="Realize Your Potential Link" onmouseover="MM_swapImage('nav','',
'images/realize.gif',1)" onmouseout="MM_swapImgRestore()" />
        <area shape="rect" coords="358,0,475,19" href=
"connection.htm" alt="Connection Link"
onmouseover="MM_swapImage('nav','','images/connections.gif',1)"
onmouseout="MM_swapImgRestore()" />
      </map>
    </div>
```

5. In each of the `<area>` tags, adjust the alt text to remove the word Link. This will just provide a more accurate description of what the image shows.

6. In each `<area>` tag, add a title attribute with the same value as the alt attribute. This addition helps people by showing tooltip text when they mouse over the image, and it also communicates the content of the link to search engines. Here's what the finished topNav `<div>` tag should look like:

```
<div id="topNav">
    <div align="right"><img src="images/header.gif" alt="Navigation
Image" name="nav" width="475" height="22" border="0" usemap=
"#NavigationMap" id="nav" />
```

```
<map name="NavigationMap" id="NavigationMap">
    <area shape="rect" coords="0,0,111,17" href="core.htm"
alt="Core Values" title="Core Values" onmouseover="MM_swapImage('nav',
'','images/coreVal.gif',1)" onmouseout="MM_swapImgRestore()" />
        <area shape="rect" coords="126,0,343,21" href="index.htm"
alt="Realize Your Potential" title="Realize Your Potential"
onmouseover="MM_swapImage('nav','','images/realize.gif',1)"
onmouseout="MM_swapImgRestore()" />
        <area shape="rect" coords="358,0,475,19" href="connection.htm"
alt="Connection" title="Connection"
onmouseover="MM_swapImage('nav','','images/connections.gif',1)"
onmouseout="MM_swapImgRestore()" />
    </map>
</div>
```

7. In the <head> tag, add a <meta> tag description of the page, containing text
   that describes the content of the site. Your code should look something
   like this:

   ```
   <meta name="Description" content="Andrew Thorn is a personal and
   executive coach, inspiring people worldwide to live better, more
   productive lives." />
   ```

8. Last, you tell the search engine spiders to use the <meta> description instead of another snippet of code when displaying the description of the
   site. Start by telling Google, Yahoo!, and MSN not to use DMOZ directory
   listings for site descriptions:

   ```
   <meta name="robots" content="noodp" />
   ```

9. Next, tell Yahoo! not to use its own directories to overwrite titles or descriptions in SERPs:

   ```
   <meta name="robots" content="noydir" />
   ```

10. Finally, tell the Google spiders not to use random HTML snippets for the
    page's description:

    ```
    <meta name="robots" content="nosnippet" />
    ```

11. When you are done, the final code should look like this:

    ```
    <!DOCTYPE html PUBLIC "-//W3C//DTD XHTML 1.0 Transitional//EN"
    "http://www.w3.org/TR/xhtml1/DTD/xhtml1-transitional.dtd">
    <html xmlns="http://www.w3.org/1999/xhtml">
    <head>
    <meta http-equiv="Content-Type" content="text/html; charset=utf-8" />
    <meta name="Description" content="Andrew Thorn is a personal and
    executive coach, inspiring people worldwide to live better,
    more productive lives." />
    <meta name="robots" content="noodp" />
    <meta name="robots" content="noydir" />
    <meta name="robots" content="nosnippet" />
    <title>Andrew Thorn</title>

    <script src="Scripts/AC_RunActiveContent.js" type="text/javascript">
    ```

```
</script>
<script type="text/javascript">
<!--
function MM_jumpMenu(targ,selObj,restore){ //v3.0
  eval(targ+".location='"+selObj.options[selObj.selectedIndex].value+"'");
  if (restore) selObj.selectedIndex=0;
}
function MM_preloadImages() { //v3.0
  var d=document; if(d.images){ if(!d.MM_p) d.MM_p=new Array();
    var i,j=d.MM_p.length,a=MM_preloadImages.arguments;
for(i=0; i<a.length; i++)
    if (a[i].indexOf("#")!=0){ d.MM_p[j]=new Image;
d.MM_p[j++].src=a[i];}}

}

function MM_swapImgRestore() { //v3.0
  var i,x,a=document.MM_sr; for(i=0;a&&i<a.length&&(x=a[i])&&x.oSrc;i++)
x.src=x.oSrc;
}

function MM_findObj(n, d) { //v4.01
  var p,i,x;  if(!d) d=document; if((p=n.indexOf("?"))>
0&&parent.frames.length) {
    d=parent.frames[n.substring(p+1)].document; n=n.substring(0,p);}
  if(!(x=d[n])&&d.all) x=d.all[n]; for (i=0;!x&&i<d.forms.length;i++)
x=d.forms[i][n];
  for(i=0;!x&&d.layers&&i<d.layers.length;i++)
x=MM_findObj(n,d.layers[i].document);
  if(!x && d.getElementById) x=d.getElementById(n); return x;
}

function MM_swapImage() { //v3.0
  var i,j=0,x,a=MM_swapImage.arguments; document.MM_sr=new Array;
for(i=0;i<(a.length-2);i+=3)
   if ((x=MM_findObj(a[i]))!=null){document.MM_sr[j++]=x; if(!x.oSrc)
x.oSrc=x.src; x.src=a[i+2];}
}
//-->
</script>
<link href="styles/main.css" rel="stylesheet" type="text/css"
media="screen" />
</head>

<body
onload="MM_preloadImages('images/coreVal.gif','images/realize.gif',
'images/connections.gif')">

<div id="header">
  <div id="logo"><a href="index.htm"><img src="images/AT_LOGO.png" name=
"Image1" width="303" height="85" id="Image1" /></a></div>
  <div id="topNav">
    <div align="right"><img src="images/header.gif" alt="Navigation Image"
name="nav" width="475" height="22" border="0" usemap="#NavigationMap" id=
```

```
"nav" />
        <map name="NavigationMap" id="NavigationMap">
            <area shape="rect" coords="0,0,111,17" href="core.htm"
alt="Core Values" title="Core Values" onmouseover=
"MM_swapImage('nav','','images/coreVal.gif',1)"
onmouseout="MM_swapImgRestore()" />
            <area shape="rect" coords="126,0,343,21" href="index.htm"
alt="Realize Your Potential" title="Realize Your Potential"
onmouseover="MM_swapImage('nav','','images/realize.gif',1)"
onmouseout="MM_swapImgRestore()" />
            <area shape="rect" coords="358,0,475,19" href="connection.htm"
alt="Connection" title="Connection"
onmouseover="MM_swapImage('nav','','images/connections.gif',1)"
onmouseout="MM_swapImgRestore()" />
        </map>
    </div>
  </div>
</div>
<div id="mainBG">
  <div id="mainFlash">
    <div id="htmlContent">
      <p>Email - <a href="mailto:andrew@andrewthorn.com"
target="_blank">andrew@andrewthorn.com</a><br />
        <br />
        Voice - 760.242.1086<br />

        <br />
        Corporate  Website - <a href="http://www.telioscorp.com"
target="_blank">www.telioscorp.com</a><br />
        <br />
        Blog - <a href="http://www.hollerinrock.com"
target="_blank">www.hollerinrock.com</a></p>
    </div>
    <div id="flashLinks">
      <script type="text/javascript">
AC_FL_RunContent(
'codebase','http://download.macromedia.com/pub/shockwave/cabs/flash/
swflash.cab#version=9,0,28,0','width','381','height','157','title',
'Connection Text (Flash)','src','connection_text','quality','high',
'pluginspage','http://www.adobe.com/shockwave/download/download.cgi?
P1_Prod_Version=ShockwaveFlash','movie','connection_text' );
//end AC code

</script><noscript><object classid=
"clsid:D27CDB6E-AE6D-11cf-96B8-444553540000"
codebase="http://download.macromedia.com/pub/shockwave/cabs/flash/
swflash.cab#version=9,0,28,0" width="381" height="157" title=
"Connection Text (Flash)">
        <param name="movie" value="connection_text.swf" />
        <param name="quality" value="high" />
        <embed src="connection_text.swf" quality="high"
pluginspage="http://www.adobe.com/shockwave/download/download.cgi?P1_
Prod_Version=ShockwaveFlash" type="application/x-shockwave-flash"
width="381" height="157"></embed>
```

```
          </object>
        </noscript>
        </div>
        </div>
      </div>

      </body>
      </html>
```

Exercise 2: Adding Searchable Text to a Poorly Optimized Site

The site *http://www.chrisorwig.com* had an interesting description of its Flash content in Google's results, and no description whatsoever in the other search engines. For that reason, the site will show up only in searches relevant to the page's title, or in searches relevant to what Google found when crawling the SWF, which currently is not useful. In this exercise, you will increase the range of searches where this site will show up by creating a search-engine-readable HTML alternate to the site's Flash content with SWFObject.

1. Open the file *index.html* in Dreamweaver or a text editor to view its contents:

```
<html xmlns="http://www.w3.org/1999/xhtml" xml:lang="en" lang="en">
<head>
<meta http-equiv="Content-Type" content="text/html; charset=
ISO-8859-1" />
<title>chris orwig photography </title>

<script language="javascript">AC_FL_RunContent = 0;</script>
<script src="AC_RunActiveContent.js" language="javascript"></script>
<style type="text/css">
<!--
body {
    margin-left: 0px;
    margin-top: 0px;
    margin-right: 0px;
    margin-bottom: 0px;
}
-->
</style></head>
<body bgcolor="#000000">
<script language="javascript">
    if (AC_FL_RunContent == 0) {
        alert("This page requires AC_RunActiveContent.js.");
    } else {
        AC_FL_RunContent(
'codebase','http://download.macromedia.com/pub/shockwave/cabs/flash/
swflash.cab#version=9,0,0,0','width','100%','height','100%','id',
'portfolio_final','align','middle','src','chris_orwig_photography',
```

```
'quality','high','scale','noscale','bgcolor','#000000','name',
'portfolio_final','allowscriptaccess','sameDomain','allowfullscreen',
'false','pluginspage','http://www.macromedia.com/go/getflashplayer',
'movie','chris_orwig_photography' ); //end AC code
    }
</script>
<noscript>
    <object classid="clsid:d27cdb6e-ae6d-11cf-96b8-444553540000"
codebase="http://download.macromedia.com/pub/shockwave/cabs/flash/
swflash.cab#version=9,0,0,0" width="100%" height="100%" id=
"portfolio_final" align="middle">
    <param name="allowScriptAccess" value="sameDomain" />
    <param name="allowFullScreen" value="false" />
    <param name="movie" value="chris_orwig_photography.swf" />
<param name="quality"
value="high" /><param name="scale" value="noscale" /><param name=
"bgcolor" value="#000000" />
<embed src="chris_orwig_photography.swf" quality="high"
scale="noscale" bgcolor="#000000" width="100%" height="100%"
name="portfolio_final"
align="middle" allowScriptAccess="sameDomain" allowFullScreen=
"false"
type="application/x-shockwave-flash"
pluginspage="http://www.macromedia.com/go/getflashplayer" />
    </object>

</noscript>

        <script type="text/javascript">
var gaJsHost = (("https:" == document.location.protocol) ?
"https://ssl." : "http://www.");
document.write(unescape("%3Cscript src='" + gaJsHost +
"google-analytics.com/ga.js'
type='text/javascript'%3E%3C/script%3E"));
</script>
<script type="text/javascript">
try {
var pageTracker = _gat._getTracker("UA-4066807-2");
pageTracker._trackPageview();
} catch(err) {}</script>
</body>
</html>
```

2. Find the name of the SWF file being used in this code and take note of it. You can find it in the `<param>` tag that has a `name` attribute value of `movie` inside the `<object>` tag. `chris_orwig_photography.swf` is the file here:

```
<param name="movie" value="chris_orwig_photography.swf" />
```

3. Delete the content in the `<body>` tag that displays the Flash content. Here's the code to delete:

```
<script language="javascript">
    if (AC_FL_RunContent == 0) {
        alert("This page requires AC_RunActiveContent.js.");
```

```
      } else {
          AC_FL_RunContent(
  'codebase','http://download.macromedia.com/pub/shockwave/cabs/flash/
  swflash.cab#version=9,0,0,0','width','100%','height','100%','id',
  'portfolio_final','align','middle','src','chris_orwig_photography',
  'quality','high','scale','noscale','bgcolor','#000000','name',
  'portfolio_final','allowscriptaccess','sameDomain','allowfullscreen',
  'false','pluginspage','http://www.macromedia.com/go/getflashplayer',
  'movie','chris_orwig_photography' ); //end AC code
          }
  </script>
  <noscript>
      <object classid="clsid:d27cdb6e-ae6d-11cf-96b8-444553540000"
  codebase="http://download.macromedia.com/pub/shockwave/cabs/flash/
  swflash.cab#version=9,0,0,0" width="100%" height="100%" id=
  "portfolio_final" align="middle">
          <param name="allowScriptAccess" value="sameDomain" />
          <param name="allowFullScreen" value="false" />
          <param name="movie" value="chris_orwig_photography.swf" />
      <param name="quality"
  value="high" /><param name="scale" value="noscale" /><param
  name="bgcolor" value="#000000" />
      <embed src="chris_orwig_photography.swf" quality="high"
  scale="noscale" bgcolor="#000000" width="100%" height="100%"
  name="portfolio_final" align="middle" allowScriptAccess=
  "sameDomain" allowFullScreen="false" type=
  "application/x-shockwave-flash"
  pluginspage="http://www.macromedia.com/go/getflashplayer" />
      </object>

  </noscript>
```

4. Delete the `<script>` tags in the `<head>` tag that make reference to the file *AC_RunActiveContent.js*. The code to delete looks like this:

```
<script language="javascript">AC_FL_RunContent = 0;</script>
<script src="AC_RunActiveContent.js" language="javascript"></script>
```

5. Above the other content within the `<body>` tag, create a `<div>` tag with an id of altContent:

```
<div id="altContent">
</div>
```

6. Inside the altContent `<div>` tag, add an `<h1>` tag for the title of the page:

```
<div id="altContent">
<h1>Chris Orwig Photography</h1>
</div>
```

7. Below the `<h1>` tag, add a description of the site in a `<p>` tag. I used a description of Chris Orwig from the About section of the site (Figure 7-10):

```
<div id="altContent">
<h1>Chris Orwig Photography</h1>
<p>Chris Orwig is a celebrated photographer, author, speaker,
```

interactive designer and on the faculty of the Brooks Institute of
Photography in Santa Barbara, California.</p>
</div>

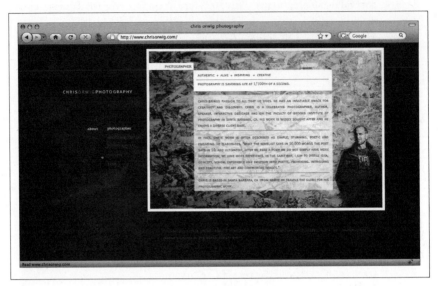

Figure 7-10. The About page from the Chris Orwig site

8. Now, use SWFObject to add the Flash content if the person viewing the
   site has the Flash Player installed. In the `<head>` tag, add the following code
   to link to the *swfobject.js* file:

   ```
   <script type="text/javascript" src="swfobject.js"></script>
   ```

9. Below the `<script>` tag you created, add another `<script>` tag, and use
   SWFObject's dynamic publishing method to embed the SWF file. Be sure
   to set the size to 100% width and 100% height to match the presentation
   of the SWF on the website:

   ```
   <script type="text/javascript">
            swfobject.embedSWF("chris_orwig_photography.swf",
   "altContent", "100%", "100%", "10.0.0", false);
   </script>
   ```

10. Now, test what search engines and people who don't have Flash will see
    when they visit this page. Temporarily disable the `swfobject.embedSWF` line
    of code by placing two forward slashes at the beginning of it:

    ```
    <script type="text/javascript">
            //swfobject.embedSWF("chris_orwig_photography.swf", "altContent",
    "100%", "100%", "10.0.0", false);
    </script>
    ```

11. Save the page and preview it in your web browser (Figure 7-11). What's wrong?

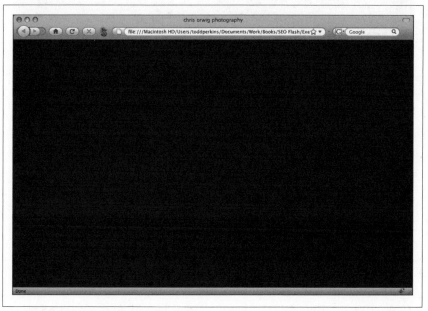

Figure 7-11. Viewing the page in Firefox

12. To test whether the text is there, choose Edit→Select All in your browser (Figure 7-12). There, you can see that the text exists, but it is hidden because it's the same color as the background. So, if anyone visiting this page has a default browser font color of black (which is the default setting in all browsers), this text will be hidden because the background is black as well.

> Text on an identical color background could be considered Black Hat SEO and get your site banned from search engines. Be sure your sites never contain text that is the same color as its background.

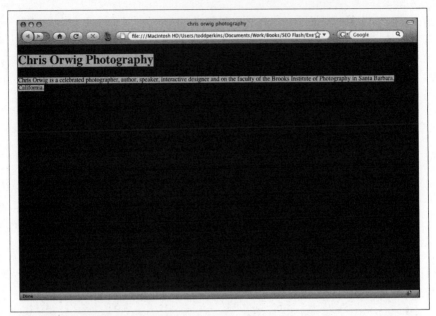

Figure 7-12. Viewing the selected black on black text

13. Now, fix the same color background issue by adding a simple CSS rule to the already existing rules for the <body> tag. Below the other rules, add a rule to set the default font color for this page to white:

```
<style type="text/css">
<!--
body {
    margin-left: 0px;
    margin-top: 0px;
    margin-right: 0px;
    margin-bottom: 0px;
    color:#FFFFFF;
}
-->
</style>
```

14. Save and test the file again to see the white text in your web browser (Figure 7-13).

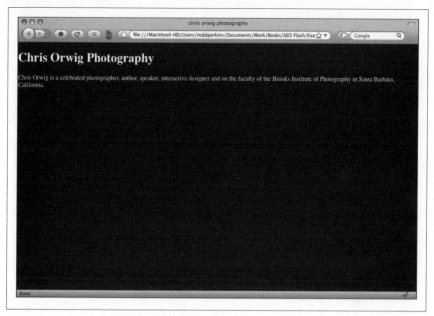

Figure 7-13. Viewing the now visible text in Firefox

15. Last, re-enable SWFObject by removing the comment you added in step 10.

```
<script type="text/javascript">
            swfobject.embedSWF("chris_orwig_photography.swf", "altContent",
"100%", "100%", "10.0.0", false);
</script>
```

16. Here's the final code for the page:

```
<html xmlns="http://www.w3.org/1999/xhtml" xml:lang="en" lang="en">
<head>
<meta http-equiv="Content-Type" content="text/html; charset=
ISO-8859-1" />
<title>chris orwig photography </title>

<script type="text/javascript" src="swfobject.js"></script>
<script type="text/javascript">
            swfobject.embedSWF("chris_orwig_photography.swf",
"altContent", "100%", "100%", "10.0.0", false);
</script>
<style type="text/css">
<!--
body {
    margin-left: 0px;
    margin-top: 0px;
    margin-right: 0px;
    margin-bottom: 0px;
```

```
        color:#FFFFFF;
}
-->
</style>
</head>
<body bgcolor="#000000">
<div id="altContent">
<h1>Chris Orwig Photography</h1>
<p>Chris Orwig is a celebrated photographer, author, speaker,
interactive designer and on the faculty of the Brooks Institute
of Photography in Santa Barbara, California.</p>
</div>
        <script type="text/javascript">
var gaJsHost = (("https:" == document.location.protocol) ?
"https://ssl." : "http://www.");
document.write(unescape("%3Cscript src='" + gaJsHost +
"google-analytics.com/ga.js'
type='text/javascript'%3E%3C/script%3E"));
</script>
<script type="text/javascript">
try {
var pageTracker = _gat._getTracker("UA-4066807-2");
pageTracker._trackPageview();
} catch(err) {}</script>
</body>
</html>
```

In this exercise, you greatly enhanced the SEO in this page. However, more improvements could still be made in terms of presentation. For example, the page layout isn't very attractive, so you could work with CSS in the altContent <div> tag to style it better in case someone viewing the page doesn't have Flash. If you're up for a challenge, try making this site look great regardless of whether the person visiting has the Flash Player or not.

 For an example of better presentation of alternate content, see the next exercise.

Exercise 3: Using XML Data with PHP to Optimize Development Time

The image galleries on Chris Orwig's site were generated using XML data. When creating alternate content, using some type of data source, like XML, makes it easy to generate an HTML alternative for Flash content. In this exercise, you use XML data to create some alternate content for his site that displays some of the images from the slideshow. You create a heading that shows a gallery's name, and thumbnail links to the full-size images, along with descriptive text.

 To see this exercise working properly, you will need to use a web server that has PHP5.

1. Copy all the files for this exercise onto your web server.
2. You start by looking at the XML data you'll be using. Open the file *data.xml* to view its contents:

```xml
<?xml version="1.0" encoding="UTF-8"?>
<gallery name="The Sojourn">
    <image>
        <file>images/images_01.jpg</file>
        <thumb>thumbnails/images_01.jpg</thumb>
        <title>Liquid Gold</title>
    </image>
    <image>
        <file>images/images_02.jpg</file>
        <thumb>thumbnails/images_02.jpg</thumb>
        <title>The Search</title>
    </image>
    <image>
        <file>images/images_03.jpg</file>
        <thumb>thumbnails/images_03.jpg</thumb>
        <title>Dreamscape</title>
    </image>
    <image>
        <file>images/images_04.jpg</file>
        <thumb>thumbnails/images_04.jpg</thumb>
        <title>Channel Islands</title>
    </image>
    <image>
        <file>images/images_05.jpg</file>
        <thumb>thumbnails/images_05.jpg</thumb>
        <title>Baja swing</title>
    </image>
    <image>
        <file>images/images_06.jpg</file>
        <thumb>thumbnails/images_06.jpg</thumb>
        <title>Tres Barcos</title>
    </image>
    <image>
        <file>images/images_07.jpg</file>
        <thumb>thumbnails/images_07.jpg</thumb>
        <title>Desert path</title>
    </image>
    <image>
        <file>images/images_08.jpg</file>
```

```
  <thumb>thumbnails/images_08.jpg</thumb>
  <title>The Sierras</title>
</image>
<image>
  <file>images/images_09.jpg</file>
  <thumb>thumbnails/images_09.jpg</thumb>
  <title>Backcountry in the Washington Cascades</title>
</image>
<image>
  <file>images/images_10.jpg</file>
  <thumb>thumbnails/images_10.jpg</thumb>
  <title>Luck to be Leafless</title>
</image>
<image>
  <file>images/images_11.jpg</file>
  <thumb>thumbnails/images_11.jpg</thumb>
  <title>Nor Cal Oak</title>
</image>
<image>
  <file>images/images_12.jpg</file>
  <thumb>thumbnails/images_12.jpg</thumb>
  <title>The journey is the destination</title>
</image>
<image>
  <file>images/images_13.jpg</file>
  <thumb>thumbnails/images_13.jpg</thumb>
  <title>Mexico</title>
</image>
<image>
  <file>images/images_14.jpg</file>
  <thumb>thumbnails/images_14.jpg</thumb>
  <title>The sound of travel</title>
</image>
</gallery>
```

3. Note that the root element, `<gallery>`, has a name attribute that contains the name of the gallery. Each image has three child elements: `<file>` represents the path to the image, `<thumb>` represents the path to the thumbnail image, and `<title>` represents descriptive text for the image.

4. Open the file *index.html* and save it as *index.php*. Note that the code in *index.php* uses an external style sheet, styles.css. These styles are used by the file *index.php* to make the display of the alternate content more attractive.

5. View the page in a web browser to see how the content is styled (Figure 7-14).

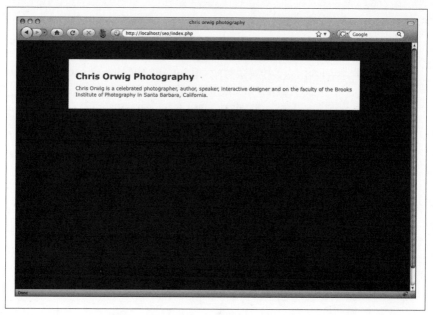

Figure 7-14. Viewing the revised page in Firefox

6. Below the content inside the `altContent` `<div>` tag, and before the closing `</div>` tag, load the file *data.xml* using PHP5's `simplexml` extension:

```
<?php
$xml = simplexml_load_file('data.xml'); ?>
```

7. Place the value of the name attribute in the XML file inside an `<h2>` tag:

```
<?php
                $xml = simplexml_load_file('data.xml'); ?>
                <h2><?php echo($xml->attributes()->name); ?></h2>
```

8. Hold the number of images in the XML file in a variable called `num_of_elements`:

```
<?php
                $xml = simplexml_load_file('data.xml'); ?>
                <h2><?php echo($xml->attributes()->name); ?></h2>
                <?php
                $num_of_elements = count($xml->image);
        ?>
```

9. Create a `for` loop that loops through each `<image>` element in the XML file:

```
<?php
                $xml = simplexml_load_file('data.xml'); ?>
                <h2><?php echo($xml->attributes()->name); ?></h2>
                <?php
                $num_of_elements = count($xml->image);
```

```
                  for($i = 0; $i < $num_of_elements; $i++)
                  {
      }?>
```

10. Inside the **for** loop, create a `<p>` tag containing the title of each image:

```
<?php
              $xml = simplexml_load_file('data.xml'); ?>
              <h2><?php echo($xml->attributes()->name); ?></h2>
              <?php
              $num_of_elements = count($xml->image);

              for($i = 0; $i < $num_of_elements; $i++)
              {?>
<p>php echo($xml->image[$i]->title);?> </p>
<?php
                  }?>
```

11. Make each image title a link to the full-size image:

```
<?php
              $xml = simplexml_load_file('data.xml'); ?>
              <h2><?php echo($xml->attributes()->name); ?></h2>
              <?php
              $num_of_elements = count($xml->image);

              for($i = 0; $i < $num_of_elements; $i++)
              {?>
<p> <a href="<?php echo($xml->image[$i]->file);?>"><?php
echo($xml->image[$i]->title);?></a> </p>
<?php
                  }?>
```

12. Before the title text and links, place the thumbnail images, assigning the **thumbnail** class to each one:

```
<?php
              $xml = simplexml_load_file('data.xml'); ?>
              <h2><?php echo($xml->attributes()->name); ?></h2>
              <?php
              $num_of_elements = count($xml->image);

              for($i = 0; $i < $num_of_elements; $i++)
              {?>
<p><img class="thumbnail" src="<?php echo($xml->image[$i]->thumb);?>"/>
<a href="<?php echo($xml->image[$i]-
>file);?>"><?php echo($xml->image[$i]->title);?></a> </p>
<?php
                  }?>
```

13. Make each thumbnail image link to the full-size image:

```
<?php
              $xml = simplexml_load_file('data.xml'); ?>
              <h2><?php echo($xml->attributes()->name); ?>
      </h2>
```

```php
<?php
$num_of_elements = count($xml->image);

for($i = 0; $i < $num_of_elements; $i++)
{?>
<p> <a href="<?php echo($xml->image[$i]->file);?>"> <img class=
"thumbnail"
src="<?php echo($xml->image[$i]->thumb);?>"/> </a> <a href="<?php
echo($xml->image[$i]->file);?>"><?php echo($xml->image[$i]->title);?>
</a> </p>
<?php
}?>
```

14. The `thumbnail` class floats the thumbnails to the left. Clear the float after each paragraph using a `<div>` tag with the class `clearFloat`:

```php
<?php
$xml = simplexml_load_file('data.xml'); ?>
<h2><?php echo($xml->attributes()->name); ?></h2>
<?php
$num_of_elements = count($xml->image);

for($i = 0; $i < $num_of_elements; $i++)
{?>
<p> <a href="<?php echo($xml->image[$i]->file);?>"> <img class="thumbnail"
src="<?php echo($xml->image[$i]->thumb);?>"/> </a> <a href="<?php echo
($xml->image[$i]->file);?>"><?php echo($xml->image[$i]->title);?></a>
</p>
<div class="clearFloat"></div>
<?php
}?>
```

15. Save the page and preview it in a browser to view the result (Figure 7-15).

16. Re-enable SWFObject by removing the comment in the `<script>` block in the `<head>` tag. It should look like this when you're done:

```
<script type="text/javascript">
         swfobject.embedSWF("chris_orwig_photography.swf",
"altContent", "100%", "100%", "10.0.0", false);
</script>
```

17. Here's the final code for *index.php*:

```
<html xmlns="http://www.w3.org/1999/xhtml" xml:lang="en" lang="en">
<head>
<meta http-equiv="Content-Type" content="text/html; charset=
ISO-8859-1" />
<title>chris orwig photography</title>
<script type="text/javascript" src="swfobject.js"></script>
<script type="text/javascript">
         swfobject.embedSWF("chris_orwig_photography.swf",
"altContent", "100%", "100%", "10.0.0", false);
</script>

<link href="styles.css" rel="stylesheet" type="text/css">
```

```
    </head>
    <body>
    <div id="altContent">
      <h1>Chris Orwig Photography</h1>
      <p>Chris Orwig is a celebrated photographer, author, speaker,
    interactive designer and on the faculty of the Brooks Institute
    of Photography in Santa Barbara, California.</p>
    <?php
                    $xml = simplexml_load_file('data.xml');
                    ?><h2><?php echo($xml->attributes()->name);
    ?></h2><?php
                    $num_of_elements = count($xml->image);

                    for($i = 0; $i < $num_of_elements; $i++)
                    {?>
    <p> <a href="<?php echo($xml->image[$i]->file);?>"> <img class=
    "thumbnail"
    src="<?php echo($xml->image[$i]->thumb);?>"/> </a> <a href="<?php echo
    ($xml->image[$i]->file);?>"><?php echo($xml->image[$i]->title);?></a>
    </p>
    <div class="clearFloat"></div>
    <?php
                    }?>
    </div>
    <script type="text/javascript">
    var gaJsHost = (("https:" == document.location.protocol) ?
    "https://ssl." : "http://www.");
    document.write(unescape("%3Cscript src='" + gaJsHost +
    "google-analytics.com/ga.js' type='text/javascript'%3E%3C/script%3E"));
    </script>
    <script type="text/javascript">
    try {
    var pageTracker = _gat._getTracker("UA-4066807-2");
    pageTracker._trackPageview();
    } catch(err) {}</script>
    </body>
    </html>
```

18. Save and close the file.

Challenge

Now that you know the main techniques for optimizing applications, you're ready to go out into the real world, applying what you've learned. The challenge I'll leave you with is to go through sites you've created and improve their SEO using what you discovered throughout this book. Have fun!

Figure 7-15. Viewing the finished page in a browser

Index

We'd like to hear your suggestions for improving our indexes. Send email to *index@oreilly.com*.

F

files
    keywords in image file names, 23
    naming, 26
    size of for HTML, 26
    syntax, 26
    uploading in ASCII, 27
Firefox
    testing JavaScript with Web Developer
        toolbar, 135
Flash, 63–84
    about, 63
    content, 66–77
    data security, 65
    defined, xxi
    exchanging data with JavaScript, 100–
        110
    indexing content, 70–75
    links, 65, 75
    summary of SEO techniques, 201–206
    SWFAddress library, 95–100
    SWFObject library, 86–95
    text in HTML code, 68
    versus Adobe Flex Builder, 145
Flash applications
    optimizing, 46–49
Flash content
    amount of, 44
Flash movies
    deep linking, 218
    indexing by Google and Yahoo!, 70
Flash Player
    data, 109
    defined, xxi
    ExternalInterface class, 101
    URLs in Flex applications, 156
flashvars parameter
    defined, 92
    using, 109
Flex (see Adobe Flex Builder)
Flex Navigator, 148
FLV (Flash Video)
    defined, xxi
folders, 62
    (see also directories)
    Flex projects, 149
    naming, 26

syntax, 26
font HTML tag, 71
font-family CSS property, 74
font-size CSS property, 74
font-style CSS property, 74
font-weight CSS property, 74
forms
    dynamic content, 129, 130
Fragment property, 169
frame labels
    deep linking with SWFAddress in
        Flash, 203
frames
    using, 44
functions
    ExternalInterface calling JavaScript
        functions, 101

G

generators
    SWFObject, 93
Google
    AdWords, 11
    Analytics, 15
    meta keywords, 24
    removing pages from, 38
    site search results, 207
    submitting sitemaps to, 33
    SWF files, xix
    Webmaster Tools, 34, 53
    Webspam, 205

H

h1, h2 and h3 HTML elements, 21
headings
    HTML code, 21
height attribute, 88
height parameter, 92
hidden pages
    dynamic content, 129
History Management
    Adobe Flex Builder, 165–168
home pages
    consolidating URLs, 56
.htaccess file
    consolidating URLs, 27
    password-protecting pages, 37

About the Author

Todd Perkins is an Adobe-Certified Flash Instructor. He has written three books on Flash, including *Adobe Flash CS3 Professional Hands-on Training* (Peachpit Press), and has recorded nearly 100 hours of Flash training, comprising over 1,000 separate lessons. He also works as a consultant and web developer.

Colophon

The animal on the cover of *Search Engine Optimization for Flash* is a long-tailed chinchilla (*Chinchilla lanigera*). One of two species of chincillas, the long-tailed chinchilla is also known as the Chilean, the Coastal, or the Lesser chinchilla. In their native habitat, chinchillas are colonial, living in the arid, rocky environments of the Andes Mountains from southern Peru to Chile. They usually hide during the day in crevices and cavities among rocks, emerging at night to feed on any available vegetation.

Long-tailed chinchillas are popular pets. They have a broad head, fairly large ears and large black eyes, a small body, and a bushy tail. Their dense, soft fur insulates them in the cold mountainous regions they inhabit. Their bodies are slender, and they have tails that can measure up to a third of the size of their body. Chinchillas have long, strong hind legs that enable them to run and jump agilely. Their dorsal side is bluish, pearl, or brownish-grey in color, and the belly is a yellowish-white color. They can weigh up to 1.8 pounds and be as long as 15 inches.

Females are mostly monogamous and bear two litters per year, with two to three young per litter. The gestation period of 111 days is a relatively long one for such a small animal. The lifespan in the wild is around 10 years, though domesticated chinchillas may live for up to 20 years.

These small mammals have been hunted for their luxurious fur since the 1900s, when around 500,000 chinchilla skins were exported annually from Chile. At that time, chinchilla populations were flourishing. Their pelts were the most valuable in the world—one could sell for as much as $100,000—and soon they were facing extinction in the wild. There are currently an estimated 10,000 chinchillas left in the Chilean mountains. Both species of chinchillas are protected by law.

The cover image is from *Cassell's Natural History*. The cover font is Adobe ITC Garamond. The text font is Linotype Birka; the heading font is Adobe Myriad Condensed; and the code font is LucasFont's TheSansMonoCondensed.

Related Titles from O'Reilly

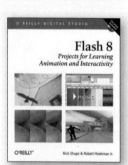

Web Authoring and Design

ActionScript 3.0 Cookbook

Ajax Hacks

Ambient Findability

Creating Web Sites: The Missing Manual

CSS Cookbook, *2nd Edition*

CSS Pocket Reference, *2nd Edition*

CSS: The Definitive Guide, *3rd Edition*

CSS: The Missing Manual

Dreamweaver 8: Design and Construction

Dreamweaver 8: The Missing Manual

Dynamic HTML: The Definitive Reference, *3rd Edition*

Essential ActionScript 3.0

Flex 8 Cookbook

Flash 8: Projects for Learning Animation and Interactivity

Flash 8: The Missing manual

Flash 9 Design: Motion Graphics for Animation & User Interfaces

Flash Hacks

Head First HTML with CSS & XHTML

Head Rush Ajax

Head First Web Design

High Performance Web Sites

HTML & XHTML: The Definitive Guide, *6th Edition*

HTML & XHTML Pocket Reference, *3rd Edition*

Information Architecture for the World Wide Web, *3rd Edition*

Information Dashboard Design

JavaScript: The Definitive Guide, *5th Edition*

JavaScript & DHTML Cookbook, *2nd Edition*

Learning ActionScript 3.0

Learning JavaScript

Learning Web Design, *3rd Edition*

PHP Hacks

Programming Collective Intelligence

Programming Flex 2

Web Design in a Nutshell, *3rd Edition*

Web Site Measurement Hacks